Biblical Discipleship:

Essential Components for Attaining Spiritual Maturity

Biblical Discipleship

Essential Components for

Attaining Spiritual Maturity

Todd M. Fink

Biblical Discipleship
Essential Components for Attaining Spiritual Maturity

by
Todd M. Fink

Published by Selah Book Press

Cover Illustration Copyright © 2016 by Selah Book Press
Cover design by Selah Book Press

Copyright © 2016 by Todd M. Fink

ISBN:
ISBN-13: 978-1-944601-01-0

Library of Congress Control Number: 2015921340

First Edition

ABBREVIATIONS

ESV	English Standard Version
NIV	New International Version
NKJV	New King James Version
NASB	New American Standard Bible
NET	New English Translation

Acknowledgement

My prayer in writing this book was that it would be something the Lord and I did together. I can honestly say that I felt God's grace and direction throughout the process. He gave me ideas and brought things to mind in such a way that let me know He was involved.

I also desired that this book would be biblically based because I wanted to allow the Lord to speak as much as possible. For this reason, this book contains a great deal of Scripture.

Thus, I want to acknowledge God for His help and give Him all the glory for this book. I believe it was He who gave me the idea to write it and the strength and grace to complete it. May He receive all the praise and glory for any role this book might have in His Kingdom.

Endorsements

As president of a Bible college and seminary, I am regularly asked if there is a discipleship book that I can strongly recommend. Thanks to Todd M. Fink, I finally have an answer. *Biblical Discipleship* addresses one of the greatest needs in the modern church. It takes into account the current cultural situation and the effects of bad theology, while suggesting practical strategies for personal growth. This book is, no doubt, going to push the ball forward.

— Dr. Braxton Hunter, Ph.D. President of Trinity
    Theological Seminary

To be a Christian is to be a disciple. To grow as a Christian demands pursuing the life of discipleship. Todd M. Fink has devoted his life to cross-cultural ministry and helping people know and grow in Christ. His many years of experience in the ministry and devotion to the Scriptures have made him a man with great wisdom on this vital topic. I'm thankful he has written this helpful resource to help God's people grow.

— Dr. Erik Thoennes, Ph.D. Professor of Theology/Chair
    Undergraduate Theology at Biola University/Talbot
    School of Theology; Pastor at Grace Evangelical Free
    Church, La Mirada, California

Todd M. Fink's *Biblical Discipleship: Essential Components for Attaining Spiritual Maturity* will prove to be a valuable resource to many who are interested in growing a deeper devotion to Christ. Fink opines an analysis of the major problems/issues in the contemporary Evangelical church that he believes are hindrances to a healthy discipleship focus. He offers a corrective vision for those who desire to go against this Evangelical sub-culture, as he describes it, and be faithful to God's call on their lives.

— Dr. David Talley, Ph.D. Professor/Chair Old Testament
    Department, Biola University

Table of Contents

Foreword

By Dr. Braxton Hunter, Ph.D.

Much of the modern church is spiritually malnourished. Contributing to this daunting dilemma are the realities of neglected, theologically corrupt, poorly devised, half-hearted and shallow forms of what some call discipleship. This is not an overstatement.

If it's not the result of an obvious human effort to distort the Christian teaching, much of the blame rests with the Western Evangelical proclivity to offer a consumer-driven church experience. Rather than choosing a local congregation based on doctrinal perspectives and spiritual growth possibilities, it's now common for individuals to join an assembly because of the amenities it offers. This sort of thinking has been suggested to the community by the local church herself. "Come visit us. We have a great _____!" One can fill in the blank with any number of services or benefits: praise band, exercise classes, gymnasium, coffee bar, and so on. It's not that there's anything wrong with these things. It's just that many local congregations have entered into an invisible contract with the community that says, "We are valuable, primarily because of these benefits," instead of one that says, "We will train you in the truth."

In other cases, the reason for this poor spiritual diet is spiritual fatigue. It seems hard enough for church leaders to care for the needs of a congregation of believers. Doing proper discipleship and training congregants to disciple each other is a time-consuming project that requires great effort and discernment. This hindrance is particularly the case for ministry leaders and churches in ministry contexts that require the majority

1

of their efforts to be spent on evangelism. However, a proper emphasis on discipleship can bolster those other efforts. More discipleship breeds more servants and more evangelism.

Nevertheless, it is often the case that the lack of rich and robust discipleship is because of an ignorance of how to accomplish it. Simply put, many ministry leaders and individuals need specific instruction on this vital matter. What they ultimately need is an explanation of how to reach spiritual maturity in their lives.

Fortunately, Todd M. Fink has provided us with just that. Though the shelves of Christian bookstores are replete with discipleship training materials, *Biblical Discipleship* is a welcome addition. It is unique in its clarity and insight. As a practical minister and an academic, I consider this book to be required reading.

Dr. Braxton Hunter, Ph.D.
President of Trinity Theological Seminary

Introduction

Today, we have many ways of defining success in life. Some define it as being a sports hero, others as being wealthy, others as being popular and well liked, and still others as being happy. How does God define success? He defines it as being spiritually mature!

How do we become spiritually mature? There's only one way, and it's called discipleship. However, statistics show that discipleship is in a state of crisis today. Many Christians are not growing in Christ and are stuck in the process of reaching spiritual maturity. A Barna study reveals that almost nine out of ten senior pastors of Protestant churches assert that spiritual immaturity is one of the most serious issues facing the church.[1]

Sadly, what discipleship meant in the time of Christ and what it means today is vastly different. Moreover, the importance Christ and the Apostles gave to discipleship is also stunningly different than the importance many Christians and churches today give it.

Unlike the disciples who had much of Scripture memorized, a whopping 81% of Christians today don't read their Bibles regularly. Unlike Christ's disciples who were "Fishers of Men," 61% of believers today have not shared their faith in the past six months. And sadly, unlike Christ and the Apostles who made discipleship the central focus of their ministries, 81% of pastors today have no regular discipleship programs in their churches. Discipleship is being neglected today, and the consequences are crippling many Christians and churches. This book hopes to change that!

---

[1] C. S. Lewis Institute, *Sparking a Discipleship Movement in America and Beyond,* cslewisinstitute.org, http://www.cslewisinstitute.org/webfm_send/210, Accessed 08/19/2015.

Chapter 1 focuses on the state of discipleship today and exposes the sad truth that it's in crisis mode. Chapter 2 reveals 13 key factors contributing to the lack of discipleship today. Chapter 3 defines biblical discipleship based on central phrases Christ used in His ministry. Chapter 4 brings to light 14 essential components of the discipleship-making process that must be understood and practiced in order to attain spiritual maturity. Chapter 5 provides practical, "how-to" help for growing in Christ. It includes self-assessment tests for measuring your level of spiritual maturity in each essential component of discipleship and gives hands-on, useful ideas for taking steps toward spiritual maturity.

This book contains a great deal of Scripture, of which some you probably have read before. However, I want to encourage you to slow down, be reflective, and allow God to speak to you afresh. God's Word is living, so no matter how many times we've read a verse, if we'll ponder and allow it to sink in, God will bring new insights and change to our lives.

Discipleship is a command for all believers and is our highest calling. This book provides biblical help for fulfilling this calling and seeks to discover what God says about genuine growth in Christ. It's both an informative book and a "how-to" book. It deals with the barriers that are hindering discipleship, and offers practical help for overcoming these barriers and attaining spiritual maturity.

So, are you ready to grow? Would you like to be pleasing to God? Would you like to fulfill the reason for which you've been created? Would you like the full blessings of God in your life? Would you like to become spiritually mature? Would you like to hear Christ's words, "Well done, good and faithful servant," when you arrive in heaven? If so, this book is for you.

Chapter 1

The State of Discipleship Today

In This Chapter

1. God's View of Discipleship Versus Today's View of Discipleship

2. The Lack of Discipleship Today

3. The Consequences of Neglecting Discipleship

1. God's View of Discipleship Versus Today's View of Discipleship

Dallas Willard, in his book *The Great Omission*, makes an incredible observation regarding the importance of discipleship when stating that the word "disciple" occurs 269 times in the New Testament, but "Christian" is only found three times.[2] Willard defines discipleship as the foundational aspect of what it means to be saved and be a true follower of Christ.

Anthony Robinson, in his article "Follow Me," picks up on Willard's statement and believes that because the word "disciple" occurs 269 times in the New Testament, it defines the mark of a genuine believer.[3] Robinson also contends that the church today is focusing primarily on conversion and neglecting the way of life here and now, which is discipleship.[4]

What Is Discipleship?

Discipleship is the process of becoming like Christ in our nature, character, values, purposes, thoughts, knowledge, attitudes, and will. In other words, it's the process of becoming spiritually mature. It lasts a lifetime and isn't relegated to a temporary study or dedicated class taken for a time and ended. Bill Hull claims, "It's not a program or an event; it's a way of life. Discipleship is not for beginners alone; it's for all believers for every day of their lives."[5]

---

[2] Dallas Willard, *The Great Omission* (HarperCollins, Kindle Edition, 2009-10-13), p. 3.
[3] Anthony B. Robinson, *The Renewed Focus on Discipleship: 'Follow Me'* (Christian Century, 124 no 18 S 4 2007, pp. 23-25. Publication Type: Article. ATLA Religion Database with ATLASerials. Hunter Resource Library), p. 23, Accessed 12/10/2014.
[4] Ibid., p. 23.
[5] Bill Hull, *The Complete Book of Discipleship: On Being and Making Followers of Christ* (The Navigators Reference Library 1, 2014, NavPress, Kindle Edition), Kindle Locations 436-437.

Discipleship Is the Only Way to Spiritual Maturity

Discipleship is the vehicle God uses to make us spiritually mature. There is no other way! It's the pathway we must follow in order to be transformed into the image of Christ and reach spiritual maturity. Through discipleship, God grants us life, love, joy, peace, healthy minds, healthy relationships, healthy families, and healthy churches. It's our life's calling and the highest purpose to which we can give ourselves.

Howard Hendricks went so far as to claim, "When a person makes a profession of faith and … is never taken through a formal discipleship process, then there's little hope of seeing genuine spiritual transformation."[6]

To the degree we are committed to discipleship will be the degree to which we attain spiritual maturity. To the degree we neglect our commitment to discipleship will be the degree to which we suffer destruction, devastation, and eternal loss.

The Role of Discipleship in the Ministry of Christ

I've had the splendid privilege of standing on the mountain where it's believed Christ gave the Great Commission. It's called Mt. Arbel and has a spectacular view of the Sea of Galilee. It's estimated that Jesus spent 70% of His ministry time around the

 Sea of Galilee, so Mt. Arbel would have been the perfect backdrop for Christ to have spoken some of His last and most important words to His disciples: "Go therefore and make

---

[6] C. S. Lewis Institute, *Sparking a Discipleship Movement in America and Beyond,* cslewisinstitute.org, http://www.cslewisinstitute.org/webfm_send/210, Accessed 08/19/2015.

disciples of all nations, baptizing them in the name of the Father and of the Son and of the Holy Spirit, teaching them to observe all that I have commanded you. And behold, I am with you always, to the end of the age" (Matt. 28:19–20).

A large part of Christ's earthly ministry entailed making disciples. During this time, He invested heavily into 12 men. Then, upon leaving, He commanded these men to go into all the world and make disciples.

The Great Commission Mandate given by Christ contains the summation of His purpose for the original disciples and all believers for all time. It would make sense then that the essential components of the discipleship-making process should be fully understood and obeyed. Unfortunately, there appears to be an immense lack of understanding in this vital area, and the gap between the command and implementation is alarmingly wide.

The Role of Discipleship in the Ministry of the Apostles

In addition to Christ's Great Commission Mandate to make disciples, the Apostle Paul sums up his, and the other Apostles' life work with the following statement: "Him we proclaim, warning everyone and teaching everyone with all wisdom that we may **present everyone mature in Christ**. For this I toil, struggling with all his energy that he powerfully works within me" (Col. 1:28–29). This verse highlights the central purpose and work of the Apostles, which was to present every person spiritually mature in Christ.

Because presenting every person mature in Christ would logically incorporate discipleship, and because the Apostles took seriously Christ's command to make disciples, it's safe to say that the summation of the Apostles' work was discipleship as well.

Therefore, in the Great Commission, we see the summation of Christ's work and purpose, and in Colossians 1:28–29 we see the summation of the Apostles' work and purpose, each focusing on

8

discipleship as its central theme. For this reason, the role of discipleship is paramount in the life of every believer and church, if we're going to be serious about becoming spiritually mature.

How Discipleship Is Viewed Today

Unlike the high priority Christ and the Apostles gave to discipleship, and despite Christ's command to be and make disciples, discipleship today is a low priority in the life of most churches and Christians. John Stott affirms this trend by acknowledging, "The state of the church today is marked by a paradox of growth without depth. Our zeal to go wider has not been matched by a commitment to go deeper."[7]

In the majority of churches today, discipleship is not a central focus nor are there clear strategies for making disciples taking place. A recent survey done by Richard J. Krejcir reveals that 81% of pastors have no regular discipleship program or effective effort of mentoring their people to deepen their Christian formation.[8]

Many of these churches seem to have the idea that discipleship isn't that important, or they hope it will somehow be fulfilled through preaching, Sunday School, home Bible studies, and small groups. However, most churchgoers aren't involved in all these activities, and even if they were, most of these activities aren't primarily focused on discipleship. The passion for fulfilling the commandment to make disciples through an intentional, strategic process seems to be lacking in the average Evangelical church today.

When the average churchgoer is asked what the discipleship process should entail, head scratching and bewilderment sets in.

---

[7] Ibid., Accessed 08/19/2015.

[8] Richard J. Krejcir, *Statistics on Pastors: What is Going on with the Pastors in America?* 2007, www.churchleadership.org/apps/articles/default.asp?articleid=42347&columnid=4545, Accessed 08/06/2015.

David Platt shares his concern about Christians today and their understanding of discipleship: "If you ask individual Christians today what it practically means to make disciples, you will likely get jumbled thoughts, ambiguous answers, and probably even some blank stares."[9]

Many believe discipleship is optional or only applies to an elite group of radical Christians. Moreover, for the average churchgoer who does believe discipleship applies to them, most think of it as general growth that takes place through casual church attendance and occasional Scripture reading. It's not thought of as a comprehensive, intentional set of disciplines that must be seriously engaged in for discipleship to occur.

There's even significant debate regarding the essential components of the discipleship-making process among leading theologians. While there has been ample discussion and much written on the topic, there's still significant confusion surrounding what discipleship should involve.

Spiritual Maturity: the Overlooked Elephant in the Room

God's purpose for us in this life is that we would be transformed into the image of Christ: "For those whom he foreknew he also predestined to be **conformed to the image of his Son**, in order that he might be the firstborn among many brothers" (Rom. 8:29). Discipleship is how God transforms us!

Sadly, for most Christians and churches, this is not their focus. As a result, the elephant in the room (what we should be focused on) is neglected and overlooked. While becoming spiritually mature should be a believer's highest goal and priority in life, for the vast majority of Christians, becoming spiritually mature isn't even on their radar screen.

---

[9] David Platt, *Follow Me* (Carol Stream, Tyndale House Publishers, 2013), p. 69.

2. The Lack of Discipleship Today

You would think that the importance of the Great
Commission Mandate to make disciples (Matt. 28:19–20), and the
focus on discipleship by the Apostles as the means to present
every person spiritually mature in Christ (Col. 1:28–29), would
bring to the forefront the importance of discipleship. However,
many adversarial winds are pushing against it, and the church is
in a perilous state of health as a result.

Bill Hull states, "I find it particularly puzzling that we
struggle to put disciple-making at the center of ministry even
though Jesus left us with the clear imperative to 'make
disciples.'"[10] Again, Hull sounds out, "Let's start with the
obvious. Discipleship ranks as God's top priority because Jesus
practiced it and commanded us to do it, and his followers
continued it."[11] However, discipleship is being neglected and
discarded by many today as optional or only for the "radical
believer." As a result, most Christians today are spiritually
immature.

Neglected Warnings

In addition to the importance Christ and the Apostles placed
on discipleship, a number of well-known pastors, authors, and
theologians have sounded the alarm over the years as well.
Unfortunately, their voices seem to be lost in our busy, fast-paced
lifestyles.

Dietrich Bonhoeffer, in his classic work *The Cost of
Discipleship*, strives to help us understand that genuine salvation

---

[10] Bill Hull, *The Complete Book of Discipleship: On Being and Making Followers of Christ*
(The Navigators Reference Library 1, 2014, NavPress, Kindle Edition), Kindle Locations
441-443.
[11] Ibid., Kindle Locations 458-459.

should include discipleship. He states, "Cheap grace is the preaching of forgiveness without requiring repentance, baptism without church discipline, communion without confession, absolution without personal confession. Cheap grace is grace without discipleship, grace without the cross, grace without Jesus Christ, living and incarnate."[12]

Bonhoeffer claims that today we often exchange discipleship with emotional uplifts instead of steadfast adherence to Christ's command regarding discipleship and its role in every believer's life.[13] Bonhoeffer cries out, "If our Christianity has ceased to be serious about discipleship, if we have watered down the gospel into emotional uplift which makes no costly demands and which fails to distinguish between natural and Christian existence, then we cannot help regarding the cross as an ordinary everyday calamity, as one of the trials and tribulations of life."[14]

Dallas Willard makes the lack of discipleship a major theme in two of his books, *The Great Omission* and *The Spirit of the Disciplines*. In *The Spirit of the Disciplines*, Willard claims, "One specific errant concept has done inestimable harm to the church and God's purposes with us—and that is the concept that has restricted the Christian idea of salvation to mere forgiveness of sins."[15] Willard also makes a bold statement regarding the importance of discipleship when he declares, "I believe there is nothing wrong with the church that a clear minded resolute application of discipleship to Jesus Christ would not cure."[16]

Bill Hull has also recently weighed in on the lack of discipleship today and states, "Unfortunately, non-discipleship

---

[12] Dietrich Bonhoeffer, *The Cost of Discipleship* (SCM Classics, Hymns Ancient and Modern Ltd., Kindle Edition, 2011-08-16), Kindle Locations 604-606.
[13] Ibid., Kindle Locations 1265-1267.
[14] Ibid., Kindle Locations 1265-1267.
[15] Dallas Willard, *The Spirit of the Disciplines* (2009-02-06, HarperCollins, Kindle Edition), p. 33.
[16] Dallas Willard, *Transformed by the Renewing of the Mind* (Lecture given at Henry Center for Theological Understanding, 2012), https://youtu.be/jkzeUcnzYbM, Accessed 10/15/2015.

'Christianity' dominates much of the thinking of the contemporary church. In addition to sucking the strength from the church, Christianity without discipleship causes the church to assimilate itself into the culture. And sadly, whenever the difference between the church's and culture's definition of morality ceases to exist, the church loses its power and authority."[17]

Hull goes on to warn, "Many mainline churches depart from orthodoxy because they reject the absolute authority of Scripture. However, many Evangelical churches pose an even more subtle danger by departing from the gospel that calls on all believers to be disciples and follow Christ in obedience."[18]

George Barna is also concerned about the lack of discipleship today. He says, "My study of discipleship in America has been eye-opening. Almost every church in our country has some type of discipleship program or set of activities, but stunningly few churches have a church of disciples. Maybe that is because for many Christians today, including Christian leaders, discipleship is not terribly important. If we can get people to attend worship services, pay for the church's buildings and salaries, and muster positive, loving attitudes toward one another and toward the world, we often feel that's good enough."[19] Barna stresses, "The strength and influence of the church are wholly dependent upon its commitment to true discipleship. Producing transformed lives and seeing those lives reproduced in others is a core challenge to believers and the local church."[20]

Greg Ogden is also troubled by the lack of discipleship today;

---

[17] Bill Hull, *The Complete Book of Discipleship: On Being and Making Followers of Christ* (The Navigators Reference Library 1, 2014, NavPress, Kindle Edition), Kindle Locations 341-344.
[18] Ibid., Kindle Locations 341-344.
[19] George Barna, *Growing True Disciples: New Strategies for Producing Genuine Followers of Christ* (Barna Reports, p. 20, 2013, The Crown Publishing Group, Kindle Edition), p. 18.
[20] Ibid., p. 21.

he says, "If I were to choose one word to summarize the state of discipleship today, that word would be superficial. There appears to be a general lack of comprehension among many who claim Jesus as Savior as to the implications of following him as Lord."[21]

Cal Thomas, a Christian syndicated columnist and social commentator, calls on Christians to look at the quality of our discipleship instead of directing our indignation at the moral decay. He writes, "The problem in our culture isn't the abortionists. It is not the pornographers or drug dealers or criminals. It is the undisciplined, undiscipled, disobedient, and biblically ignorant Church of Jesus Christ."[22]

[21]Greg Ogden, *Transforming Discipleship: Making Disciples a Few at a Time* (2010, InterVarsity Press, Kindle Edition), p. 21.
[22]Ibid., p. 22.

3. The Consequences of Neglecting Discipleship

The level of spiritual maturity among many Christians today is extremely concerning. This is primarily due to the misunderstanding of what discipleship entails and the neglect of an intentional, strategic plan for making disciples. While there are many positive things happening in the church today, there's a grave concern in the area of discipleship. According to recent statistics, the state of the average Christian and Evangelical church of the Western world today is in crises mode and suffering the consequences of neglecting discipleship. Consider the following stats:

- Only 19% of Christians read their Bibles daily or regularly (this means 81% don't read their Bibles daily or regularly).[23]
- About 40% of Evangelical Christians rarely or never read their Bibles.[24]
- Most Christians are biblically illiterate. Fewer than half of all adults can name the four Gospels, and many Christians cannot identify more than two or three of the disciples.[25]
- Atheists, agnostics, and Mormons scored better on biblical literacy than Evangelical Christians (Pew Research).[26]
- Of self-identified Christians, 27% believe Jesus sinned while on earth (Barna).[27]
- 61% of Christians have not shared their faith in the last six

---

[23] Russ Rankin, *Study: Bible Engagement in Churchgoer's Hearts, Not Always Practiced,* Nashville, 2012, http://www.lifeway.com/Article/research-survey-bible-engagement-churchgoers, Accessed 07/23/2015.
[24] Ibid., Accessed 07/23/2015.
[25] Albert Mohler, *The Scandal of Biblical Illiteracy: It's Our Problem,* Christianity.com, http://www.christianity.com/1270946, Accessed 08/18/2015.
[26] C. S. Lewis Institute, *Sparking a Discipleship Movement in America and Beyond,* cslewisinstitute.org, http://www.cslewisinstitute.org/webfm_send/210, Accessed 08/19/2015.
[27] Ibid., Accessed 08/19/2015.

months.[28]

- 48% of Christians have never invited a friend to church.[29]
- Only 25% of church members attend a Bible study or small group at least twice a month.[30]
- The average Christian prays somewhere between 1–7 minutes a day.[31]
- 81% of pastors have no regular discipleship program or effective effort of mentoring their people to deepen their Christian formation.[32]
- 20% of Christians say they rarely or never pray for the spiritual status of others.[33]
- 42% of Christians say they find it difficult to find time on a regular, disciplined basis to pray and read the Bible.[34]
- 18% of Christians say they don't have a fixed pattern of prayer, but only pray when the chance or need arises.[35]
- 60% of Christians pray on the go.[36]

[28] Jon D. Wilke, *Churchgoers Believe in Sharing Faith, Most Never Do,* 2012, Lifeway.com, http://www.lifeway.com/Article/research-survey-sharing-christ-2012, Accessed 08/19/2015.
[29] Ibid., Accessed 08/04/2015.
[30] Richard J. Krejcir, *Statistics on Pastors: What is Going on with the Pastors in America?* 2007, www.churchleadership.org/apps/articles/default.asp?articleid=42347&columnid=4545, Accessed 08/06/2015.
[31] Deborah Beeksma, *The Average Christian Prays a Minute a Day; Prayer by the Faithful Helps Their Relationships,* GodDiscussion.com, 2013, Accessed 07/27/2015. Victory Life Church, VictoryLifeChurch.org, *Intercessory Prayer—Praying Always,* http://www.victorylifechurch.org/pdf/Intercessory_Praying_Always.pdf, Accessed 08/19/2015.
[32] Richard J. Krejcir, *Statistics on Pastors: What is Going on with the Pastors in America?* 2007, www.churchleadership.org/apps/articles/default.asp?articleid=42347&columnid=4545, Accessed 08/06/2015.
[33] Jon D. Wilke, *Churchgoers Believe in Sharing Faith, Most Never Do,* 2012, Lifeway.com, LifeWay Research, http://www.lifeway.com/Article/research-survey-sharing-christ-2012, Accessed 08/19/2015.
[34] Cath Martin, Evangelicals Admit Struggling to Find Time for Daily Bible Reading and Prayer, 2014, Christianity Today, www.christiantoday.com/article/daily.bible.reading.and.prayer.is.a.struggle.for.aany.evangelicals/36765.htm, Accessed 08/18/2015.
[35] Ibid., Accessed 08/19/2015.
[36] Ibid., Accessed 08/19/2015.

- Only 26% of Christians feel they have been equipped by their church to share their faith with others.[37]
- Numerous studies show that self-identified Christians are living lives indistinguishable from non-Christians (Jim Houston).[38]
- Only half of Christians believe in absolute moral truth (Barna).[39]
- 5% of Evangelical Protestants are living with their partner outside of marriage.[40]
- 14% of Evangelical Protestants are divorced or separated.[41]
- 39% of Protestant pastors believe it's okay to get a divorce if a couple no longer loves one another.[42]
- Church discipline, an intensive form of discipleship for believers involved in serious sin, is virtually non-existent.[43]
- Churches today are often growing without depth (John Stott).[44]

Now to be fair, some of these stats fluctuate between various studies, but if they are even remotely accurate, the problem is still alarming. The stats reveal that the spiritual state, as a whole, of Evangelical churches and Christians in the Western world today is

---

[37] Ibid., Accessed 08/19/2015.
[38] C. S. Lewis Institute, *Sparking a Discipleship Movement in America and Beyond,* cslewisinstitute.org, http://www.cslewisinstitute.org/webfm_send/210, Accessed 08/19/2015.
[39] Ibid., Accessed 08/19/2015.
[40] Pew Research Center, *Evangelical Protestant,* Pewforum.org, http://www.pewforum.org/religious-landscape-study/religious-tradition/evangelical-protestant, Accessed 08/19/2015.
[41] Ibid., Accessed 08/19/2015.
[42] LifeWay Research, *Views on Divorce Divide Americans,* 2015, LifeWayResearch.com, http://www.lifewayresearch.com/2015/08/12/views-on-divorce-divide-americans, Accessed 08/19/2015.
[43] R. Albert Mohler Jr, The Disappearance of Church Discipline—How Can We Recover? Part One, 2005, AlbertMohler.com, www.albertmohler.com/2005/05/13/the-disappearance-of-church-discipline-how-can-we-recover-part-one, Accessed 08/20/2015.
[44] C. S. Lewis Institute, *Sparking a Discipleship Movement in America and Beyond,* cslewisinstitute.org, http://www.cslewisinstitute.org/webfm_send/210, Accessed 08/19/2015.

very troublesome and distant from what God intended. Michael Ramsden is disturbed about this and claims, "The American church is dying, not from the lack of evangelism, not from lack of resources, but from lack of effective discipleship."[45]

According to the stats, we're reaping damaging consequences for neglecting discipleship. As a result, most Christians are stuck in their growth in Christ and are failing to reach spiritual maturity. Dennis Hollinger cries out, "I'm convinced that what the world needs is not just more converts, but men and women who are authentic disciples of Christ, who love Christ with their whole being, and who will take their faith into the trenches of every sphere of life."[46]

Some things we can neglect and not adversely affect our spiritual health, but some things are foundational and critical to get right: understanding discipleship and the essential components of the discipleship-making process must be gotten right. Therefore, it's paramount we understand what's negatively affecting our commitment to discipleship. By neglecting discipleship, we reject God's nature and image, choosing instead to retain the image of sin and remain spiritually immature.

We can be certain that if the summation of Christ's and the Apostles' ministries was the command to make disciples, then Satan and his demonic cohort will do all they can to confuse and deter us in the process. We must not let them succeed!

Conclusion to Chapter 1

In this chapter, we analyzed the state of discipleship and spiritual maturity today, concluding that they're in critical condition and being grossly neglected. In the next chapter, we'll investigate 13 key factors contributing to this neglect.

---

[45] Ibid., Accessed 08/19/2015.
[46] Ibid., Accessed 08/19/2015.

Chapter 2

Key Factors Contributing to the Neglect of Discipleship Today

In This Chapter

1. The Distractions and Cares of Life

2. Materialism and the Pursuit of Wealth

3. The Refusal to Pay the Cost of Discipleship

4. The Lack of the Fear of the Lord

5. Being Ashamed of Total Devotion to Christ

6. The Effects of Prosperity Gospel Theology

7. Misunderstanding Heavenly Rewards

8. Misunderstanding the Purpose of Discipleship

9. The Lack of Church Discipline

10. The Belief in Salvation Without Discipleship

11. The Belief in Salvation Without Obedience

12. The Belief in Salvation Without Works

13. The Belief in Grace Without Effort

In chapter 1, we analyzed the state of discipleship and spiritual maturity today, concluding that they're in critical condition and being grossly neglected. In this chapter, we'll investigate 13 key factors contributing to this neglect. This will be a hard-hitting chapter, so prepare yourself to be challenged!

1. The Distractions and Cares of Life

Many Christians today are not devoted disciples of Christ because there are way too many distractions in their lives. They claim they just don't have the time for the level of dedication that discipleship requires. People are busy these days with important things in their lives: work, school, getting ahead, acquiring an attractive home, having nice cars, sports, enjoying the pleasures of life, and so forth. While these things are not necessarily bad in and of themselves, they can be if they are getting in the way of being a devoted disciple of Christ.

Many of these good and important things can also be thorns in our lives that choke out the Word of God and His plans for us. Christ told a story about four kinds of soils (four kinds of responses from people who hear His Word). Upon each soil (heart), fell God's Word, and each heart had a different response:

> And he told them many things in parables, saying: "A sower went out to sow. And as he sowed, some seeds fell along the path, and the birds came and devoured them. Other seeds fell on rocky ground, where they did not have much soil, and immediately they sprang up, since they had no depth of soil, but when the sun rose they were scorched. And since they had no root, they withered away. **Other seeds fell among thorns, and the thorns grew up and choked them**. Other seeds fell on good soil and produced grain,

20

some a hundredfold, some sixty, some thirty. He who has ears, let him hear" (Matt. 13:3–9).

A few verses later, Christ clarifies that the thorny soil represents the cares of this life that choke out the Word of God: "As for what was sown among thorns, this is the one who hears the word, **but the cares of the world and the deceitfulness of riches choke the word, and it proves unfruitful**" (Matt. 13:22).

Notice that the seed (the Word of God) which fell among the rocky ground and thorny ground did show life for a while, but then died out. Only the last soil produced fruit. Notice too, that for those who did produce fruit, some produced less than 100%. It's very likely that even among the good soil (lives of committed believers), the reason they only produced 30% or 60% was due to the thorns (distractions) in their lives that inhibited their fruitfulness.

This parable reveals the importance of God's Word as the key to fruitfulness in a Christian's life. However, many Christians are too busy to read it because of busyness. We should take a serious inventory of the distractions in our lives that are choking out God's Word and causing us to produce little or no fruit and eliminate them.

Today, We Have Unprecedented Distractions Pulling Us Away from Christ

In our age, we have a record amount of options facing us. Gone are the days when life was simpler, less tangled, and had fewer details and problems. We're now faced with countless impulses and stimuli from things like sports, social media, texting, phone calls, emails, Internet, TV, magazines, billboards, friends, work, entertainment, and on and on. People have a hard time focusing on God because they are "on" and connected all the time.

Television alone has revolutionized the Western world in staggering ways. Here are recent statistics on how much the average person in the U.S. watches TV:[47]

- Average time spent watching television per day ~ 5 hours and 11 minutes
- Years the average person will have spent watching TV in their lifetime ~ 9 years
- Percentage of U.S. homes with three or more TV sets ~ 65%
- Number of minutes per week the average child watches TV ~ 1,480 (24.66 hours)
- Percentage of Americans that regularly watch TV while eating dinner ~ 67%
- Hours per year the average American youth watches TV ~ 1,200
- Number of violent acts seen on TV by age 18 ~ 150,000
- Number of 30 second TV commercials seen in a year by an average child ~ 16,000

In addition to TV, we have countless other distractions in our lives. Many of these things are not wrong in and of themselves; it's just that we allow them into our lives in an excessive amount so that they choke out discipleship and fruitfulness. Consider the following items:

- Work
- Wealth
- Large homes
- Nice cars
- Possessions
- Hobbies
- Entertainment
- Facebook
- Social Media
- Internet
- Pleasure
- School & excessive homework
- Retirement
- Sports

---

[47] Statistic Brain Research Institute, *Television Watching Statistics*, 2015, www.statisticbrain.com/television-watching-statistics, Accessed 08/07/2015.

These, among others not listed, can take us away from our priority in life of being disciples of Christ. They are activities that can choke out God's Word and thus become thorns. They are choices we make that result in "saving our lives" instead of losing them for Christ.

It's obvious, according to the statistics, that we have time for the activities we love, but often don't make time for discipleship. The problem is that we're making soft choices. We're saying yes to the thorns and cares of this world instead of saying yes to Christ and discipleship.

Now it should be mentioned that "losing our lives" is where we find true life. The thorns are what actually rob our attention from laying up treasures in heaven. They are things that distract us from eternal rewards and cause us to focus on temporal pleasures instead.

By utilizing just a portion of time many Christians spend on activities like TV, sports, hobbies, entertainment, and social media, they could easily take Bible courses or get an online Bible degree. This would position them to be much more fruitful for Christ, which would result in storing up riches in heaven instead of on earth. Instead of frittering away their lives, they could invest them in eternal matters.

If we're wise, we'll say no to the thorns (distractions) of this life and say yes to losing our lives for Christ. If we do so, we'll not only find our lives in this life, but in the one to come as well. You see, happiness is a byproduct of serving and pleasing God. If we make happiness our primary goal, we'll never be happy because we'll be "saving our lives." However, if we lose them for Christ, then He will add joy to our lives despite the suffering, persecution, and trials we may endure for His sake.

Happiness and Entertainment: the Gods of the 21st Century

Many Christians today need to make some radical changes to

their lifestyles and priorities in order to be obedient disciples of Christ. The lofty place they give to pleasure and entertainment is crippling them. Many are not engaged in serious discipleship because they are distracted by the pleasures of life. The gods of our day are happiness and entertainment, and many Christians are lost in the pursuit of them. If it's not fun, thrilling, and exciting, they want no part of it.

It's almost become standard procedure today that everything we do must first be run through the filter of pleasure and convenience or we want no part of it. Many would even try to run discipleship through this same filter. They ask themselves, "How can we make it fun, exciting, attractive, thrilling, entertaining, and convenient?"

It's just not realistic to think we can make the cost of discipleship that involves denying yourself, taking up your cross, losing your life, dying to self, hating your life, and being persecuted for Christ convenient and entertaining. I fear we've become "lovers of pleasure rather than lovers of God," and we're trying to import our fun and entertainment syndrome into the discipleship-making process.

Happiness and Obedience

Some Christians even think it's okay to disobey certain commands of Scripture as long as it makes a person happy. They view happiness as supreme. They believe God wants us to be happy, so even if our lifestyles don't quite harmonize with Scripture, it's okay to disobey because God will forgive. They've bought into the lie that God's primary goal for us is happiness. This should be of no surprise as the message many pastors preach today is a continual focus on the blessings of God while neglecting the cost of following Him.

Today, the scales are so tilted towards happiness that many believe it's their Christian right. They fail to understand that God hasn't called us to be happy and entertained, but devoted and fruitful. God wants to replace our pursuit of happiness and pleasure with genuine joy and purpose. He wants us to lose our lives for Him so we can find them.

Entertainment and Spiritual Battles

Many Christians are ignorant of the spiritual battles being waged in high places because following the news and keeping up with current events is not fun or entertaining. They are blind to what's happening in the spiritual realm of the political arena and how it's affecting the moral fabric of our culture. They are unaware of the currents of philosophy spoken of in the last days and the dangers of the Great Apostasy. Many don't keep up on the news, don't vote, don't care, and have basically "checked out" regarding most things that aren't fun or thrilling.

Entertainment and the Last Days

Life for many Christians is primarily about entertainment, thrill, and having a good time, and if it's not, they have no interest. Essential godly character like self-discipline, responsibility, hard work, patience, endurance, suffering, faithfulness, and service are lacking in the lives of many. We're living in the last days as described in 2 Timothy 3:1–5:

> But understand this, that in the last days there will come times of difficulty. For people will be **lovers of self, lovers of money**, proud, arrogant, abusive, disobedient to their parents, ungrateful, unholy, heartless, unappeasable, slanderous, without self-control, brutal, not loving good, treacherous, reckless, swollen with conceit, **lovers of pleasure rather than lovers of God**, having the appearance of godliness, but denying its power. Avoid such people.

> This pretty well sums up our culture today, and

25

unfortunately, it's affecting the lives of Christians as well. Many believers are "lovers of pleasure rather than lovers of God."

We must understand that discipleship is not necessarily fun. Denying yourself is not a great thrill. Taking up your cross is not that exciting. Losing your life for the cause of Christ is not the latest fad. Suffering family division because of Christ is painful. Being ridiculed by society for holding to biblical truth is hard. Training yourself in godliness is not popular. Exercising self-discipline for the purpose of discipleship takes patience and fortitude. Not following the winds of modern day morality is challenging. Reading the Bible instead of watching TV takes self-discipline. Praying requires commitment and patience, and losing friends because of Christ is lonely.

However, these challenges are the core principles of discipleship that bring deep, genuine joy and eternal rewards in heaven. Those who are wise will choose the eternal riches over the fleeting pleasures of our day. They will be like Moses who, "When he was grown up, refused to be called the son of Pharaoh's daughter, choosing rather to be mistreated with the people of God than to **enjoy the fleeting pleasures of sin**" (Heb. 11:24–25).

Entertainment and the Church

In many churches today, there's a strong focus on entertainment. They ask how the music, preaching, adult, youth, and children's ministries can be entertaining so people will attend.

I am all for making church as attractive and professional as possible, but I don't think we should alter our message or promote the concept that "if it's not fun and exciting, we don't do it." Church is not a theater, a club, a sports activity, or a show where the goal is to entertain. Its purpose is to glorify God through preaching His Word, making disciples, and worshipping Him in Spirit and truth.

I don't believe we should get caught up in the entertainment trap. Attempting to eliminate the reality that discipleship is costly and inconvenient is deceitful. We need to be careful we don't join in the modern day belief that following Christ is supposed to be entertaining. If we build on this flawed foundation, we'll produce weak followers who will be the first to bail when they encounter any hardship.

Some churches are trying to satisfy the culture's appetite for entertainment and are incorporating a high dose of amusement into their church services to draw a crowd. They make sermons humorous, entertaining, upbeat, lighthearted, and short. What kind of disciples are these churches producing, and are they subtlety teaching their followers to "save their lives" instead of losing them?

Modern Day Conveniences and Discipleship

We live in an unparalleled time in the history of mankind. Advancements in technology have given us every modern convenience under the sun. While there are positives to these advancements, there are negatives as well. On the downside, in our effort to make life easier, we've become a soft and tender society. Toughness, suffering, hard work, endurance, self-discipline, and perseverance are lacking commodities.

My folks are from the Great Plain States of Nebraska and South Dakota. They grew up without electricity, indoor bathrooms, and running water in their homes. They had to walk or ride a horse to school, had no air conditioning during the hot, blistering summers, and didn't have heating throughout their uninsulated homes during the sub-zero winters. My mother tells of how she took a heated rock to bed at night to stay warm and milked 26 cows before and after school. My father was extremely poor, worked hard, and was raised on side pork (the trash meat from pigs). He milked several cows twice daily and rode a horse 10 miles to school. My parents were tough, rugged, disciplined, hardworking folks who knew how to suffer and endure hardship, and it was the same for many others in their day as well.

Discipleship Is Not Convenient

I fear that a great negative of our modern day conveniences is that we've become spoiled, soft, and tender. We know little about suffering hardship and going without. Today, if we have an inconvenience in our lives, we buy something to fix it or take a pill to make us feel better. We're not tough soldiers for Christ, but generally delicate and weak.

About the only thing left today that requires much hardship in life is sports. Other than that, almost everything else is convenient and easy. Unfortunately, the side effects of our conveniences are producing a soft and fragile society.

I believe our modern conveniences are also affecting our Christian lives. We don't like to be inconvenienced. We like instant gratification, ease, fun, and entertainment. Without realizing how much we've become products of our culture, deep within our subconscious mind is the belief that if something is hard we need to find a way to alleviate it.

Unlike what many would like, this attitude doesn't apply to discipleship and the Christian life. There's a cost to discipleship, and it's not convenient! It takes self-discipline, commitment, toughness, endurance, patience, and long-suffering. There's no modern convenience that can make discipleship easy. We can't throw disciples in the microwave for a few minutes and pop out mature believers. Spiritual maturity had a cost during the time of Christ, and it has a cost today. It has never been, and it will never be, convenient!

Busyness: an Enemy of Discipleship

People's lives are extremely occupied with countless activities and stimuli each day. In fact, many are addicted to it, and it has

28

become their god. Cath Martin reveals that, because of our modern day busyness, many Christians are even trying to sustain their relationships with God while on the move: "In the face of busy lives, many evangelicals are doing faith 'on the go' and utilizing digital media to help them maintain their spiritual lives. A third of these busy Christians now use Bible apps, with daily devotional apps and the Book of Common Prayer app among the popular choices."[48]

Many Christians say they don't have time for discipleship because they're too busy, yet they have plenty of time for all their other activities. Why is this so? The stats show that it's because many Christians are saying no to Christ and discipleship and are saying yes to their own desires and plans. Putting God first is sacrificed or eliminated, while other activities are kept intact and prioritized.

Adding to all of the pleasure-oriented stimuli available to us today is the pursuit of wealth, power, and prestige that we believe bring pleasure and happiness. In many households, both father and mother are working long hours in order to have large homes, nice cars, good retirement, vacations, and a host of other pleasures money can bring. The time in which we live is marked by busyness and the motto of our day is activity.

Even though spending time with God and His Word is critical for growth in Christ, busyness distracts many away. A recent Barna Group survey reveals this startling fact: "Like all other forms of analog media, the Bible is pushed to the side in part because people are just too busy. Among those who say their Bible reading decreased in the last year, the number one reason was busyness: 40% report being too busy with life's

---

[48] Cath Martin, *Evangelicals Admit Struggling to Find Time for Daily Bible Reading and Prayer*, 2014, Christianity Today, www.christiantoday.com/article/daily.bible.reading.and.prayer.is.a.struggle.for.many.evangel icals/36765.htm, Accessed 08/18/2015.

responsibilities (job, family, etc.), an increase of seven points from just one year ago."[49]

Boredom Is at an All-Time High

Despite all our busyness and activity, boredom is at an all-time high. Why is this so? Why do children, students, and adults feel unsatisfied today? If busyness and pleasure bring happiness, why is boredom plaguing many today? It's because God made us to serve Him and not ourselves. Until we understand this, we can gain the whole world and all its pleasures, but still be empty.

Distractions in the Formative Years

As a former youth pastor, I remember the difficulty I had with some of my students. It was a struggle getting them to youth group, to church, and to discipleship activities because they just didn't have the time. They were too busy with school, sports, and jobs. Youth group and discipleship were in competition with their other pursuits, and unfortunately, most of the time the spiritual activities lost out. Growth in Christ and discipleship just weren't as high a priority. The good things in their lives were in the way. And sadly, most of their parents supported them and made schooling, sports, and jobs a priority for them over youth group and discipleship.

I often felt like I was fighting a losing battle and was grieved by their lack of growth. I've been able to trace the lives of many of these youth over the past 30 or so years, and today, many of them who made God and discipleship a low priority have paid a heavy price. Some no longer even walk with the Lord. The eternal consequences of the busyness in their lives have been, and will always be, an enormous cost to them.

---

[49] Barna Group, *The State of the Bible: 6 Trends for 2014,* 2014, https://www.barna.org/barna-update/culture/664-the-state-of-the-bible-6-trends-for-2014#.VdNGKTZRGUk, Accessed 08/18/2015.

In order to grab their attention, I often threatened to give these students a spiritual grade—a grade like they received in school for classes they attended. After all, they earned grades in school for how well they performed. What if I gave them a spiritual grade to help them see how well they were doing spiritually? Unfortunately, many would have flunked out.

Today, the average student spends around 7–8 hours in school a day, an hour or two on homework, an hour or two on extracurricular activities like sports, and then some have jobs on top of it all. And of course, we can't leave out TV, video games, and social media. When do they have time for God? Their lives are so stuffed full of other activities that being a disciple of Christ is shoved to the wayside.

The average person will spend a year or so in kindergarten, 12 years in primary and secondary education, and four years in college. During these years, the amount of time spent learning about earthly knowledge is astronomical. However, the time spent learning about biblical knowledge is minuscule and scarcely measurable in comparison. We've elevated secular knowledge to such a high degree that we feel justified in sacrificing eternal knowledge on its altar.

I believe God is in favor of us being responsible in school, but I can't help but think He's more concerned that we acquire eternal knowledge so we can build our lives on a solid foundation, and not on sand.

Building Upside Down

In biblical times, secular knowledge was built upon the foundation of Scripture. Critical factors like character, honesty, respect, self-discipline, diligence, hard work, and responsibility formed the foundation upon which secular knowledge rested.

Today, we have it backward. We make secular knowledge the foundation of life and demote eternal, biblical knowledge as subservient. In other words, we build biblical knowledge on the foundation of secular knowledge instead of building secular knowledge on the foundation of biblical knowledge. We give secular knowledge priority and, if we have time, squeeze in a little Bible knowledge.

For example, how many parents "stress out" if their children don't spend time studying their Bible like they do if they don't spend time doing their homework? Most parents are responsible regarding their children's secular knowledge, but irresponsible regarding their children's biblical knowledge! We're doing just the opposite of the biblical model and then wonder why our sons and daughters aren't serious about their relationships with Christ. We wonder why, according to Rainer Research, "approximately 70% of American youth drop out of church between the age of 18 and 22."[50] Moreover, the Barna Group estimates that "80% of those reared in the church will be 'disengaged' by the time they are 29."[51]

Our priorities are backward, and we're paying a high price. By elevating secular knowledge over biblical knowledge and discipleship, many parents are participating in damaging their children's spiritual future, which will have consequences, not only in this life, but in eternity as well.

Today, we're building on a shallow foundation. Many are building their houses on the sand. The state of the family is in disarray, our lives are harried and scarred, we're busy going every direction under the sun, and much of the free time we do have is spent on pleasure and entertainment. I'm afraid the average Christian today is falling far short of what Christ calls us to be.

Many are more concerned about their careers than Christ;

---

[50] Drew Dyck, *The Leavers: Young Doubters Exit the Church,* 2010, ChristianityToday.com, www.christianitytoday.com/ct/2010/november/27.40.html, Accessed 09/28/2015.
[51] Ibid., Accessed 09/28/2015.

more concerned about their earthly home than their eternal home; more concerned about sports activities than godly activities; more concerned about secular knowledge than Biblical knowledge; more concerned about their physical condition than their spiritual condition; and more concerned about their present life than their eternal life.

Getting Rid of Unnecessary Weights

Many Christians today need to lighten up! They have too many activities — even good ones — in their lives that are distracting them away from discipleship. Scripture calls these activities "weights." It says, "Therefore, since we are surrounded by so great a cloud of witnesses, let us also lay aside every **weight**, and sin which clings so closely, and let us run with endurance the race that is set before us" (Heb. 12:1).

In this verse, two things can deter us from our commitment to discipleship: sin and weights. Weights refer to the activities in life that are not bad but take away our time. God wants us to slim down in these areas so we can have more time for discipleship and attaining spiritual maturity.

When we give priority to the "weights" in our lives, we have less time to give God our best. As a result, we wind up giving God our leftovers: leftover time, leftover energy, and leftover service. When Christ called the original disciples, He didn't call them to give Him their leftovers. Today, Christ doesn't call us to give Him our leftovers either. He calls us to put Him first and give Him our best.

Distractions and Discipleship

In 1 Corinthians 7, God reveals how He feels about all the distractions in life that take us away from Him and discipleship:

But I want you to be free from concern. One who is

unmarried is concerned about the things of the Lord, how he may please the Lord; but one who is married is concerned about the things of the world, how he may please his wife, and his interests are divided . . . This I say for your own benefit; not to put a restraint upon you, but to promote what is appropriate and to **secure undistracted devotion to the Lord** (1 Cor. 7:32–35, NASB).

In this passage, the Apostle Paul is promoting the benefits of singleness. While he clearly states in the context that marriage is honorable and desirable, he also highlights how God feels about the distractions of life that can draw us away from Him.

Christ gave a warning as well about the distractions of life that would affect many in the last days: "But watch yourselves lest your hearts be weighed down with dissipation and drunkenness and **cares of this life**, and that day come upon you suddenly like a trap" (Luke 21:34).

God desires that we might be free from the distractions and concerns of the world so we can focus more fully on Him and discipleship. I wonder how He feels about us today?

Conclusion

Never in the history of any civilization have there been so many stimuli and activities available. How is this affecting Christians and discipleship? It's reeking catastrophic consequences according to the state of the average Christian today.

My mother made a wise statement about time management many years ago, saying, "We always have time for what's important to us." I believe she's right! It's not that we don't have time; it's that our priorities are out of line. We're so caught up in the distractions of our current age that we don't take time for Christ and discipleship.

2. Materialism and the Pursuit of Wealth

In Christ's call to discipleship, He exposes a trap that hinders many Christians from being fully devoted disciples of Christ and reaching spiritual maturity. They are being sucked into the deception that materialism, pleasure, and prestige are the true riches of life, not discipleship and living for Christ.

The fact that 81% of Christians don't regularly read their Bibles, 61% of believers have not shared their faith in the last six months, and the average Christian prays between 1-7 minutes a day reveals that many Christians are lost in materialism and neglecting discipleship.

Many believers are invested so heavily in this life that they're blind to eternity. They are working so hard to have a pleasant and enjoyable life now that spiritual maturity and the things of God are neglected. They have the eye impediment of shortsightedness. In our unprecedented age of materialism and consumerism, we're more susceptible than ever to this danger.

In Christ's call to follow Him, He bluntly states that materialism is an enemy of discipleship. We must choose one or the other, for no one can serve two masters (Matt. 6:24).

Following Christ means He has complete priority over our pursuit of materialism and pleasure. It means He is number one in our life, and not just in theory, but in reality. However, if we choose materialism over Christ, we might enjoy this life now, but will lose many of our rewards in heaven and fall into countless temptations and snares in the meantime.

Most Christians would strongly argue that their possessions aren't more important than God. However, the time they spend devoted to them reveals just the opposite.

Physical possessions are nothing more than what allows us to exist, and our purpose for existing is to know God and attain spiritual maturity, not getting lost in materialism. If our possessions become more important than God, then they are out of balance and can become our modern day idols.

Loving the World More Than God

We live in wonderful times with abundant luxuries and blessings. However, many are lost in the blessings and love this world too much. We need to heed God's warning: "Do not love the world or the things in the world. If anyone loves the world, the love of the Father is not in him. For all that is in the world — the desires of the flesh and the desires of the eyes and pride of life — is not from the Father but is from the world. And the world is passing away along with its desires, but whoever does the will of God abides forever" (1 John 2:15-17).

While our earthly activities aren't wrong in and of themselves, they can be if we're so occupied with them that we don't have time for following Christ and discipleship. If we're so absorbed in worldly activities that we have little time for eternal matters, then we love this world more than we should.

God loves to bless us and richly provides us with everything to enjoy (1 Tim. 6:17). However, if we focus more on the blessings of God rather than on God Himself, then it indicates we love the blessings more than God. We can become guilty of worshipping the idols of wealth, fame, and pleasure instead of God. As a result, we fail to be rich toward God and invest in our eternal home. We might be rich in earthly possessions but poor in heavenly riches.

Many Christians today are poor spiritually. They are like the lukewarm Christians in the church of Laodicea: "For you say, I am rich, I have prospered, and I need nothing, not realizing that you are wretched, pitiable, poor, blind, and naked" (Rev. 3:17). Many Christians are blind to their spiritual poverty, having no idea of their condition before God and of their possible loss of eternal rewards in heaven. Their eyes are locked on this world and are honed in on storing up their treasures here. As a result, they are poor and naked but don't know it.

The Cost of Materialism

Christ told a parable that perfectly illustrates the foolishness of being so absorbed in materialism and the pleasures of this life that eternal riches are neglected:

> And he said to them, "Take care, and be on your guard against all covetousness, for one's life does not consist in the abundance of his possessions." And he told them a parable, saying, "The land of a rich man produced plentifully, and he thought to himself, 'What shall I do, for I have nowhere to store my crops?' And he said, 'I will do this: I will tear down my barns and build larger ones, and there I will store all my grain and my goods. And I will say to my soul, 'Soul, you have ample goods laid up for many years; relax, eat, drink, be merry.' But God said to him, 'Fool! This night your soul is required of you, and the things you have prepared, whose will they be?' So is the one who lays up treasure for himself and is not rich toward God" (Luke 12:15–21).

This rich man had it all. He worked hard to have a good life. In fact, he worked so hard that he reached the point of retirement where he thought it was time to reap the rewards of his labor. He said to himself, "Soul, you have ample goods laid up for many years; relax, eat, drink, and be merry."

His desire is really the inner desire of us all. We long for the time when we can kick back, relax, eat, drink, and be merry.

In our Western culture, retirement is elevated as the time to eat, drink, and be merry. We're told to work hard so we can "kick back" and enjoy life during retirement. We need to be careful not to buy into our culture's message and neglect serving God in our latter years, or we might end up being fools like the rich man.

Those in retirement have the most wisdom, time, and experience to offer, yet many are eating, drinking, and being merry instead of serving God.

Modern Day Fools

Christ calls those who focus primarily on this life and aren't rich toward God, "Fools"! They work hard at acquiring a good life; they get a large house, nice cars, a good job, a good education, and gain recognition and status before others. However, they are poor in the eyes of God and will pay the consequences for all eternity. They give more importance to this life than heaven. Their aim is to accumulate money, influence, recognition, and happiness. They believe, as the rich man, that these are the true riches of life, but Jesus says to those who pursue them and neglect serving God, "You fool"!

The unbelievable oversight of this rich man was that he was so invested in this life that he completely overlooked eternity. He was like a story told by Steven Cole:

> In 1981, a man was flown into the remote Alaskan wilderness to photograph the natural beauty of the tundra. He had photo equipment, 500 rolls of film, several firearms, and 1,400 pounds of provisions. As the months passed, the entries in his diary, which at first detailed the wonder and fascination with the wildlife around him, turned into a pathetic record of a nightmare. In August, he wrote, "I think I should have used more foresight about arranging my departure. I'll soon find out." He waited and waited, but no one came to his rescue. In November, he died in a nameless valley, by a nameless lake, 225 miles northeast of Fairbanks. An investigation revealed that he had carefully provided for his adventure, but he had

made no provision to be flown out of the area.[52]

What a tragedy! This man prepared for everything but his departure. His story applies to many Christians today. We're so focused on this life that we forget to plan for our departure. We're not focused on eternity, but on our jobs, education, homes, cars, hobbies, sports, pleasures, activities, TV, Internet, Facebook, and on and on. We have time for all these activities, but don't have much time for reading our Bibles, serving the Lord, leading Bible studies, being Sunday School teachers, sharing Christ, developing our gifts and abilities, and deepening our knowledge of God.

Getting Our Priorities Right

Many believers are doing the same as the rich man and are neglecting the call of discipleship because they'd rather eat, drink, and be merry. They prefer enjoying the pleasures of life rather than pursuing spiritual maturity. For this reason, Christ told us not to worry or be so engrossed in materialism and the pleasures of this life that we neglect His eternal kingdom:

> Therefore, I tell you, **do not be anxious about your life**, what you will eat or what you will drink, nor about your body, what you will put on. Is not life more than food, and the body more than clothing? Look at the birds of the air: they neither sow nor reap nor gather into barns, and yet your heavenly Father feeds them. Are you not of more value than they? And which of you by being anxious can add a single hour to his span of life? And why are you anxious about clothing? Consider the lilies of the field, how they grow: they neither toil nor spin, yet I tell you, even Solomon in all his glory was

---

[52] Steven J. Cole, *Why You Should Hate Your Life.* Bible.org. 2014, bible.org/seriespage/lesson-67-why-you-should-hate-your-life-john-1224-26, Accessed 08/11/2015.

not arrayed like one of these. But if God so clothes the grass of the field, which today is alive and tomorrow is thrown into the oven, will he not much more clothe you, O you of little faith? Therefore, **do not be anxious**, saying, "What shall we eat?" or "What shall we drink?" or "What shall we wear?" For the Gentiles seek after all these things, and your heavenly Father knows that you need them all. But **seek first the kingdom of God** and his righteousness, and all these things will be added to you (Matt. 6:25–34).

Notice that Christ doesn't say that earning a living and working hard are wrong. In fact, the Book of Proverbs is loaded with verses that speak of being responsible and hard working. Also, the Apostle Paul says, "For even when we were with you, we would give you this command: If anyone is not willing to work, let him not eat" (2 Thess. 3:10). Moreover, Paul includes, "But if anyone does not provide for his relatives, and especially for members of his household, he has denied the faith and is worse than an unbeliever" (1 Tim. 5:8).

God expects us to be responsible, diligent, and hardworking in providing for our families, and if we don't, we are worse than unbelievers. However, Christ's call to "Seek first the Kingdom of God" is not in conflict with working hard and providing for our families. What God is against is the excessive pursuit of materialism that causes us to neglect being fully devoted disciples of Christ. We can be responsible and seek first the Kingdom of God at the same time.

We are commanded to give the Kingdom of God our highest priority. For Christians who make materialism their priority instead of being disciples of Christ, they'll miss out on the life God intended now and have few rewards in heaven.

Are We Too Involved in Materialism and Pleasure?

How do we know if we're too involved in materialism? Here's a simple answer: if we don't have time to read and study our Bibles, don't have time to pray, don't have time to evangelize and make disciples, don't have time to develop our gifts, don't have time to deepen our knowledge of God, don't have time to serve God and others, don't have time to faithfully attend church, then we're too busy with the affairs of this life and are not seeking first the Kingdom of God.

Preoccupation with this life is robbing many of the priority of discipleship and the treasures it brings.

Consumerism and Our Modern Day Culture

The day in which we live is unlike any other time in history. We're called consumers and for good reason. Virtually every advertisement we hear, every commercial we see, every billboard we drive by, every magazine we pick up, and every newspaper we read is screaming at us to buy their stuff. We're told that without their products we're unhappy, but with them, the happiness we've always longed for can be ours. We're told by friends, acquaintances, and the world that happiness is found in possessions.

Our society is drowning in a sea of materialism, but most can't see the danger. From early childhood we're indoctrinated in the belief that earthly possessions bring happiness, so we get on board the train early and ride it till death—never realizing that there's a life much richer, much deeper, with more purpose and meaning, and with the promise of eternal rewards. It's called the life of discipleship and is God's best.

Only What's Done for Christ Will Last

Being a disciple is where true life and meaning reside. It's our life's calling and the highest purpose to which we can give ourselves. It's the vehicle through which life and spiritual maturity are attained. However, it has a cost, and the cost is seeking first God's Kingdom.

Seeking God's Kingdom first means that we put God as the highest priority in our lives. It means we are fruitful and productive in His Kingdom, not absorbed and lost in acquiring worldly possessions. Because materialism is an enemy of discipleship, God warns of its danger:

> But godliness with contentment is great gain, for we brought nothing into the world, and we cannot take anything out of the world. But if we have food and clothing, with these we will be content. But those who desire to be rich fall into temptation, into a snare, into many senseless and harmful desires that plunge people into ruin and destruction. For the love of money is a root of all kinds of evils. **It is through this craving that some have wandered away from the faith and pierced themselves with many pangs** (1 Tim. 6:6–10).

The only thing we're going to take out of this life is our works and service for Christ. As a stanza from the popular poem by C. T. Studd says:

> Only one life, yes only one,
> Soon will its fleeting hours be done;
> Then, in "that day" my Lord to meet,
> And stand before His Judgement Seat;
> Only one life, twill soon be past,
> Only what's done for Christ will last.[53]

If we're rich in good works for Christ, faithful as His disciples, committed to the priority of seeking His Kingdom first,

---

[53] C. T. Studd, *Only One Life Twill Soon Be Past,* http://hockleys.org/2009/05/quote-only-one-life-twill-soon-be-past-poem, Accessed 08/27/2015.

and devoted to serving Him no matter the cost, then we will be rewarded richly in heaven. But if we're lazy servants who are neglecting these commitments, then we'll suffer loss and have few or no rewards. We will have spent our lives lost in materialism and blind to eternity's riches, choosing a few fleeting years of pleasure at the expense of endless, eternal rewards in heaven.

Conclusion

The lure of the world and materialism is calling at every corner, countless voices all singing the same song. All are drawing our attention to the pleasures of this life and dulling God's voice that calls us to follow Him and store our riches in heaven. The wise person will listen to God's voice and choose the eternal riches over the temporal. Unfortunately, many won't.

Sadly, many Christians are being deceived by materialism and believe it will fulfill the deep longings of their souls. Instead, God tells us that joy and purpose are found in our commitment to discipleship and following Him.

We're consumers! Consumers of materialism, consumers of pleasure, and consumers of entertainment. Unfortunately, many Christians aren't consumers of God's Word or seriously involved in discipleship. Materialism and the pursuit of wealth are weeds choking out discipleship in our lives today, and most don't realize the severity of the problem. In fact, we're so busy we don't even know there is a problem!

3. The Refusal to Pay the Cost of Discipleship

In today's world, everyone wants a bargain. The cost of living drives us to be discount consumers. We're trained early in life to cut costs, be frugal, look for the best deal, and stretch our money.

We also look for the easiest and most efficient way to accomplish tasks. In fact, virtually all inventions have been born out of the desire to reduce work and make life easier. This mentality works fine in the physical realm but creates havoc in the spiritual realm.

It's great to enjoy the blessings of modern technology in our physical lives, but this same desire for ease can be a curse in our spiritual lives. Christ clearly highlighted the cost of discipleship, and there's no modern invention to make it easier. There's only one way to spiritual maturity, and it's by paying the cost of discipleship.

Christians Today and the Cost of Discipleship

In 1937, Dietrich Bonhoeffer produced a classic book called *The Cost of Discipleship*. In it, he addressed those within Christianity that he felt embraced "easy Christianity" or "cheap grace" in the Western world. Even in Bonhoeffer's day, he felt many Christians were neglecting discipleship and seeking a bargain spiritually. They wanted spiritual maturity without discipleship, heavenly rewards without serving, salvation without obedience, and the blessings of God without submission to Him.[54]

Today, not much has changed. The reason many Christians don't embrace discipleship is because they frankly don't want to pay the price. For them, the cost of spiritual maturity is too high.

---

[54] Dietrich Bonhoeffer, 2011-08-16, *The Cost of Discipleship*, SCM Classics Hymns Ancient and Modern Ltd. Kindle Edition.

They'd rather watch TV, play video games, spend time on their electronic devices, and do something fun rather than invest in discipleship. Scripture would define them as lazy servants who are lovers of pleasure rather than lovers of God (2 Tim. 3:4).

Many Christians Today Are Spiritually Lazy

Christ told a parable about spiritual laziness to show its devastating effects on our lives. In the Parable of the Talents, Christ gave talents to three different servants, and then called each into account for how they used them. Two of the servants used their talents wisely and were rewarded. However, one servant didn't use his talent but wasted it. To this servant, Christ said, **"You wicked and lazy servant!"** (Matt. 25:26, NKJV). Christ expects us to use our talents in serving Him, and He'll call us into account at the end of our lives for how we did. Christ called the servant who didn't use his talents "wicked and lazy," making it very clear how He feels about laziness.

The talents Christ gives us represent our time, abilities, resources, money, spiritual gifts, knowledge of God, skills, and so on. Unfortunately, many Christians waste much of their time on pleasure instead of developing and using their talents. They are highly adept at mastering video games, are extremely knowledgeable about TV and movies, are sports buffs and up to date with the latest fads and viral videos. However, they are not adept with God's Word, are unskillful in using their spiritual gifts, and uninvolved in ministry.

It's easy in our day to succumb to spiritual laziness and not be engaged in discipleship as Christ commanded. Laziness is destructive to discipleship and brings with it a high price in this life, and an even higher price in eternity.

Many Christians Are Undisciplined

Christians today, by and large, are undisciplined. Most know what they should do, but don't have the self-discipline to do it. The word "disciple" is related to the root word "discipline." Therefore, a believer must possess self-discipline in order to be a disciple.

Dallas Willard claims, "Full participation in the life of God's Kingdom and in the vivid companionship of Christ comes to us only through appropriate exercise in the disciplines for life in the spirit."[55] And Bill Hull sums up the thinking of many when he says, "Most of us want to reap the harvest of discipline while living a life of relative sloth."[56]

Spiritual maturity is unattainable without self-discipline. Therefore, if we expect to get anywhere in the Christian life and be the kind of disciples Christ calls us to be, we must begin by building discipline into our lives. We need to heed God's counsel in 1 Timothy 4:7-8: "Rather **train yourself for godliness**; for while bodily training is of some value, godliness is of value in every way, as it holds promise for the present life and also for the life to come."

The Cost of Non-Discipleship

For those unwilling to pay the cost of discipleship, they might feel they are getting a bargain by taking the easy road, but in the end, they'll pay a higher price for non-discipleship than discipleship. Dallas Willard claims, "The cost of non-discipleship is far greater — even when this life alone is considered — than the price paid to walk with Jesus, constantly learning from Him."[57]

Willard continues, "Non-discipleship may very well cost a Christian such things as abiding peace, a life penetrated throughout by love, faith that sees everything in the light of God's

---

[55] Dallas Willard, 2009, *The Spirit of the Disciplines* (HarperCollins, Kindle Edition), p. 26.
[56] Bill Hull, *The Complete Book of Discipleship: On Being and Making Followers of Christ* (The Navigators Reference Library 1, 2014, NavPress. Kindle Edition), Kindle Locations 451-452.
[57] Dallas Willard, *The Great Omission* (HarperCollins, Kindle Edition, 2009), p. 9.

overriding governance for good, hopefulness that stands firm in the most discouraging of circumstances, and power to do what is right and withstand the forces of evil. In short, non-discipleship costs you exactly that abundance of life Jesus said He came to bring (John 10:10)."[58]

Willard concludes, "The cost of discipleship, though it may take all we have, is small when compared to those who don't accept Christ's invitation to be a part of His company in The Way of life."[59] The cost of non-discipleship is greater than the cost of discipleship, and if we're discerning believers, we'll take it to heart. We'll choose the road that leads to life and spiritual maturity rather than the easy road many Christians are traveling today.

Conclusion

The reason many Christians don't embrace discipleship is because they frankly don't want to pay the price. For them, the cost of spiritual maturity is too high.

Christ clearly highlighted the cost of discipleship, and there's no modern invention to make it easier. There's only one way to spiritual maturity, and it's by paying the cost of discipleship.

---

[58] Ibid., p. 9.
[59] Dallas Willard, *The Spirit of the Disciplines* (Harper Collins, Kindle Edition, 2009), Kindle Location 170.

4. The Lack of the Fear of the Lord

What does the fear of the Lord have to do with a lack of discipleship? Doesn't it seem a little out of place here?

It can be strongly argued from Scripture that the fear of the Lord is the foundation upon which discipleship rests and is its number one requirement. In fact, a compelling case can be built that the fear of the Lord is not only the foundation for discipleship, but for salvation and every other aspect of the Christian life. God says, "The fear of the Lord is the beginning of wisdom; all those who practice it have a good understanding" (Ps. 111:10).

To the degree a person fears the Lord is the degree to which they will even care about discipleship in the first place. And to the degree a person fears the Lord is the degree to which they will be very careful to obey God and all His commands, despite what family, friends, and society say.

The fear of the Lord is the value we give God and the perspective from which we look at Him. It sets our worldview and establishes our priorities in life. It's a major theme and doctrine of Scripture that is extremely positive and healthy. It's a fountain of life, brings riches, honor, and wealth, and endures forever.

Because the fear of the Lord is so foundational to discipleship and has been greatly overlooked, I believe it deserves some time and attention.

Defining the Fear of the Lord

Considerable controversy over the past 40 or so years has arisen regarding what the fear of the Lord means. There are four main interpretations:

48

1. Some define the fear of the Lord as soft or nonexistent. They believe God loves us and is not to be feared. God is our friend, and we're on a buddy system with Him. As Roger Barrier points out, "Too many Christians want, in fact, not so much a Father in Heaven as a 'Grandfather in Heaven' — a senile benevolence who, as they say, 'liked to see young people enjoying themselves' and whose plan for the universe was simply that it might be truly said at the end of each day, 'a good time was had by all.'"[60]

2. Others would define the fear of the Lord as simply respect for God. JoHannah Reardon responds to this view by saying, "I often hear people explain the fear of the Lord as a mere respect or reverence. But the Bible uses the word *fear* at least 300 times in reference to God, so we make a mistake when we downplay it."[61] Reardon continues, "While respect is definitely included in the concept of fearing God, there is more to it than that. A biblical fear of God, for the believer, includes understanding how much God hates sin and fearing His judgment on sin — even in the life of a believer."[62]

3. Others would define the fear of the Lord as reverence and awe of God. They believe Hebrews 12:28–29 provides a good description of its meaning: "Therefore, since we are receiving a kingdom that cannot be shaken, let us be thankful, and so worship God acceptably with **reverence and awe**, for our God is a consuming fire." This reverence and awe is believed by some to be exactly what the fear of the Lord means and is the motivating factor for us to surrender to God. One author

---

[60] Roger Barrier, *What Does it Mean to "Fear the Lord?"* 2013, Crosswalk.com, http://www.crosswalk.com/church/pastors-or-leadership/ask-roger/what-does-it-mean-to-fear-the-lord.html, Accessed 08/15/2015.
[61] JoHannah Reardon, *What Does It Mean to Fear God?* ChristianityToday.com, Accessed 08/15/2015.
[62] Ibid., Accessed 08/15/2015.

elaborates on this view by stating, "Each of us will give an account of our lives to God, and He is fully aware of everything we think, desire, speak, and do. The fear of the Lord is an awareness of these truths. It can be defined as a continual awareness that you are in the presence of a holy, just, and almighty God, and that every motive, thought, word, and action is open before Him and will be judged by Him."[63]

4. And still others would see the fear of the Lord as a much stronger term synonymous with extreme fear or terror of God. They believe that there are other words in Hebrew and Greek for mere respect, reverence, or honor that God could have used if the fear of the Lord meant to simply respect or revere Him. As one scholar states, "With this distinction in both Hebrew and Greek, some still assert that fear merely means reverence. As if God through His Spirit could not select the right word hundreds of times! Some would prefer to believe this than to understand that God really ought to be feared. Why is it we will not accept the fear of God? Why do we try to 'explain away' the fear of God in Scripture?"[64]

Which of these four interpretations is correct? I believe the biblical evidence supports interpretations three and four.

The Meaning of the Fear of the Lord in Hebrew and Greek

The word "fear" in the phrase "fear of the Lord" comes from the Hebrew word *yirah* (transliterated), and means "to be terrified" (Jonah 1:10), "to be in awe" (1 Kings 3:28), and "to have

---

[63] Institute in Basic Life Principles, *What is the Fear of the Lord?* Iblp.org, http://iblp.org/questions/what-fear-lord, Accessed 08/15/2015.
[64] Acts 17:11 Bible Studies, *The Fear of God,* http://www.acts17-11.com/fear.html, Accessed 08/17/2015.

respect" (Lev. 19:3).[65]

"The fear of the Lord is the reverence one would pay to a king because he is the majesty. But if one has offended the king and punishment is coming, the fear of the king's wrath in Hebrew is *yare*. *Yare* is used in the phrase "fear the Lord" 31 times in the Old Testament."[66]

In summary, *yare* and its variant forms mean: to fear, revere, be afraid, to stand in awe of, be awed, honor, respect, to be fearful, be dreadful, to cause astonishment and awe, be held in awe, to inspire reverence or godly fear or awe, to make afraid, and terrify.[67]

The use of the Greek word *phobo* carries the same meaning as the Hebrew word *yare* (Matt. 28:4; 1 Pet. 2:17).

Biblical Texts on the Fear of the Lord

The following are key verses that explain the meaning of the fear of the Lord:

- **Hebrews 12:28:** "Therefore let us be grateful for receiving a kingdom that cannot be shaken, and thus let us offer to God acceptable worship, with **reverence** and **awe**."

- **Jeremiah 5:22:** "Do you not **fear** me? Declares the Lord. Do you not **tremble** before me?"

- **Psalm 2:11:** "Serve the Lord with **fear**, and rejoice with **trembling**."

- **Matthew 10:28:** "And do not **fear** those who kill the body but cannot kill the soul. But rather **fear** him who can destroy both soul and body in hell."

---

[65] Neverthirsty.org, *Bible Questions & Answers*, http://www.neverthirsty.org/pp/corner/read2/r00664.html, Accessed 08/15/2015.

[66] Ibid., Accessed 08/15/2015.

[67] Lumina.bible.org, https://lumina.bible.org/bible/Deuteronomy+10, Accessed 08/16/2015.

These verses support the interpretation that the fear of the Lord is much more than simple respect or reverence. It carries the sense of awe, deep reverence, extreme wonder, dread, and trembling.

What Does the Fear of the Lord Mean?

The "fear of the Lord" is a common term Scripture uses to define the value and worth we should give God in our lives. For the person who fears the Lord, they will be extremely careful to love and obey God as they should. For the person who does not fear the Lord, they will care little or nothing about God. They are a hard-hearted person who can know what God wants them to do but could care less about doing it.

Is There a Conflict Between Fearing the Lord and Loving the Lord?

Some believe the fear of the Lord no longer applies to us today, but just the love of the Lord. They cite 1 John 4:16–18 as the text that nullifies the command to fear the Lord:

> So we have come to know and to believe the love that God has for us. God is love, and whoever abides in love abides in God, and God abides in him. By this is love perfected with us, so that we may **have confidence for the day of judgment**, because as he is so also are we in this world. There is no fear in love, but perfect love casts out fear. For fear has to do with punishment, and whoever fears has not been perfected in love.

According to this passage, some claim that it's wrong to fear the Lord, and if we do, we don't understand God's love correctly. However, what about the other 300 references to the fear of the Lord we find in Scripture, of which many are direct commandments? How do they fit with 1 John 4:16–18?

Additionally, Christ says that if we obey and keep His Word, then our love for Him is perfect:

> And by this we know that we have come to know him, if we **keep** his commandments. Whoever says, "I know him" but does not **keep** his commandments is a liar, and the truth is not in him, but whoever **keeps** his word, in him truly the love of God is perfected (1 John 2:3–5).

God's Love Does Not Remove Accountability

First of all, it should be noted that God's love does not remove our accountability to Him for our actions in this life. God is clear that both the non-believer and the believer will give an account to Him for how they lived their lives.

1 John 4:16-18 talks about how we can have confidence before God on the Day of Judgment, not that there will be no judgment. It speaks of how we can be perfected in love so we don't have to fear punishment, not that there will be no punishment.

With this being said, what does the Day of Judgment mean in this passage and how can we have confidence on that day?

For the believer, the glorious good news is that their sins have been forgiven in Christ and **no condemnation** awaits them. Therefore, they have nothing to fear regarding hell and God's wrath upon them. They need not fear punishment because they have placed their faith in Christ and have passed from death to life. They have responded to God's love and can now have full confidence that they are saved and will not incur God's wrath. For this reason, God's love should cast out any fear of His judgment and punishment upon them.

However, believers will still give an account for how they served God with their lives. The Apostle Paul gives reference to this when addressing believers. Note how he even includes himself in this time of accountability:

For we must all appear before the judgment seat of Christ, so that each one may receive what is due for what he has done in the body, whether good or evil (2 Cor. 5:10).

At this place, the believer is not judged as to whether or not they will be saved and going to heaven, but judged based on how they used their talents and served Christ in this present life.

How We Can Have Confidence at the Judgment Seat of Christ

The love of the Lord motivates us to live in obedience to God, and as we do, we are filled with peace and confidence before the Lord. While we aren't perfect, we can rest assured that if we're seriously following Christ and have no major sins in our lives, then we have nothing that would cause us to fear anything when we give account to the Lord. Once again, this doesn't mean we will be perfect or perfectly love and obey God, but it refers to the overall joy and peace a believer has when they know they are sincerely following the Lord with all their heart and are being pleasing to Him.

To the degree that we love God and keep His commandments will be the degree to which we'll have no fear when we give account at the Judgment Seat of Christ. We'll have peace and confidence regarding this day because we are loving God and being obedient to Him.

For the believer who is living a casual Christian life or living in unrepentant sin, they will not have the peace that things are right between them and the Lord, and in their case, they should rightly be concerned about how it will go for them when they give account to Christ. Their concern should not be about judgment and hell, but about losing heavenly rewards and being displeasing to the Lord.

In summary, we as believers should have a deep reverence and awe of God, giving Him the value and worth He deserves.

We should be extremely careful to love and obey Him as we should, being very attentive to please Him in every aspect of our lives. We should understand that nowhere in Scripture are we commanded **not** to fear the Lord. But just the opposite is true. Countless times we are directly commanded to fear the Lord and give Him the worth and value He demands.

The Fear of the Lord Applied to the Non-Believer

For the non-believer, there ought to be an expectant horror, terror, trembling, and dread before God for the judgment and wrath that awaits them. The reality of spending eternity in hell should shake them to their core.

For those who trample underfoot the sacrifice of Christ, and turn their back on Him and His salvation, they should shudder and tremble before God Almighty:

> For if we go on sinning deliberately after receiving the knowledge of the truth, there no longer remains a sacrifice for sins, but a fearful expectation of judgment, and a fury of fire that will consume the adversaries. Anyone who has set aside the Law of Moses dies without mercy on the evidence of two or three witnesses. How much worse punishment, do you think, will be deserved by the one who has trampled underfoot the Son of God, and has profaned the blood of the covenant by which he was sanctified, and has outraged the Spirit of grace? For we know him who said, "Vengeance is mine; I will repay." And again, "The Lord will judge his people." **It is a fearful thing to fall into the hands of the living God** (Hebrews 10:26–31).

Therefore, for the non-believer who could care less about God and does not give Him the worth and value He deserves, there ought to be an expectant horror, terror, trembling, and dread before God for the judgment and wrath that awaits them.

Fearing the Lord and Loving the Lord

The phrases "fear the Lord" and "love the Lord" go hand in hand. To love the Lord is to fear Him, and to fear the Lord is to love Him: "For as high as the heavens are above the earth, so great is his **steadfast love** toward those who **fear him**" (Ps. 103:11). "But the steadfast **love of the Lord** is from everlasting to everlasting on those who **fear him**, and his righteousness to children's children" (Ps. 103:17). These verses show that the fear of the Lord and the love of the Lord are harmonious, not conflictive truths.

Christ defines, in large part, what it means to love God. He says, "Whoever has my commandments and keeps them, he it is who loves me. And he who loves me will be loved by my Father, and I will love him and manifest myself to him" (John 14:21).

Keeping God's commandments is the mark of a person who truly loves and fears the Lord. Words are cheap; obedience is costly. A person who truly loves the Lord will not only say so, but will show it through obedience.

How the Fear of the Lord Is Viewed by Many Today

Many Christians and churches have a strong focus on the love of God, and a weak or practically non-existent focus on the fear of God. Just ask yourself if you've recently heard an entire message devoted to the topic of hell or the fear of the Lord? Then ask yourself if you've recently heard a message about the love of God?

If you're like most, the messages you've heard about the love of God versus the messages about the judgments of God and hell are extremely disproportional. Our focus today is on the love and grace of God. The fear of the Lord is unpopular and viewed negatively, while love and grace are viewed as far more appealing and positive.

Yet, when analyzing Christ's message in the Gospels, we see that He talked far more about the judgments of God and hell than about heaven. He did just the opposite of what most do today.

Now to clarify, God is love, and His love is an overarching truth of Scripture, but God is also a just God and will punish those who reject His love. To only focus on His love and omit His justice is not a balanced treatment of Scripture. We see this in the following text: "The Lord is slow to anger and **abounding in steadfast love**, forgiving iniquity and transgression, but **he will by no means clear the guilty**, visiting the iniquity of the fathers on the children, to the third and the fourth generation" (Num. 14:18).

The Biblical View of the Fear of the Lord

As mentioned, the "fear of the Lord" is a common term Scripture uses to define the value and worth we should give God in our lives. For the person who fears the Lord, they will be extremely careful to love and obey God as they should. For the person who does not fear the Lord, they will care little or nothing about God.

We can measure how much we fear the Lord by measuring how concerned we are about carefully obeying and loving Him. If we have areas in our lives where we are not fully obeying God, then this reveals a lack of the fear of the Lord on our part. For example, when 81% of Christians today are not regularly reading their Bibles, this reveals that they do not fear the Lord much.

There are few themes in Scripture that speak of such rich blessings in the believer's life as the fear of the Lord. Rather than being viewed as something negative, God views it as exceedingly positive. Consider the following verses that speak of the benefits and blessings the fear of the Lord brings to our lives:

- **The fear of the Lord brings church growth, discipleship, peace, and comfort:** "So the church throughout all Judea and Galilee and Samaria had peace and was being built up. And walking in the fear of the Lord and in the comfort of the Holy Spirit, it multiplied" (Acts 9:31). Contrary to most popular church growth philosophies, the fear of the Lord was a central cause of growth in the early church.

- **The fear of the Lord is the whole purpose of mankind:** The summation of our purpose in life is summed up at the end of the Book of Ecclesiastes: "The end of the matter; all has been heard. Fear God and keep his commandments, for this is the whole duty of man" (Eccl. 12:13).

- **The fear of the Lord brings riches, honor, and life:** "The reward for humility and fear of the Lord is riches and honor and life" (Prov. 22:4).

- **The fear of the Lord motivates us to know Scripture:** "Then they will call upon me, but I will not answer; they will seek me diligently but will not find me. Because they hated knowledge and did not choose the fear of the Lord" (Prov. 1:28).

- **The fear of the Lord causes us to live carefully:** "Now then, let the fear of the Lord be upon you. Be careful what you do, for there is no injustice with the Lord our God, or partiality or taking bribes" (2 Chron. 19:7).

- **The fear of the Lord causes us to be faithful:** "And he charged them: 'Thus you shall do in the fear of the Lord, in faithfulness, and with your whole heart'" (2 Chron. 19:9).

- **The fear of the Lord is wisdom:** "And he said to man, 'Behold, the fear of the Lord, that is wisdom, and to turn away from evil is understanding'" (Job 28:28).

- **The fear of the Lord is clean and endures forever:** "The fear of the Lord is clean, enduring forever; the rules of the Lord are true, and righteous altogether" (Ps. 19:9). Interestingly, the fear of the Lord is an eternal reality that will always be a part of God's Kingdom.

- **The fear of the Lord brings understanding**: "The fear of the Lord is the beginning of wisdom; all those who practice it have a good understanding. His praise endures forever" (Ps. 111:10).

- **The fear of the Lord is to hate evil:** "The fear of the Lord is hatred of evil. Pride and arrogance and the way of evil and perverted speech I hate" (Prov. 8:13).

- **The fear of the Lord is a fountain of life:** "The fear of the Lord is a fountain of life, that one may turn away from the snares of death" (Prov. 14:27).

- **The fear of the Lord brings life and satisfaction:** "The fear of the Lord leads to life, and whoever has it rests satisfied; he will not be visited by harm" (Prov. 19:23).

- **The fear of the Lord is required by God:** "And now, Israel, what does the Lord your God require of you, but to fear the Lord your God, to walk in all his ways, to love him, to serve the Lord your God with all your heart and with all your soul" (Deut. 10:12).

- **The fear of the Lord brings blessings:** "Blessed is the man who fears the Lord, who greatly delights in his commandments" (Ps. 112:1).

- **The fear of the Lord brings friendship with God:** "The friendship of the Lord is for those who fear him, and he makes known to them his covenant" (Ps. 25:14).

- **The fear of the Lord causes us to turn from evil:** "By steadfast love and faithfulness iniquity is atoned for, and by the fear of the Lord, one turns away from evil" (Prov. 16:6).

- **The fear of the Lord brings the love of God in our lives:** "But the steadfast love of the Lord is from everlasting to everlasting on those who fear him, and his righteousness to children's children" (Ps. 103:17).

- **The fear of the Lord motivates us to evangelize:** "Therefore, knowing the fear of the Lord, we persuade others" (2 Cor. 5:11).

- **Those who fear the Lord lack nothing:** "Oh, fear the Lord, you his saints, for those who fear him have no lack!" (Ps. 34:9).

- **God hears the prayers of those who fear Him:** "He fulfills the desire of those who fear him; he also hears their cry and saves them" (Ps. 145:19).

- **The Lord takes pleasure in those who fear Him:** "But the Lord takes pleasure in those who fear him, in those who hope in his steadfast love" (Ps. 147:11).

As these verses indicate, the fear of the Lord is a positive doctrine that brings some of the deepest blessings known to mankind. It's a theme pastors should be promoting and elevating in their churches, a doctrine that should run throughout all preaching and teaching. Discipleship rests on the foundation of the fear of the Lord and instead of avoiding it, Christians and churches today should be embracing it. But for some reason, they are reluctant and afraid to do so. I hope they are doing it out of ignorance, not because they fear man more than God.

The Fear of Judgment and the Human Heart

Interestingly, we get a glimpse into how God made the human heart by noting the way He uses the fear of judgment in dealing with mankind.

When the children of Israel entered the Promised Land, they

gathered at Shechem to renew their covenant with the Lord (Deut. 27, 28). Half of the tribes of Israel stood on Mt. Gerizim to pronounce blessings for obedience to God's commands (Deut. 28:1–14) and the other half stood on Mt. Ebal to pronounce curses for disobedience to God's commands (Deut. 28:15–68).

The tribe of Levi had a separate role in that they pronounced pure curses for disobedience, with no mention of blessings (Deut. 27:9–26).

In total, God spoke 65 verses (83%) that dealt with curses for disobedience and 14 verses (17%) that dealt with blessings for obedience. This significant difference should cause reflection. Why would God be so imbalanced in the attention given to the curses over the blessings? He also used this same tendency throughout the rest of the Old Testament.

We see a similar pattern in the life of Christ as well. He spoke overwhelmingly more about hell than heaven, and the judgments of God were a continual theme in His preaching. In fact, Christ is the leading voice on the subject of hell and spoke of it more than any other New Testament figure.

What do the themes of curses and blessings found in Deuteronomy, and the strong focus on judgment and hell in Christ's preaching, teach us about the human heart? It seems to indicate that the human heart is created in such a way by God that it responds better to the fear of judgment than the reward of blessings. It doesn't mean that blessings don't have an impact, as God did refer to them quite a bit.

Speaking About the Judgments of God

God made us and knows we respond better to judgment than blessings. We can take or leave blessings, but we can't take or leave judgment for disobedience. In other words, blessings are optional, but judgment is not.

If Christians and pastors don't speak of the judgments of

God, people may only choose to obey God if they think His blessings are worth the effort. If they don't think they are worth it, they'll "pass" on them as they'll have no fear of judgment for doing so. In other words, if judgment is removed from the table and blessings are the only option from which to choose, then people will just decide whether the blessings are worth it or not. If they decide the blessings aren't worth it, then in their minds they'll have nothing to lose but the blessings. For example, a child might choose to take or leave a reward for good behavior, but they can't choose whether or not they might be disciplined for bad behavior. It's the same with us.

However, when judgment is brought into the equation and put on the table, then people are faced with the realization that their misbehavior will incur God's judgment. By communicating clearly the reality of the judgments of God, people will realize they have two options. For the non-believer, they'll have to decide whether or not they want to pay the eternal price of suffering in hell for rejecting Christ. And for the believer, they'll have to decide whether or not disobedience to God is worth incurring His discipline in their lives, the loss of fellowship with Him, and the loss of eternal rewards.

Because it seems clear that the human heart responds better to judgment than blessings, it's imperative that we include the judgments of God in communicating Scripture to others.

Prophecy and the Fear of the Lord

One of the principle purposes of prophecy is to help us see the coming judgment that awaits those who don't fear the Lord. Unfortunately, books of the Bible that are prophetic in nature are largely overlooked today.

The Book of Revelation is unique in this aspect as it dramatically reveals the sobering reality of God's wrath upon those who reject Him and sell themselves to sin instead. For this reason, it's the only book in the Bible that begins with a promise for reading and hearing it: "Blessed is the one who reads aloud the words of this prophecy, and blessed are those who hear, and who keep what is written in it, for the time is near" (Rev. 1:3).

Most pastors and Christians feel the Book of Revelation is too difficult to understand, so they neglect it. Rather than mining its rich treasures, they disregard it because to them it's not worth the effort. However, in so doing, they disregard one of the most powerful books of the Bible.

The Fear of the Lord and the Gospel

The avoidance of the fear of the Lord affects the message of salvation. Today, in an attempt to eliminate negativity from the church atmosphere, many evangelistic salvation calls soften or pass over the sinfulness of mankind, the consequences of sin, judgment, and hell. They primarily focus on the love of God and His blessings.

A gospel that omits the sinfulness of mankind and the judgments of God is an incomplete gospel. It fails to clarify the reality of coming judgment and the consequences of sin. It's like hiding the truth from a cancer patient that they are sick and will die without treatment.

Hiding the truth about judgment presents a gospel that views the judgment of God as non-existent or as not that important. It's a gospel very different from that which Christ and the Apostles preached.

Consequences for Neglecting the Judgments of God

If the theme of judgment and hell is neglected or not taught, then there can be severe consequences. In addition, if there's an unbalanced focus on the love and grace of God, and little on the judgment and justice of God, then we can cause great deceit and destruction in the lives of many.

If we lead non-Christians to believe that there are basically no consequences for rejecting God, then we will have participated in the greatest deception of all time, and our omission of the truth can result in their eternal damnation.

I believe that if we leave out the hard truths of Scripture, we'll answer to God for doing so. This is why James 3:1 gives us this warning: "Not many of you should become teachers, my brothers, for you know that **we who teach will be judged with greater strictness.**"

If we leave out the sinfulness of mankind and the judgment of hell, then we can promote a false gospel that encourages non-believers to continue in their sin, and as a result, sends them to hell. The neglect of the judgment of God can lead others to believe that it doesn't really matter how they live their lives because God's love and grace will remove all the consequences for their disobedience to Him. To promote this mentality is not love, but deception.

Conclusion

The fear of the Lord is a foundational doctrine that applies to both the believer and non-believer. For the non-believer, there should be an expectant horror, terror, trembling, and dread before God for the eternal judgment that awaits them in hell.

For the believer, it's a theme that provides some of the deepest and richest blessings found in life. It endures forever and will never fade. Believers should not fear the judgment of hell, but the consequences a lack of the fear of the Lord produces. Consequences such as:

- The lack of discipleship
- Failing to reach spiritual maturity
- Sinful or poor choices
- The discipline of the Lord for serious unrepentant sin

- The loss of fellowship with God
- The loss of blessings
- The loss of eternal rewards

The fear of the Lord is the value and worth we should give God. It is developed as we grow in understanding and applying the Bible to our lives. It's God's gift to us and brings life, blessings, and rewards. It casts out the fear of judgment and gives us peace and confidence before the Lord.

The fear of the Lord can be summarized as having a right view of God, putting Him first, loving Him more than anything and anyone, and living in reverent awe and wonder at who He is and all He's done.

As mentioned, pastors and Christians today should not avoid its theme, but instead, should run to it and embrace it. After all, the fear of the Lord is what brings church growth, discipleship, and comfort to the church: "So the church throughout all Judea and Galilee and Samaria had peace and was being built up. And walking in the **fear of the Lord** and in the comfort of the Holy Spirit, it multiplied" (Acts 9:31).

Contrary to most popular church growth philosophies, the fear of the Lord is healthy and is one of the foundational truths that should be taught in churches today. It's one of the most important factors in discipleship and without it, very little, if any, will happen.

5. Being Ashamed of Total Devotion to Christ

"For whoever is **ashamed of me and of my words** in this adulterous and sinful generation, of him will the Son of Man also be ashamed when he comes in the glory of his Father with the holy angels" (Mark 8:38).

There's a growing hostility towards Christians today, and our culture now sees biblical principles as politically incorrect. Rather than stand against the turning tide, many Christians are instead choosing a path of peace and conformity to our culture's declining values.

It's not popular to be totally devoted to Christ as that's viewed as too radical and extreme. Moreover, for the person who holds to the truths of Scripture, they are often considered abrasive, hateful, intolerant, and judgmental.

How is being ashamed of Christ and His words affecting discipleship? Many Christians are ashamed to be fully devoted disciples for fear they'll become outcasts and marginalized among their friends and families. They prefer a kind of Christianity where they can enjoy all the blessings of God and those of their culture at the same time. They want the best of both worlds. In order to get the best jobs, gain recognition, be popular, and fit in, many Christians choose to avoid being devoted disciples as this would disrupt their world. They fear losing friends, family members, and general status in life so being a fully devoted Christian is avoided, and discipleship is glossed over and neglected.

Signs of the Times

Scripture clearly teaches that in the last days there will be a great falling away from the truth. People won't tolerate sound doctrine; there will be a great rebellion against God, and the times will be like the days of Sodom and Gomorrah. Even the church will be affected as many church members will prefer messages that are positive and upbeat rather than the truth of Scripture. "For the time is coming when people will not endure sound teaching, but having itching ears they will accumulate for themselves teachers to suit their own passions, and will turn away from listening to the truth and wander off into myths" (2 Tim. 4:3–4). Unfortunately, this verse describes the state of many Christians and churches today.

How should we deal with the mounting pressure to conform to our culture's increasing immorality, political correctness, and false philosophies of the last days?

For roughly 1,850 years of church history, there was solidarity on most moral issues. Yes, there was disagreement regarding some major doctrinal matters, resulting in the Reformation, but largely, on the moral issues, there was unified agreement.

However, moral tenants of the faith that began to erode in the Enlightenment Period — increased in pace during the 1850s, when science and evolution came to the forefront — have gained further acceleration since the 1960s. Scriptural morals are now being challenged on every front, and there's a new progressive move to radically alter civilization as we know it and usher in an entirely new morality. This morality is really nothing new; it's just the unleashing of the same old dark and twisted immorality of the sinful nature moved by the currents of Satan and the demonic realm.

How are Christians today responding to this challenge? Sadly, not very well according to the statistics. Rather than holding to the traditional moral values of Scripture the church has embraced for thousands of years, many are throwing much of it out the window and embracing the new "progressive" moral standards our culture is adopting.

With a scarce 19% of Evangelical Christians reading their

Bibles regularly, it's easy to see why evangelicalism is in trouble and we're caving into our culture's values. Many Christians are just simply ignorant and naive regarding what Scripture says about many of the moral issues of our day.

Key Issues Facing Christians Today

Some of the biggest issues facing Christians today are homosexuality, transgender issues, gender roles, abortion, divorce, sex outside of marriage, and childrearing philosophies. Many Christians hold views on these matters that are contrary to Scripture. Do they do this because they are ignorant of God's Word and simply don't know what it says, or do they love their culture and friends more than Christ? Are they ashamed to be totally devoted to Christ and His Word?

Many pastors today are also avoiding these key issues because they don't want to offend church attenders who have adopted our culture's values. Many churches now permit divorce with no biblical reasons, marry divorced people who are not biblically free to remarry, approve of homosexuality, overlook premarital sex, and wink at other questionable behavior. They believe the church today should just accept and support any lifestyle that both the Christian and non-Christian choose to embrace despite the clear teaching of Scripture that these acts are sinful.

Being Ashamed to Speak the Truth

Some Christians today propose a version of love they believe is best expressed by accepting, embracing, supporting, and celebrating certain sinful lifestyles that, according to God's Word, are immoral and wrong. I believe Scripture teaches that love is best expressed by telling the truth, not by allowing a person to continue in a destructive lifestyle for which they will destroy their lives, the lives of those around them, and incur the judgment of

God.

The moral issues of our day are nothing new, and the Apostle Paul had to confront them as well. Instead of approving, celebrating, remaining silent, or overlooking these issues, he dealt with them head on by stating the truth: "Or do you not know that the unrighteous will **not inherit the kingdom of God?** Do not be deceived: neither the sexually immoral, nor idolaters, nor adulterers, nor men who practice homosexuality, nor thieves, nor the greedy, nor drunkards, nor revilers, nor swindlers will inherit the kingdom of God" (1 Cor. 6:9).

Approving of the sinful choices of those involved in these sins would be similar to supporting an alcoholic's damaging lifestyle. We love best by speaking the truth, not by enabling people to continue their destructive activities. Unfortunately, many Christians are ashamed of the truth, remain silent, and shy away from being fully devoted disciples of Christ for fear of losing their status or popularity.

Being Ashamed to Choose Christ over Our Culture

Many Christians and churches today lag behind adopting the values of their culture by just 10 or so years. They change their message, morals, and values in order to fit in and not lose respect. Are they doing this because they are ashamed of being totally devoted to Christ and His words?

The pressure to conform to the values of our families, friends, and culture is a mounting force many Christians and churches are fiercely battling. It's a battle between staying true to God's Word despite the pressure or making concessions in order to alleviate it.

To relieve this tension, many pastors and churches are choosing a path of peace and positivity over conflict and strife. They don't want negativity in their churches, so they try to create a positive atmosphere that's loving and upbeat. They might have good motives, but are they ashamed to be fully devoted followers of Christ and His Word? Are they compromising and passing over certain hard truths and sins because they don't want any negativity in their churches? Are they afraid of offending church attenders and visitors who have adopted the values of their culture and would think they are crazy for truly preaching the hard truths of the Bible?

The call to discipleship is a call to total devotion to Christ. However, many churches are setting a poor example of discipleship because they are ashamed to fully obey the truths of Scripture that are not politically correct. While these churches may say discipleship is important, their example says something different. It says that they are ashamed of being fully devoted followers of Christ.

Being Ashamed to Address Gender Role Issues

Since the 1960s, the societies of the Western world have undergone major transformations regarding gender roles. In all fairness, I believe some of these modifications have been positive. However, some of these changes are highly concerning from a strictly biblical perspective. These changes deal with a new view of the gender roles in the church and family that our culture now embraces.

For almost two millenniums, the church understood the gender roles very clearly. They unanimously believed that Scripture taught clear distinctions regarding the roles of men and women within the church and home. But things have changed drastically in recent years.

Egalitarianism (the belief that men and women share the exact same roles in both the church and home) believes there is no distinction anymore regarding gender roles. This was not the case during four millenniums of Old Testament history and two millenniums since the New Testament. Therefore, for around six millenniums, believers understood clear distinctions in the gender roles, and there are virtually no examples to the contrary.

It's logical to ask why this change has all of a sudden occurred in correlation with the changes in our culture. Why were believers blind to the teachings of egalitarianism for almost six millenniums if they are found in Scripture? If there were sufficient biblical evidence supporting egalitarianism, then it should have surfaced eons ago. But why hasn't it? We should also see numerous examples of egalitarianism in church history as well. But we don't. Why is this so?

I believe it's because there's little support for it in Scripture. I've done significant research on this topic, and the evidence is overwhelmingly clear from Scripture that egalitarianism has very weak arguments supporting it. That's why, during the whole history of the church, we find virtually no support or examples upholding its position.

It appears, from an unbiased perspective, that Christians embracing our society's new values may be going to Scripture looking for wiggle room to support their beliefs instead of honestly going to the text and letting the text say what it says.

What has changed over the last six millenniums that would now cause us to question everything? The only thing that has changed is the values of our culture within the past 50 or so years that now challenge the gender roles and many other social issues.

Being Ashamed to Be Salt in Our Culture

Christ calls us to be salt in the world: "You are the salt of the earth, but if salt has lost its taste, how shall its saltiness be restored? It is **no longer good for anything** except to be thrown out and trampled under people's feet" (Matt. 5:13). What was the purpose of salt in Christ's day? It had three main functions: (1) to preserve food, (2) to add flavor, and (3) to provide minerals for bodily health.

Today, we are salt by preserving the truth of God's Word

71

instead of sacrificing it on the altar of political correctness. We are salt by adding flavor to life through demonstrating what it means to follow Christ's commands in all areas of our lives. And we are salt by providing health to the world as we speak the truth about the destructiveness and eternal consequences of sin. However, many Christians are ashamed to say anything and go against the tide of our culture's values.

Being Ashamed to Be Light in Our Culture

We're also called to be lights in the world: "You are the light of the world. A city set on a hill cannot be hidden. Nor do people light a lamp and put it under a basket, but on a stand, and it gives light to all in the house. In the same way, let your light shine before others so that they may see your good works and give glory to your Father who is in heaven" (Matt. 5:14–16). We are called to live in such a way that others can see the difference in our lives from that of the world.

What difference should they see? They should see believers who are living pure lives according to the commandments of God, who don't just say one thing and do another, but are genuine followers of Christ. They are not hypocrites, but practice what they preach. However, numerous studies show that "Self-identified Christians are living lives indistinguishable from non-Christians."[68]

The purpose of light is to illuminate and break the darkness. We're called to be lights by knowing God's Word and shining it into our culture. We're not to join the works of darkness, but reveal the evil deeds of our culture by shining God's Word upon it. "For at one time you were darkness, but now you are light in the Lord. Walk as children of light (for the fruit of light is found in all that is good and right and true), and try to discern what is

---

[68] C. S. Lewis Institute, *Sparking a Discipleship Movement in America and Beyond,* cslewisinstitute.org, http://www.cslewisinstitute.org/webfm_send/210, Accessed 08/19/2015.

pleasing to the Lord. Take no part in the unfruitful works of darkness, but instead, **expose them**" (Eph. 5:8–11).

Rather than celebrate, support, or approve the works of darkness, we should expose them. We should speak the truth in love, but nonetheless, we must speak the truth. However, many Christians are not living the truth and are not shining the light of God's Word upon the values of their culture. They are afraid and remain silent. And sadly, some join in the works of darkness, celebrating them rather than exposing and standing against them like the great prophet Isaiah did when he said, "Woe to those who call evil good and good evil, who put darkness for light and light for darkness who put bitter for sweet and sweet for bitter" (Isa. 5:20).

Being Ashamed to Speak for God

Scripture is full of examples of those who chose to please their families, friends, and culture rather than obey God. For example, Pilate chose to offer Christ up to be crucified in order to please a crowd, and Peter chose to deny Christ instead of acknowledging Him before His accusers.

On the other hand, God provides us with many examples of those who didn't bow to political pressure despite the enormous tension to do so. Among them is the Prophet Micaiah. Even though he was under extreme pressure to gloss over the Word of God to protect his life, he chose to obey God instead. His incredible story is recounted in 1 Kings 22.

During Micaiah's day, King Ahab (a wicked king over the 10 northern tribes of Israel) invited King Jehoshaphat (the king of Judah, who was a godly king) to go with him to war to take the city of Ramoth-gilead, a city once belonging to Israel but now lost to another nation.

King Jehoshaphat asked King Ahab to inquire of the Lord to see whether or not God would bless their plans. So King Ahab gathered all the prophets of Israel together, and these prophets unanimously affirmed God's blessing to bring victory if they went to battle.

King Jehoshaphat, for some reason, still had doubts and asked if there was any other prophet who could inquire of the Lord about their mission. King Ahab said, "There's this prophet Micaiah, but he never prophesies anything good from the Lord concerning me." Nonetheless, King Jehoshaphat insisted that this man be brought forth.

An officer, sent to summon Micaiah, warned the prophet not to stir up trouble by saying anything that differed from what the other prophets had already spoken. Micaiah responded, "As the Lord lives, what the Lord says to me, that I will speak" (1 Kings 22:14).

So Micaiah stood in the presence of King Ahab, King Jehoshaphat, all the prophets of Israel, all the officials of the two king's royal courts, and probably many army officials and commanders as well. All the power of two kingdoms were represented in this gathering. What would Micaiah do? What would he say? Would he be loyal to God and speak His words or yield to the pressure of those present and save his life? What would you do?

Micaiah chose to speak the truth of God's Word into his culture and as a result, was scorned and beaten by the other prophets, and then thrown into a dungeon by King Ahab. Nonetheless, Micaiah's words came true, and King Ahab lost his life because he refused to listen to Micaiah and the Word of the Lord.

Many other prophets in the Old Testament also spoke the Word of God to their culture and were beaten, persecuted, and killed. And the greatest example of all is Christ. He spoke the truth of God's Word into His culture and lost His life as a result. In addition, the Apostle Paul, the Apostles, and many others in

Scripture suffered great persecution for standing up for God and the truth. We applaud and admire them!

However, when it gets closer to home and affects us, many run from persecution and choose the values of our culture instead of standing with Christ. It's hard to stand against the tide of our culture, and it's especially hard to stand against family and friends. It's also hard for pastors and church leaders to stand against some within their congregations as they don't want a church split, lose members, see giving and tithes reduced, and have conflict.

Nonetheless, we have a choice to make. We can be like Micaiah, who chose to speak the Word of the Lord regardless of the cost, or we can choose the safe, easy route and appease our culture. What choice will you make?

Being Fearful of Losing Family and Friends

We naturally love our family, friends, and church family, and don't want to lose them. They provide us with the relationships we so desperately need. However, we must make a choice. Will we love family, friends, and our culture's values more than God? Will we remain silent on biblical issues out of fear of losing relationships? Will we conform to our society instead of being conformed to Christ? Will we fear being labeled intolerant, judgmental, dogmatic, and even hateful for speaking the truth? Will we be ashamed of what God says about moral issues and biblical truth, or will we speak the truth in love to our culture?

Recall what Christ said, "For whoever is **ashamed of me and of my words** in this adulterous and sinful generation, of him will the Son of Man also be ashamed when he comes in the glory of his Father with the holy angels" (Mark 8:38).

Unless we want to suffer shame and embarrassment before Christ, we need to be faithful in saying what God says about our culture. We're His mouth and voice. Unfortunately, many

Christians are ashamed to be fully devoted disciples as it causes problems in their relationships.

One of the ways we show our love and devotion to Christ is by being faithful to what He teaches in His Word. By holding fast to His teachings, regardless of the pressure to do otherwise, we demonstrate our love and devotion to Christ. Christ said, "Whoever has my commandments and keeps them, he it is who loves me" (John 14:21). If we don't keep Christ's commands, we have little right to claim we love Him. We can raise our hands in church, close our eyes in worship, and say whatever we want, but it's in our actions and commitment to keep Christ's commandments that we truly display our love for Him.

Being Ashamed to Be Small "p" Prophets to Our Culture

We are supposed to be like Christ and genuinely love people by telling them the truth. We also, in a sense, are called to be similar to the prophets of old. These prophets were called to speak God's Word into their culture. However, their hearers didn't want to hear their words and most of the prophets suffered great persecution or were killed for speaking the truth.

Today, I believe we're called to be like the prophets and speak the Word of God into our culture. However, the words we speak are the words of God already revealed in Scripture. Let me be clear: we don't speak our own words, but the words of Scripture! They are the only authoritative and inspired words known to mankind. Sadly, our culture, like the culture of the prophets, doesn't want to hear that they are sinners and their lifestyles are wrong.

Instead of hearing God's Word with open arms and repenting, our culture tends to get angry and attack the messenger. Nonetheless, our calling is to be small "p" prophets. We don't make up new Scripture, we just faithfully repeat what has already been revealed. We are also not to water it down, change its nuances, alter it, or adapt it so that it blends in with our culture's values. Instead, we are to speak the truth in love. We don't concern ourselves with how those in our culture might respond. How they do so is between them and God. We are called to be like the Prophet Ezekiel:

> So you, son of man, I have made a watchman for the house of Israel. Whenever you hear a word from my mouth, you shall give them warning from me. If I say to the wicked, O wicked one, you shall surely die, and you do not speak to warn the wicked to turn from his way, that wicked person shall die in his iniquity, but his blood I will require at your hand. But if you warn the wicked to turn from his way, and he does not turn from his way, that person shall die in his iniquity, but you will have delivered your soul (Ezek. 3:17–19).

God told Ezekiel that He would hold him accountable if he didn't faithfully warn the wicked people of his day to turn from their sins. I believe God will hold us accountable as well if we don't do the same. If we smooth over the sins of our culture, or remain silent because we're afraid, then I believe God will hold us accountable.

Why do many Christians remain silent and don't speak the words of God into their culture? Possibly, it's because they fear being labeled intolerant, judgmental, dogmatic, or hateful. Certainly that's what every culture in the Bible said to those who spoke God's Word to them as well. Whether it was the Prophets, Christ, the Apostles or us, it always has been and will always be the same.

A sinful society just doesn't want to be told that what they are doing is wrong and sinful. Therefore, when we speak God's words to them, they will naturally respond by accusing us of being intolerant, judgmental, dogmatic, or hateful. They'll attack the messenger who bears the message instead of heeding their warnings and repenting.

Sadly, many Christians are choosing to go along with our culture's sinful lifestyles because they are unwilling to be different and stand with God. Rather than being fully devoted followers of Christ, they settle for a mild version of Christianity that complies with their culture's values.

Being Ashamed to Use Good Judgment

One of the most misunderstood verses in the Bible is "Judge not that you be not judged" (Matt. 7:1). It's spoken so frequently that many believe we can't say anything contrary about anyone's sinful behavior or we're guilty of judging them. They claim it doesn't matter what God's Word might say; we have no right to weigh in on any matter.

What does this verse about judging really mean? We must see it in its context to fully understand it, as a verse taken out of context becomes a pretext. In other words, a verse lifted out of the other verses around it becomes what we want it to say rather than what it truly says. Here's the context:

> Judge not, that you be not judged. For with the judgment you pronounce you will be judged, and with the measure you use it will be measured to you. Why do you see the speck that is in your brother's eye, but do not notice the log that is in your own eye? Or how can you say to your brother, "Let me take the speck out of your eye," when there is the log in your own eye? You hypocrite, first take the log out of your own eye, and **then you will see clearly to take the speck out of your brother's eye** (Matt. 7:1–5).

First of all, it's true that our role is not to pass sentence upon another, that's God's job. However, in this passage, Jesus is not saying that we should never make any judgment about right and wrong. He means that we should not do it in a hypocritical

78

manner.

God clearly calls us to use good judgment about right and wrong. Note how the passage ends: "You hypocrite, first take the log out of your own eye, and then you will **see clearly** to take the speck out of your brother's eye" (Matt. 7:5).

Therefore, this passage is **not** saying we are not to use good judgment, but instead, that we are **not** to use our good judgment hypocritically. We shouldn't say, "Don't do that," while we do the very same thing. It's failing to practice what we preach.

The point of this verse is to teach us how to judge correctly, not that we can't speak the truth of Scripture regarding sinful matters. For this reason, we are given the responsibility to judge between right and wrong, but must first get the beam out of our own eye in order to **see** clearly.

There are other verses in Scripture that also teach we have a responsibility to judge correctly using the Word of God in dealing with others. Consider the following verses:

- **Galatians 6:1:** "Brothers, if **anyone is caught in any transgression,** you who are spiritual **should restore him** in a spirit of gentleness. Keep watch on yourself, lest you too be tempted."

- **1 Corinthians 5:11–13:** "But now I am writing to you not to associate with anyone who bears the name of brother if he is guilty of sexual immorality or greed, or is an idolater, reviler, drunkard, or swindler — not even to eat with such a one. For what have I to do with judging outsiders? Is it not those inside the church **whom you are to judge?** God judges those outside. Purge the evil person from among you."

These verses affirm that we have a responsibility to evaluate right and wrong in order to minister God's Word to others.

We must remember that to simply repeat what God says is not being judgmental. We are not passing judgment on others when we proclaim what God's Word says to them; it is God's Word that is passing the judgment. Therefore, we must not be ashamed to exercise good judgment in order to help others. We are to be like doctors who prescribe medicine (God's truth) based upon our patient's needs.

Being Ashamed to Confront Our Inconsistencies

When we tell others that they are wrong while we're committing the same sin, we are inconsistent and guilty of being hypocritical. This can be done on an individual or a church-wide level. The world often claims we say one thing and do another, or that we single out some sins and pass over others.

For example, they see Christians speaking out against society's sins while at the same time, overlooking divorce, sexual immorality, etc., among their own church members. They see anger against some sins, but apathy toward others. They see these inconsistencies in our conduct, and as a result, say we're judgmental. Unfortunately, they have a point. We have no right to say one sin is wrong if we turn right around and allow other sins in our midst without confronting them.

Some years ago, David Kinnaman wrote a book called *Un Christian*. It highlighted the belief that many non-Christians view Christians as hypocritical. [69]

While the church never has and never will be perfect—and we would have no right to say anything if perfection was the standard bearer—when the gap is significantly wide between what we say and what we do, then we simply lose our moral authority and become guilty of hypocrisy in the world's eyes. We preach, "Thus says the Lord," yet we don't practice what we preach.

The importance of speaking a clear, biblical message and

---

[69] David Kinnaman and Gabe Lyons, *Un Christian*, (Grand Rapids, MI, 2007).

practicing what we preach is paramount if we want to have any influence and moral voice in our culture.

Misunderstanding the Nature of Truth

We must understand that truth by its nature is intolerant, judgmental, dogmatic, and absolute. Sadly, however, only half of Christians believe in absolute moral truth (Barna).[70] This reveals that for around half of Christians our culture's values have more influence over them than Scripture.

If I were to say, "Gravity exists, and if you jump out a window you will fall," that statement would be intolerant, judgmental, dogmatic, and absolute. However, even though some might think my statement is too dogmatic and absolute, what they think doesn't change the reality that gravity exists, and if you jump out a window, you will fall. My statement simply defines the essence of gravity.

And so it is with the essence of truth. Truth cannot be truth if it's not absolute. However, in our day of relativism (the belief that there are no absolutes), truth doesn't fit well. Nonetheless, it doesn't matter at all if the majority of people think gravity doesn't exist—it still exists. And it doesn't matter what they say or how angry they may get, gravity is an absolute, intolerant, dogmatic reality. Truth is the same!

If we repeat the words of Christ, "I am the way, and the truth, and the life. No one comes to the Father except through me" (John 14:6), we are repeating an intolerant, judgmental, dogmatic, and absolute statement. However, we are not passing judgment and setting up our own standard of right and wrong, but just simply repeating God's divinely revealed truth.

---

[70] C. S. Lewis Institute, *Sparking a Discipleship Movement in America and Beyond*, cslewisinstitute.org, http://www.cslewisinstitute.org/webfm_send/210, Accessed 08/19/2015.

Building a Crowd Instead of a Church

Some churches soften or eliminate the hard truths of Scripture in their desire to be more appealing to non-believers and grow their churches. This can be a form of deception as it hides and distorts the truth. In so doing, they can subtly communicate that they are ashamed of being totally devoted to Christ and His words. They could be more concerned about building a crowd than building a church.

As a result, non-believers may respond to God in an entirely different way than they should because they've been misled. Richard J. Krejcir comments, "I need to make this clear; in my many years of research (since the late 1970s), the churches that do and/or want to water down the message to attract more people make a huge mistake. They neuter the power and purpose of the Church to which Christ called us."[71]

Krejcir continues, "It's imperative we understand that growth statistics are just one aspect of an indicator of a healthy church. True success is being obedient to what God has called us to do and realizing that although we're responsible to serve, we're not responsible for the results. Our surrender to the will of God over our will and desires equals success; we are called to have the focus that God has and the passion and prayer to follow through. These are the marks of a successful church leader."[72]

Our faithfulness to God is determined by the degree to which we choose to obey His Word over pleasing others. We must realize that our priority in life is to love God more than our family, friends, and culture. We're called to be disciples who speak the truth of Scripture, not take the liberty to alter it because

---

[71] Dr. Richard J. Krejcir, *Statistics and Reasons for Church Decline*, 2007, Church Leadership.org, http://www.churchleadership.org/apps/articles/default.asp?articleid=42346&columnid=4545, Accessed 08/07/2015.
[72] Ibid., Accessed 08/07/2015.

we're ashamed to be fully devoted followers of Christ.

Being Ashamed of the Gospel

Today, some Christians and churches are ashamed of the gospel of Jesus Christ. For this reason, they omit parts of it that are unappealing to non-Christians. Aspects that are largely omitted or neglected include truths like the sinfulness and depravity of mankind, the consequences of sin, confession of sin, repentance, the judgments of God, the fear of the Lord, discipleship, denying self, taking up your cross, and hell. They pass over these uncomfortable truths and rush to the blessings of salvation instead. They focus on the benefits of receiving Christ, but leave out the consequences of rejecting Him.

Are they ashamed of Christ and attempting to remove the "offense of the gospel"? Interestingly, unlike many churches today, Christ focused more on the judgments of God and the cost of following Him than blessings.

The Apostle Paul was persecuted all over the known world because the gospel he preached was offensive: "But if I, brothers, still preach circumcision, why am I still being persecuted? In that case, the **offense of the cross** has been removed" (Gal. 5:11). When Christ and the Apostles preached the gospel, it was very offensive to many at that time.

The gospel was offensive to the Jews who believed that following the Law brought salvation. It was offensive to the Romans who believed in many false gods, and therefore, rejected the claim that salvation was found only in Christ. The gospel was folly to the secular mind who considered it ridiculous (1 Cor. 1:18). It was foolish to the Greeks who thought salvation came through wisdom and knowledge, and it's offensive to our culture today for many of the same reasons. There's no way to remove the offense of the Cross except by changing it to appease others. Unfortunately, some Christians and churches are doing just that.

However, in so doing, they are proclaiming a different gospel.

According to Scripture, a gospel that omits or alters the sinfulness of mankind, who Christ is, the judgment of God, and hell is an incomplete gospel. It's a false gospel that fails to communicate that from which a person is saved. It's a false gospel similar to cults like the Jehovah Witnesses, Mormons, Seventh-Day Adventists, and others who don't believe in the judgments of God and hell.

Conclusion

Being ashamed of total devotion to Christ affects discipleship and causes us to choose a path of peace and conformity instead of obedience and transformation. It allows the fear of losing family, friends, status, and popularity govern our lives instead of Christ. It opts for a version of Christianity that stands with our culture instead of standing with Christ. It causes us to be ashamed of full devotion to Christ because that would make us stand out and be different—something many Christians are unwilling to choose.

6. The Effects of Prosperity Gospel Theology

I believe another factor affecting the lack of discipleship today is the teachings of the Prosperity Gospel movement. Much of what they promote is now creeping into the Evangelical church.

There has been considerable debate in recent decades over what many have labeled the "Prosperity Gospel" or the "Health and Wealth Gospel" (also known by other phrases such as, "Name It and Claim It," "Confess It and Possess It," and "Word of Faith"). Their theological views vary from a more radical version to a softer, lighter version.

Beliefs of the Radical Version of the Prosperity Gospel

This version of the Prosperity Gospel believes God wants us to be rich, healthy, and happy, so we should partner with Him in faith to pursue these things. It teaches that Christians should expect miracles to provide physical healing and material riches. In addition, it claims Christians have a right to prosperity, money, wealth, big houses, expensive cars, large bank accounts, and profitable investments. It believes that our financial and health problems can be solved by sending "seed-faith" contributions to faith healers. Moreover, it teaches that if we do experience suffering or hardship, it's because we're guilty of sin and have a lack of faith.[73] The Prosperity Gospel movement began in the 1970s and has grown extensively over the years.

Beliefs of the Softer Version of the Prosperity Gospel

In recent years, there has been a more modern version of the Prosperity Gospel that is making its way into mainstream

---

[73] David E. Pratte, *Does God Promise Miracles to Give Us Healing and Prosperity?* 2011, Light to My Path Publications, www.gospelway.com/god/health-wealth.php, Accessed 08/22/2015.

Christianity. What began in the 1970s is gaining steam today. This softer version is more dangerous than ever because it contains subtler lies in its message. It promotes half-truths as whole truths, and a half-truth presented as a whole truth becomes an untruth.

When talking about the attraction and longevity of the Prosperity Gospel, Kate Bowler notes a major change that has extended its longevity: "The ascent of a smoother, more sophisticated 'soft prosperity' message — touted by more relaxed, corporate figures like Joel Osteen, Joyce Meyer, and Paula White — replaced the more theologically — explicit 'hard prosperity' teachings of an earlier generation. This helped the movement's appeal within a more therapeutic, secular context."[74]

A recent scholar has noted, "In the Prosperity Gospel, the believer is told to use God, whereas the truth of biblical Christianity is just the opposite — God uses the believer. Prosperity Theology sees the Holy Spirit as a power to be put to use for whatever the believer wills."[75] The main premise of the Prosperity Gospel is that God exists to serve mankind rather than mankind existing to serve God. It believes God's main purpose is to make us happy, healthy, and wealthy.

John Piper calls the Prosperity Gospel deceitful and deadly: "Luring people to Christ to get rich is both deceitful and deadly. It's *deceitful* because when Jesus himself called us, he said things like: 'Any one of you who does not renounce all that he has cannot be my disciple' (Luke 14:33). And it's *deadly* because the desire to be rich plunges 'people into ruin and destruction' (1 Tim. 6:9)."[76]

---

[74] Larry Eskridge, *The Prosperity Gospel Is Surprisingly Mainstream*, 2013, ChristianityToday.com, http://www.christianitytoday.com/ct/2013/august-web-only/prosperity-gospel-is-surprisingly-mainstream.html, Accessed 08/22/2015.
[75] Gotquestions.org, *What Does the Bible Say About the Prosperity Gospel?* http://www.gotquestions.org/prosperity-gospel.html, Accessed 08/22/2015.
[76] John Piper, *Prosperity Preaching: Deceitful and Deadly*, 2007, Desiring God, DesiringGod.org, http://www.desiringgod.org/articles/prosperity-preaching-deceitful-and-deadly, Accessed 08/23/2015.

The Preaching Style of the Prosperity Gospel

The Prosperity Gospel's preaching focuses on "felt need" messages about success, encouragement, positivity, wealth, health, happiness, blessings, purpose, love, and relationships. Preaching is nearly exclusively positive and upbeat, entertaining, and with virtually nothing negative mentioned.

The sinfulness and depravity of mankind, confession of sin, repentance, the judgments of God, the fear of the Lord, discipleship, denying self, taking up your cross, losing your life, suffering, church discipline, transformation through trials and suffering, and hell are virtually omitted and considered negative themes.

It's important to note that, biblically speaking, God does desire to bless us, and there's nothing wrong with positive, encouraging messages, but when parts of the gospel are eliminated or passed over because they are viewed as too negative, then this is where the great error exists. The main problem lies in what's eliminated, not so much in what's included.

Theological Problems of the Prosperity Gospel

While there are elements of truth within the Prosperity Gospel movement, much of their beliefs are only half-truths. The following are key issues that are problematic and untrue:

- **It omits many truths from the gospel:** Its biggest problem is not what it includes but what it excludes. While some of what it includes is unbalanced and twisted, it still does contain some truth. However, its omission of foundational truths is what's extremely concerning and leads it to be classified by many (myself included) as a false gospel. It virtually omits the sinfulness and depravity of mankind, the consequences of sin, and hell.

87

- **Salvation means something entirely different:** The Prosperity Gospel's version of salvation is salvation from poverty, sickness, failure, and unhappiness, not salvation from sin and hell.

- **It teaches we can have God's blessings without following His principles and commands:** It promotes a "lazy man's" approach to acquiring blessings as it advocates a "fast track" approach that eliminates the need for discipleship. Instead of attaining God's blessings through a lifelong, faithful application of God's principles, Prosperity Theology believes blessings can be attained immediately and miraculously without much effort on our part.

- **It teaches wealth and health are guarantees:** It treats God like an ATM Who is obligated to give us what we want when we want it. It diminishes His personhood and turns Him into a machine, making Him our servant rather than us being His servants.

- **It teaches happiness can be acquired without departing from sin:** The sinfulness of mankind is passed over and in its place is preached success, happiness, prosperity, positivity, health, etc. People are taught they can attain all the blessings of God while, at the same time, violating God's call for purity, confession of sin, holy living, and fellowship with God in the inner heart.

- **It reveals a shallow and ignorant understanding of the Word of God:** For the student of Scripture, it becomes quickly apparent that the beliefs of the Prosperity Gospel movement come up short. Verses are taken out of context and omitted, biblical themes are overlooked, and many verses are twisted and changed. It's clear they have gone to Scripture with the intent of making it say what they want instead of letting the

Scriptures say what they really say.

- **It fails to understand that God's main purpose for our life is that we would be transformed into His image, not have an easy life (Rom. 8:28–29):** In order to transform us into His image, God uses trials (James 1:2–3), suffering (2 Cor. 4:16–18), and pain. Prosperity Theology bypasses this truth and focuses on that which satisfies many of the desires of the sinful nature instead. Purpose and success are defined as being wealthy, healthy, and happy.

- **It wrongly defines God's blessings:** Instead of allowing God to define what His blessings are, Prosperity Theology defines them for Him. Proponents cherry pick the blessings they like and omit the ones they don't. Among their handpicked favorites are happiness, wealth, ease of life, health, and success. To the astute believer, it can be seen that some of these so-called "blessings" are just a dressed up version of what the Bible calls "fleshly" and "worldly" desires.

The True Blessings of God

God defines His blessings much differently than what Prosperity Theology advocates. Consider the following verses:

- **Matthew 5:3:** "Blessed are the **poor in spirit**, for theirs is the kingdom of heaven."

- **Matthew 5:4:** "Blessed are those **who mourn**, for they shall be comforted."

- **Matthew 5:5:** "Blessed are the **meek** [teachable], for they shall inherit the earth."

- **Matthew 5:6:** "Blessed are those who **hunger and thirst for righteousness**, for they shall be satisfied."

- **Matthew 5:7:** "Blessed are the **merciful**, for they shall receive mercy."

- **Matthew 5:8:** "Blessed are the **pure in heart**, for they shall see God."

- **Matthew 5:9:** "Blessed are the **peacemakers**, for they shall be called sons of God."

- **Matthew 5:10:** "Blessed are those who are **persecuted** for righteousness' sake, for theirs is the kingdom of heaven."

- **Matthew 5:11–12:** "Blessed are you when others **revile you** and **persecute you** and **utter all kinds of evil against** you falsely on my account. Rejoice and be glad, for your reward is great in heaven, for so they **persecuted** the prophets who were before you."

As can be seen, God's blessings are much deeper and broader than the limited, selfish ones of the Prosperity Gospel.

Prosperity Gospel's Intrusion into Mainline Evangelicalism

Unfortunately, the Prosperity Gospel has made inroads into mainline Evangelical Christianity, and some of its seeds are sprouting up and growing among many Evangelical churches.

How can we know if some of the beliefs and philosophies of the Prosperity Gospel are influencing us? By carefully analyzing and asking ourselves what truths of the gospel we are omitting or neglecting.

Do we promote a version of salvation, like that of the Prosperity Gospel, which is salvation from problems, failure, and unhappiness, not salvation from sin and hell? Do we neglect the sinfulness of mankind, confession of sin, the consequences of sin, repentance, the judgments of God, the fear of the Lord, church discipline, the role of trials and suffering in the transformation process, discipleship, or hell? Moreover, are we so overly concerned about being positive and entertaining that we neglect the purity of the church and the truth of the gospel? If so, it's very likely the seeds of the Prosperity Gospel have crept into our midst and are influencing us.

Conclusion

In summary, there are two core concerns about Prosperity Gospel Theology: (1) the truths of the gospel it twists and excludes, and (2) the role of discipleship.

By omitting or twisting key truths of the gospel, many can be deceived and could very well wind up in hell.

By omitting or neglecting discipleship, it can severely diminish the avenue by which God transforms us into His image, presents us mature in Christ, and grants us His true blessings. If we neglect the role of discipleship, then we reject God's nature and image, choosing instead to retain the image of sin and remain spiritually immature.

Unlike Prosperity Gospel Theology, there are no shortcuts to acquiring God's blessings. They are not instantaneously acquired by miraculous methods, but conversely, come through a life-long perseverance of living out God's principles and commands through discipleship.

7. Misunderstanding Heavenly Rewards

"Do not lay up for yourselves treasures on earth, where moth and rust destroy and where thieves break in and steal, **but lay up for yourselves treasures in heaven**, where neither moth nor rust destroys and where thieves do not break in and steal. For where your treasure is, there your heart will be also" (Matt. 6:19–21).

When we fail to understand the big picture of life, it greatly affects discipleship. We wind up storing our riches on earth rather than in heaven.

God has given abundant revelation about heavenly rewards in Scripture. Running throughout its pages are rich illustrations and ample verses regarding this doctrine. In fact, it's a foundational theme of Scripture and one affiliated with the justice of God. It's only right that we are rewarded based on our actions and choices in this present life. Scripture teaches that according to how we live this life, we will be rewarded or punished in the next.

The Theme of Rewards in Scripture

The word "reward" or its variant is mentioned around 82 times in Scripture. In the Sermon on the Mount, which was Christ's longest and most famous sermon, He spoke about rewards nine times. In it, He emphasized the importance of storing up riches in heaven rather than on earth.

The Parable of the Talents also unfolds the truth of rewards (Matt. 25:14–30). In this parable, Christ gave certain individuals talents (abilities, gifts, time, resources, etc.) and then went away on a long journey. Upon returning, He settled accounts with those to whom He gave the talents. Some of these servants served well and doubled their talents. To them were given rewards based on their efforts and faithfulness. For the person who was lazy and chose not to serve God — even though he knew he would incur judgment—he was punished and sent to hell. This parable teaches that God will reward those who faithfully serve Him and punish those who don't.

At the end of the Book of Revelation, Christ talks about how He will bring rewards with Him upon His return: "Behold, I am coming quickly, and **My reward is with Me**, to render to every man according to what he has done" (Rev. 22:12, NASB).

The doctrine of rewards teaches that how we use the abilities, gifts, time, and resources that God gives us in this life will determine the rewards we will have in the next.

Christians and the Judgment Seat of Christ

Scripture teaches that all Christians will give an account for how they used their talents and served God at a place called the Judgment Seat of Christ. At this place, the believer is not judged as to whether or not they will be saved and going to heaven, but judged based on how they used their talents and served Christ in this present life. "For we must all appear before the judgment seat of Christ, so that each one may **receive what is due for what he has done** in the body, whether good or evil" (2 Cor. 5:10). This passage reveals the reality that each believer will stand before Christ and give an account for how they served Him in this life, and based upon how they served Him will determine the rewards they will receive in heaven.

There's another passage that sheds light on the Judgment Seat of Christ and what will take place there. It deserves a close look as it contains sobering words we should carefully ponder:

> According to the grace of God given to me, like a skilled master builder I laid a foundation, and someone else is building upon it. Let each one take care how he builds upon it. For no one can lay a foundation other than that which is laid, which is Jesus Christ. Now if anyone builds on the

foundation with gold, silver, precious stones, wood, hay, straw — each one's work will become manifest, for the Day will disclose it, because it will be revealed by fire, and the fire will test what sort of work each one has done. **If the work that anyone has built on the foundation survives, he will receive a reward. If anyone's work is burned up, he will suffer loss, though he himself will be saved, but only as through fire** (1 Cor. 3:10-15).

This passage teaches that some Christians will suffer loss when they appear before Christ to be judged for how they lived their lives and used the talents given them. They will still be saved and go to heaven, but they will suffer a loss of some kind. Some of these Christians might suffer loss because they served out of self-glory or wrong motives, and some might suffer loss because of laziness and unfruitfulness as seen in the parable of the talents.

Scripture teaches that heavenly rewards will be given to believers based upon their service to Christ. For those who have been diligent in serving and focused upon storing their riches in heaven, they will enjoy them forever. For those who lived carelessly, they will be saved, but will suffer loss of some kind.

The Difference Between a Gift and a Reward

What is the difference between a gift and a reward? A gift is something freely received and isn't based upon our effort or works but upon the kindness and love of another. However, a reward is given based on our efforts and works.

Scripture clearly teaches that salvation is a gift and is not based on works or effort in any way: "For by grace you have been saved through faith. And this is not your own doing; it is the gift of God, **not a result of works**, so that no one may boast" (Eph. 2:8-9). The only thing we must do to receive Christ's gift of salvation is to accept it.

Rewards, on the other hand, are given by God based upon

our efforts and service to Him. This is why the theme of rewards is found so abundantly throughout Scripture, and why Christ so emphatically encouraged us to lay up riches in heaven.

Misunderstanding Heavenly Rewards

I believe there are five main misunderstandings today negatively affecting the doctrine of heaven and rewards. These beliefs affect the role of discipleship and the eternal state of all believers. They are:

1. The belief that we can be saved by mere belief in God without producing fruit or showing any evidence of salvation.

2. The belief that heaven, and the rewards given there, will be the same for everyone despite how we live our lives on earth.

3. The belief that God's grace will wipe away all the consequences of choices made in this life so we can live negligently without suffering any eternal ramifications.

4. The belief that a Christian's freedom in Christ means they have the liberty to sin without any eternal consequences and accountability.

5. The misunderstanding or denial that all believers will give an account at the Judgment Seat of Christ for how they served God with their lives and used the talents He gave them.

These five misunderstandings are detrimental to discipleship. At stake are not trivial matters, but the loss of rewards that will affect our eternal state.

Consequences of Misunderstanding Heavenly Rewards

Because many believe in some or all five theological fallacies mentioned, they run the danger of doing just enough to get by in their Christian lives in the present. They conclude that they are going to heaven, and heaven will be the same for everyone, so why sacrifice this life's pleasures? In their view, the important thing is just making it to heaven. So, they'll tend to do just enough to get to heaven, but live their lives as they wish in the present.

I believe this mentality is seriously affecting the role of discipleship today, and for this reason, there are few strategic discipleship programs in our churches and little personal discipleship taking place. It might explain why 81% of Evangelical Christians don't read their Bibles regularly, why 61% of believers have not shared their faith in the last six months, and why the average time spent in prayer is 1–7 minutes a day.

After all, if how we serve God in this life doesn't really affect our life and rewards in heaven, then many will take the soft and pleasurable road instead. They'll just be content with going to heaven; believing it will be the same for everyone. As a result, the role of discipleship will be neglected because it's built on the premise that the sacrifice and effort invested in serving Christ in this life will be rewarded in heaven.

How Many Rewards Do You Want?

The sobering reality exists that each one of us has been granted the freedom to choose the amount of rewards we will have in heaven. It's not God's choice, but ours! He will simply be faithful in rewarding us based on how we used our talents in serving Him. Some will have many rewards and enjoy them for eternity, while others will have few or no rewards and live with that reality forever. Heaven will be wonderful and be the same place for every believer, but not all will enjoy the same amount of rewards there.

There are eternal consequences to the belief held by many that heaven and the eternal rewards given there will be the same for everyone. However, according to the Parable of the Talents (Matt. 25:14–30) and the Parable of the Minas (Luke 19:11–27), heaven will be the same place for all who enter, but it will not be the same experience. Some will have many rewards and be given oversight over much, while some will have few rewards and be given oversight over little or, possibly, nothing.

We Serve God Because We Love Him: Not Just to Get Rewards

I need to make it emphatically clear that we should not serve God just for His rewards, but because we genuinely love Him. God will only reward us if our motives are pure and we serve Him with grateful, overflowing love for all He has done for us.

Conclusion

We know that heaven will be wonderful for all who enter, and God will wipe away all tears there. However, I don't believe that when we are in heaven, He will blind our eyes to the clear reality that some will have few rewards while others will have many. That reality will be obvious and will last for all eternity. For those who suffer loss (1 Cor. 3:15), they will live with that consequence forever. They will miss out on the rewards they could have had if they had not been so distracted in this present life with laying up treasures on earth instead of in heaven. This is a sobering thought that should give us great pause.

When we enter heaven, what we did in this life and how we lived it will be locked in place for all eternity. We won't be able to go back and relive our lives and lay up riches in heaven like we should have just because we were foolish and didn't take time for God. After we realize our great error, it will be too late.

The misunderstanding of heavenly rewards has huge ramifications for our eternal state. As a result, many will be deeply regretful when they appear before the Judgment Seat of Christ and suffer loss, or receive few or no rewards.

8. Misunderstanding the Purpose of Discipleship

Many Christians misunderstand the purpose of discipleship, which in turn, leads to its neglect. They view it as applying primarily to "super Christians" and not to them. However, based on the texts of Scripture discussed so far, we can strongly contend that a person who is genuinely saved is also a disciple. The variant of the word "disciple" is mentioned 269 times in the Bible and the word "Christian," a scant three times. Therefore, the word "disciple" best fits the description of what a Christian is.

The purpose of discipleship is to become like Christ in our nature, knowledge, thoughts, desires, and purposes. It is God's plan for developing us into spiritually mature Christians and is not optional, but a command for all. Unfortunately, many Christians don't see it that way.

Discipleship is God's only plan for conforming us into His image. He has no plan "B"! He just doesn't wave a magical wand over us that produces instant maturity in our lives. On the contrary, God expects us to participate in the process of discipleship in order to become like Him. By neglecting discipleship, we are rejecting God's nature and image, choosing instead to retain the image of sin and remain spiritually immature.

The Neglect of Discipleship and the Great Falling Away

God warns that in the last days there will be a great falling away by many who claim to be believers. Christ said, "And then **many will fall away** and betray one another and hate one another. And many false prophets will arise and **lead many astray**" (Matt. 24:10–11). Moreover, Paul alerted, "Now the Spirit expressly says that in later times **some will depart from the faith** by devoting themselves to deceitful spirits and teachings of demons" (1 Tim. 4:1). The Great Falling Away will significantly affect Christians and churches who are neglecting discipleship because they won't have the discernment needed to recognize the false messages of our day.

Many Christians don't know what they believe because they don't read their Bibles. Also, many sermons today have a weak focus on the Bible because they are topical and primarily deal with felt needs. As a result, the foundational doctrines of Scripture are being neglected or viewed as impractical.

When asked to defend key doctrines like the truthfulness of Scripture, who God is, who Christ is, who the Holy Spirit is, what the essence of the gospel is, what the purpose of the church is, the events of the last days, the judgements of God, and moral issues, many Christians are hard pressed to provide answers. Moreover, many think that some cults are equal or similar to Christianity in their doctrinal positions.

Confusion and ignorance reign because discipleship is not encouraged, and most churches have no strategy for making disciples where these foundational doctrines could be taught. Many churches are more interested in gathering a crowd than in making disciples. They are more interested in meeting people's felt needs than their doctrinal and spiritual needs. As a result, doctrine and hard topics are ignored in an attempt to remove any negativity from the church atmosphere. Many churches want an atmosphere that is positive, uplifting, happy, and where people leave feeling upbeat and warm, so their preaching focuses more on the felt needs of their hearers than on doctrine.

Sound Doctrine and the Church Today

Although the focus God gives in the Pastoral Letters (1 and 2 Timothy and Titus) highlight the importance of sound doctrine (its theme is mentioned about 20 times), the focus today is more on topical messages that deal with felt needs. While preaching on felt needs is not bad in and of itself, it can produce weak believers who are ignorant of sound doctrine if it's their main diet. These believers can also become shallow and selfish, thinking that God and others primarily exist to meet their felt needs. In addition, they'll be more susceptible to the growing number of false prophets who are arising, and will continue to arise in the last days. It's not uncommon today for Christians to spend years in some churches and have no idea what they believe because they are rarely, if ever, exposed to doctrinal teaching.

I believe the neglect of discipleship and the disregard of doctrine will be the main causes for the Great Falling Away in the last days. People will simply have little biblical discernment to recognize the false doctrines that will creep in due to their ignorance of truth. Therefore, they will be easy prey for Satan and his lies. With the majority of Christians being biblically illiterate and knowing little about doctrine, they'll be easy targets for false teachers with fine sounding messages. Unfortunately, these false teachers will preach half-truths that will go unnoticed by many.

Conclusion

The purpose of discipleship is to become spiritually mature. How do we become spiritually mature? There's only one way, and it's called discipleship. It's not a game God wants us to play because He has nothing better for us to do; instead, it's His life vest that will rescue us from the raging waves of Satan's lies and protect us from the Great Apostasy of the last days. It will usher us into the abundant life, transform our nature, and give us wisdom and discernment to choose the best things in life instead of the good things. Moreover, it's the means whereby we will store up treasures in heaven and prepare for our eternal home.

By neglecting discipleship, we are rejecting God's nature and image, choosing instead to retain the image of sin and remain spiritually immature.

9. The Lack of Church Discipline

Most Christians would not associate church discipline with discipleship, but they are closely related. Discipleship entails both a forward and backward looking focus. It encourages believers who are right with God to move forward in their journey toward spiritual maturity, and it looks backward to seek out believers who are left behind in the process due to their involvement in sin. Church discipline is part of the "seeking out" aspect that rescues believers who are left behind and is an integral part of discipleship. When we overlook church discipline, we overlook a critical aspect of discipleship.

Sadly, the vast majority of Evangelical churches today do not practice church discipline. Albert Mohler comments on this trend by saying, "The decline of church discipline is perhaps the most visible failure of the contemporary church. No longer concerned with maintaining purity of confession or lifestyle, the contemporary church sees itself as a voluntary association of autonomous members, with minimal moral accountability to God, much less to each other."[77]

Today, we have a low view of the seriousness of sin! Immorality in the world is in a state of freefall, and Christians aren't that far behind. Why is this so? I believe one of the reasons is that there's no longer any consequences or accountability in the church for Christians who get involved in serious sin. As a result, sin runs rampant and is viewed as permissible. We have cancer in our church bodies, and most are content with allowing it to exist and even grow.

A permissive mentality that overlooks the seriousness of sin

---

[77]Albert Mohler, *The Disappearance of Church Discipline–How Can We Recover? Part One,* 2005, AlbertMohler.com, http://www.albertmohler.com/2005/05/13/the-disappearance-of-church-discipline-how-can-we-recover-part-one, Accessed 08/21/2015.

negatively affects discipleship because sin and disobedience are viewed as acceptable, with no negative consequences.

While the intent of this book is not a full treatment on church discipline, nonetheless, we'll look at a few principles about the role of church discipline in relation to discipleship.

What Is Church Discipline?

Church discipline can be described as a form of "intensive care" for **unrepentant church members who claim to be Christians**, but are involved in serious sin. Let me be clear; church discipline is **not** for unbelievers. It is also **not** for believers who repent and turn from their sins. Church discipline is only for **unrepentant church members who claim to be Christians**, but are involved in serious sin.

In order to rescue these unrepentant believers, serious measures should be undertaken to save them from destruction and devastation. It's an aspect of discipleship designed by God to be exercised when all other measures fail. It's an expression of genuine love and is to be administered in a loving, but firm manner. J. Hampton Keathley III, states, "Though church discipline appears unloving and harsh, it nevertheless rests upon the divine authority of Scripture and is vital to the purity, power, progress, and purpose of the church."[78]

Keathley adds, "The responsibility and necessity for discipline is not an option for the church if it obeys the Word of God, but a church must be equally concerned that Scripture is carefully followed in the practice of church discipline."[79]

John MacArthur affirms, "The purpose of church discipline is the spiritual restoration of fallen members and the consequent

---

[78] J. Hampton Keathley III, *Church Discipline*, Bible.org, https://bible.org/article/church-discipline, Accessed 10/08/2015.
[79] Ibid., Accessed 10/08/2015.

strengthening of the church and glorifying of the Lord. When a sinning believer is rebuked, and he turns from his sin and is forgiven, he is won back to fellowship with the body and with its head, Jesus Christ."[80]

Today, Many View Church Discipline as an Act of Hate

It's sad that the very means God has instituted for rescuing believers involved in serious sin from the grips of spiritual death is viewed as hate, rather than love. What a tragedy! As a result, the "Intensive Care Unit" of most churches is out of order, and numerous believers are dying spiritual deaths because its doors are closed.

Most would agree that God wants us to discipline our children so they grow up to be responsible and respectable. They understand this form of love when applied to children, yet for some reason, many Christians do just the opposite with fellow believers engaged in serious sin. They stand by and allow them to destroy their lives, damage the testimony of the church and of Christ, and do nothing. I don't believe that's true love. It might appear like love, but it allows destruction, not restoration, and how can allowing destruction be defined as love?

God disciplines those He loves and so should we: "My son, do not regard lightly the discipline of the Lord, nor be weary when reproved by him. For the Lord disciplines the one he loves, and chastises every son whom he receives" (Heb. 12:5).

Church Discipline in the Old Testament

We see the principle of church discipline in the Old Testament in the commands given to the nation of Israel to discipline and punish sin in its midst. In some cases, because of rebellion or lack of obedience to God's laws, individuals were

---

[80] John MacArthur, Grace to You, *Church Discipline*, www.gty.org/resources/distinctives/DD02/church-discipline, Accessed 10/08/2015.

excommunicated from being part of God's chosen people. This was a strong deterrent against sin: "But the person who does anything with a high hand, whether he is native or a sojourner, reviles the Lord, and that person shall be cut off from among his people. Because he has despised the word of the Lord and has broken his commandment, that person shall be utterly cut off; his iniquity shall be on him" (Num. 15:30–31).

Jesus and Church Discipline

Jesus said, "If your brother sins against you, go and tell him his fault, between you and him alone. If he listens to you, you have gained your brother. But if he does not listen, take one or two others along with you, that every charge may be established by the evidence of two or three witnesses. If he refuses to listen to them, tell it to the church. And if he refuses to listen even to the church, **let him be to you as a Gentile and a tax collector**" (Matt. 18:15–17).

Gentiles and tax collectors were people the Jews repudiated, avoided contact with, and viewed as sinful and unclean. When Christ told the Jews to treat an unrepentant brother involved in serious sin as a Gentile or tax collector, He was communicating the same concept as excommunication in the Old Testament.

The New Testament and Church Discipline

- **1 Corinthians 5:11–13:** "But now I am writing to you **not to associate** with anyone who **bears the name of brother** if he is guilty of sexual immorality or greed, or is an idolater, reviler, drunkard, or swindler — **not even to eat with such a one**. For what have I to do with judging outsiders? Is it not those inside the church whom you are to judge? God judges those outside. **Purge the evil person from among you.**"

  Here we see an example of church discipline wherein a Christian was having sexual relations with his father's wife, and the church in Corinth stood idly by, doing nothing (1 Cor. 5). Under the Holy Spirit's and the Apostle Paul's command, the Corinthian Church exercised church discipline on this sinful member. This discipline might seem harsh, but we see in 2 Corinthians that this man repented and was restored to fellowship with both God and the church (2 Cor. 2:5-8). Can you imagine the joy this brought to God and the Corinthian Church? Can you imagine the health it brought to countless lives by protecting them from sin's cancerous poison?

- **2 Thessalonians 3:14-15:** "Take special note of anyone who does not obey our instruction in this letter. **Do not associate with them, in order that they may feel ashamed**. Yet do not regard them as an enemy, but warn them as you would a fellow believer." This passage deals with believers who are unwilling to obey the clear commands of Scripture.

- **1 Timothy 5:19-21** (NASB): "Do not receive an accusation against an elder except on the basis of two or three witnesses. **Those who continue in sin, rebuke in the presence of all, so that the rest also will be fearful of sinning**. I solemnly charge you in the presence of God and of Christ Jesus and of His chosen angels, to maintain these principles without bias, doing nothing in a spirit of partiality." Here we see church discipline applied to leaders. Those who continue in sin are to be rebuked in the presence of all so that the rest will be fearful of sinning.

When we eliminate church discipline, we eliminate the fear of sinning. We remove a consequence God intended the church to exercise for deterring sin. As a result, sin can run rampant in our churches and grow like cancer, bringing destruction and death in its wake.

How to Treat Non-Christians Involved in Serious Sin

Many pastors and Christians seem confused regarding the difference between how God commands us to treat non-believers and believers involved in grievous sin. They lump both categories together and treat them the same. They fail to understand that God makes a clear distinction in Scripture between non-Christians and Christians, and has clear distinctions regarding His expectations of them.

For the non-Christian involved in serious sin (which is somewhat normal), God commands us to love and welcome them into our lives and churches. The doors of our lives and churches should be open to ministering to sinners just like Christ did. He was called "A friend of sinners" (Luke 7:34), and we should be too. However, we should not be friends with sinners to support them in their sin, but instead, we are to share Christ's Word with them and do everything possible to convince them to turn to Christ and repent of their sins.

God commands us to love all people, but He does not command us to love their sinful activities. In fact, He says just the opposite. The good news is that all sins can be forgiven through Christ's death on the Cross. However, these activities are still sinful. To tell people practicing sinful activities that their sin is okay is not love, but misleading. If we mislead them into believing a lie, then we'll give an account to God for doing so. Therefore, we are to love sinners and share Christ with them, but not endorse, celebrate, or support them in their sin.

How to Treat Christians Involved in Serious Sin

How should we deal with unrepentant Christians involved in serious sin? We treat them very differently than non-believers. It's different because, unlike a non-Christian, the Christian is born-again, knows God, has His Spirit and power within them — enabling them to do right — has God's Word that instructs them against sin, and has the church and believers guiding and helping them.

The non-Christian is dead in their trespasses and sins and unable to change without Christ's help. The Christian is alive in Christ and is blessed with all spiritual blessings in heavenly places (Eph. 1:3). Believers, therefore, have no excuse for falling into serious sin.

For those who call themselves believers, yet are involved in deep sin with no willingness to change, the church, and every Christian, should follow God's will in exercising loving church discipline in their lives (1 Cor. 5:11). This is God's remedy for rescuing hardened Christians who are involved in sin. It's a form of "intensive care" discipleship to be used for saving a sick believer who is in the grips of spiritual death.

Unfortunately, many Christians hold the view that we should treat non-believers and believers the same when they are involved in deep sin. They believe in a version of love that calls for just accepting, loving, encouraging, and praying for them.

Now while we are commanded to love, encourage and pray for our Christian brothers and sisters involved in serious sin, what do we do when they refuse to change? In their case, God commands us to exercise a different kind of love. It's a form of love that is disciplinary, a kind of love that seeks to save and redeem. It's called church discipline and is designed by God to rescue a hardened, unrepentant Christian from their sinful choices so that they don't destroy their lives, damage the testimony of the church, bring reproach to Christ, and fall into greater judgment from God.

John MacArthur states, "The goal of church discipline, then, is not to throw people out of the church or to feed the self-righteous pride of those who administer the discipline. It is not to embarrass people or to exercise authority and power in some unbiblical manner. The purpose is to restore a sinning believer to holiness and bring him back into a pure relationship within the assembly."[81] It's a form of discipleship for the purpose of restoration.

Misunderstanding Church Discipline

Probably the most misunderstood concept about church discipline is the belief that it's not love. But just the opposite is true! Church discipline, if carried out in a biblical manner, is a deep expression of love. It's love applied to a wayward sheep in order to bring them back to the fold. In the same way God disciplines those He loves, the church should also discipline those it loves. To not discipline is to not love.

Some Christians and churches feel that all an unrepentant believer needs is more knowledge, not church discipline. Their reasoning is based on the assumption that if we can just help them know more, then surely they'll come to their senses. They fear that if we exercise church discipline, then we'll surely lose them. This philosophy sounds loving and reasonable, but I don't believe it's the correct biblical response. What unrepentant Christians need is not more knowledge, but the willpower to obey what they already know. Church discipline helps provide the willpower they need.

For an unrepentant believer who knows the truth and is hardened in their sin, the only remedy left for them is church discipline. This discipline also involves the rest of the church's participation by stepping up the pressure on the unrepentant believer to repent and obey God. And as mentioned, it's a form of intensive-care discipleship for rescuing unrepentant believers from spiritual death.

In the same way we shouldn't stand by and watch a loved one in a boat go over a waterfall to their death, we shouldn't stand by and allow a brother or sister in Christ to fall to their spiritual

---

[81] John MacArthur, Grace to You, *Church Discipline,*
www.gty.org/resources/distinctives/DD02/church-discipline, Accessed 10/08/2015.

death as well. To allow them to continue in their sin, damage the testimony and purity of the church, and bring reproach to the name of Christ is not biblical love. I believe it's biblical irresponsibility.

The Main Purpose of Church Discipline

Another critical misunderstanding about church discipline is the failure to realize that its main purpose is to protect the rest of the church from the cancer of sin and rebellion. It exists to rescue the unrepentant believer, but its primary function is to keep the rest of the church healthy: "Do you not know that a **little leaven leavens the whole lump**? Cleanse out the old leaven that you may be a new lump, as you really are unleavened" (1 Cor. 5:6–7). If sin in the church is allowed to spread, then the purity of Christ's church is affected.

Also, the destruction and pain the rest of the church can fall into by copying the behavior of an unrepentant sinner can be devastating. By exercising church discipline, we make a bold statement to the church that sin is serious and has no place in a believer's life. By not exercising church discipline, we allow just the opposite. Church discipline brings a cleansing effect on the church that is healthy; allowing serious sin to go undealt with and grow like cancer is not healthy. Many pastors are reluctant to exercise church discipline, thinking it will harm their churches, but just the opposite is true; it will bring health.

In Scripture, God reveals three main reasons why He is so concerned about purity, and therefore, commands us to exercise church discipline: (1) it rescues individual Christians from sin, (2) it protects the church from sin's destruction, and (3) it allows the church to have a greater witness to the world regarding who God is and how He desires mankind to live. When serious sin is allowed by those claiming to be His followers, God's message is damaged because the world sees no difference between how they and God's people live.

Conclusion

The lack of discipleship today in most Evangelical churches is affecting the level of spiritual depth among many believers. This in turn produces Christians who are more susceptible to being judgmental and hypocritical because their lives don't match their words. It then leads to the diminishing power of the church to speak out against society's sins because Christians are caught up in the very same sins that should be condemned.

We need to recognize that discipleship is what develops within us spiritual maturity. Without it, we'll be less effective in reaching the world as our message will be hindered by our lack of example.

Being a disciple of Christ is a call to obey His commands. If we fall into serious sin, then we should expect to be lovingly confronted by mature believers who love us enough to tell us so. When the church lovingly confronts sin in its ranks, it is not being hateful or judgmental, but loving.

Discipleship entails both a forward and backward looking focus. It encourages believers who are right with God to move forward in their journey toward spiritual maturity, and it looks backward to seek out believers who are left behind in the process due to their involvement in sin. Church discipline is part of the "seeking out" aspect that rescues believers who are left behind and is an integral part of discipleship. When we overlook church discipline, we overlook a critical aspect of discipleship.

10. The Belief in Salvation Without Discipleship

A proper understanding of discipleship begins with a proper understanding of salvation. If the true essence of salvation is misunderstood, then the importance and role of discipleship will be misunderstood as well. Many contributing factors are affecting the neglect of discipleship, but one of the most significant seems to be the misunderstanding of the relationship between salvation and discipleship.

Our actions and lifestyles are built upon our belief systems; therefore, if we have a faulty belief system, our actions will naturally follow.

Is Discipleship Optional?

Today, many Christians view discipleship as optional. Despite the fact that it was the central focus of Christ's and the Apostles' ministries, things have changed over the years. What does Christ teach about salvation and discipleship? Is the belief in salvation without discipleship biblical?

Dallas Willard claims that today Christianity as a whole tends to believe salvation is good enough to get us to heaven and discipleship is optional.[82] Willard elaborates on the state of Christianity today when he says, "For at least several decades the churches of the Western world have not made discipleship a condition of being a Christian. One is not required to be, or to intend to be, a disciple in order to become a Christian, and one may remain a Christian without any signs of progress toward or in discipleship."[83] In addition, John MacArthur believes that the contemporary teaching that separates discipleship from salvation

---

[82] Dallas Willard, *The Great Omission* (HarperCollins. Kindle Edition, 2009-10-13), p. 4.
[83] Ibid., p. 4.

springs from ideas foreign to Scripture.[84]

The Calls of Christ to "Follow Me" Combine Salvation and Discipleship into One Act

In the accounts where Christ uses the term "Follow Me," they include both a salvation and discipleship call. While some would like to separate Christ's call to salvation from His call to discipleship, they seem to be one in the same according to Jesus. In other words, salvation and being a disciple go hand in hand. Notice how Christ combines salvation and discipleship together:

> And calling the crowd to him with his disciples, he said to them, "If anyone would come after me, let him deny himself and take up his cross and follow me. For whoever would save his life will lose it, but whoever loses his life for my sake and the gospel's will save it. For what does it profit a man to gain the whole world and forfeit his soul? For what can a man give in return for his soul?" (Mark 8:34–37).

There are four other parallel passages where Christ makes the similar or same call to follow Him (Matt. 10:38–39, 16:24–26; Luke 9:23–25; John 12:25–26). In each call, Christ is addressing two groups: the crowd following Him and His disciples.

In Mark 8:34–37, Christ makes a sweeping statement to all, "If anyone would come after me, let him deny himself and take up his cross and follow me." These words would be argued by some to be a call to discipleship only. However, in the same call, Christ uses the terms "lose your life" and "lose your soul."

How would the terms "lose your life" and "lose your soul" relate to discipleship only? Losing your life and losing your soul would only make sense if the terms refer to salvation, for how could a disciple who is obediently following Christ through

---

[84] John MacArthur, *The Gospel According to Jesus* (Grand Rapids, Michigan, Zondervan Publishing House, 1988), p. 196.

denying themself and taking up their cross lose their soul? It
seems clear that Christ combines both salvation and discipleship
together into one call. He doesn't see two distinct aspects to the
Christian life, but one. His call to salvation was a call to
discipleship. Therefore, to be a follower of Christ is to be a
disciple.

It would appear, then, that it's unlikely that one can be saved
without being a disciple. Salvation, according to Jesus, seems to
include much more than mental acquiescence to certain truths
about God. It involves an active faith that expresses itself in
following Christ. Therefore, salvation and discipleship are one
and the same. To be saved is to be a disciple. To be a disciple is to
be saved. Unlike some who would like to separate salvation from
discipleship, in the calls of Christ to follow Him, they were not
separated but combined.

A "Two-Tier" Form of Christianity

Bill Hull, who has written one of the most extensive books on
discipleship called *The Complete Book of Discipleship: On Being and
Making Followers of Christ,* is deeply concerned about the growing
number of Christians who believe that discipleship is optional.

Hull asserts that we've established a "two-tier" state of
Christianity. The first level is for those who believe in Christ and
then "live primarily as they please," and the second level is for
"serious followers" who choose the option of being devoted
disciples.[85] He claims, "The church culture in the Global North—
along with Australia, New Zealand, and South Africa—has
largely accepted the idea of non-discipleship Christianity: people
can be Christians without making any effort to submit to and

[85] Bill Hull, *The Complete Book of Discipleship: On Being and Making Followers of Christ*
(The Navigators Reference Library 1, 2014, NavPress. Kindle Edition), Kindle Locations
700-703.

follow Christ."[86]

Hull continues, "The fact that we've developed this two-tier state of Christianity forces us to retrace our theological footsteps back to the actual message we proclaim. We need to ask ourselves, 'What kind of person does non-discipleship Christianity produce?'"[87]

Hull then elaborates on his claim by stating, "This common teaching is that a Christian is someone who by faith accepts Jesus as Savior, receives eternal life, and is safe and secure in the family of God; a disciple is a more serious Christian active in the practice of the spiritual disciplines and engaged in evangelizing and training others. But I must be blunt: I find no biblical evidence for a separation of Christian from disciple."[88]

As a result of the belief in a "two-tier" form of Christianity, many view discipleship as optional. Hull alleges, "They believe they can be saved without being a disciple because by and large, the modern gospel teaches that faith equals agreement with a set of religious facts. The problem is that believing in Jesus has no meaning if we don't follow Him in discipleship. Believing without discipleship is not believing; it is agreeing to a set of facts about a religious figure."[89]

Hull claims that preaching a gospel that excludes discipleship is a different gospel: "But because we've preached a different gospel, a vast throng of people think they are Christian/saved/born again when they really aren't! We've made the test for salvation doctrinal rather than behavioral, ritualizing it with walking the aisle, praying to receive Christ, or signing a doctrinal statement."[90]

David Platt shares this similar concern by stating, "Churches

---

[86] Ibid., Kindle Locations 700-703.
[87] Ibid., Kindle Locations 700-703.
[88] Ibid., Kindle Locations 572-575.
[89] Ibid., Kindle Locations 718.
[90] Ibid., Kindle Locations 740-742.

today are filled with supposed Christians who seem content to have a casual association with Christ while giving nominal adherence to Christianity. Scores of men, women, and children have been told that becoming a follower of Jesus simply involves acknowledging certain facts or saying certain words."[91]

From a biblical perspective, this view can run the risk of promoting a form of conversion that can easily produce false salvation and a lack of discipleship. It can give the appearance that we can be saved and then live our lives as we please. This mentality leads to the conclusion that we can have the desires of the flesh and heaven too — that we don't need to give up much to be saved. It violates the call of Christ to follow Him in discipleship because discipleship is viewed as optional. Consequently, the state of evangelicalism is suffering as a result, and today we have many spiritually immature Christians.

The Problem with Separating the Gospel into Parts

I admire those who separate the gospel into parts in order to better understand it. However, discipleship has been negatively affected as a result.

Instead of viewing the gospel as a complete process, there's a desire to separate the initial stage of salvation (belief and faith) from its other parts such as repentance, obedience, and fruit. In so doing, faith and belief are often elevated and clarified, while the expression of salvation as evidenced by repentance, obedience, and fruit, is overlooked or misunderstood as works. Instead of viewing the gospel in its entirety, it's divided up and dissected.

While careful analyzation of each part has its role, we can run the risk of losing sight of the big picture because we're so focused on the details. Therefore, it's important to look at the entirety of the salvation process to understand what it entails, not just one

---

[91] David Platt, *Follow Me* (Carol Stream, Tyndale House Publishers, 2013), p. 3.

part of it.

The gospel is only the gospel when it functions in its entirety. On the contrary, the gospel is not the gospel if only part of it is believed and practiced.

Conclusion

How does the belief that we can be saved without being a disciple affect discipleship? If we believe there are two aspects of salvation and that we can choose the salvation aspect but omit the discipleship aspect, then discipleship will be viewed as optional.

I believe being saved and being a disciple are one and the same. It's like a two-sided coin: on one side is faith in Christ and on the other side is following Christ. The act of following Christ is the biblical expression of genuine salvation.

I believe if we primarily focus on one side of the coin (belief only) and omit the other side of the coin (being a disciple), we can promote a false gospel. Both sides of the coin represent the coin in its entirety. Discipleship is the "following Christ" side of the coin. Naturally, if we omit the "following Christ" side of the coin we omit discipleship. This is the great danger of the belief in salvation without discipleship.

11. The Belief in Salvation Without Obedience

I believe the misunderstanding of salvation in relation to obedience is another central factor contributing to the neglect of discipleship today. As a result, many Christians are not engaged in discipleship because they believe they can be saved without obedience or submission to Christ. Is salvation without obedience biblical?

Dallas Willard quotes a statement by A. W. Tozer concerning the belief in salvation without obedience: "A notable heresy has come into being throughout Evangelical Christian circles – the widely accepted concept that we humans can choose to accept Christ only because we need him as Savior and that we have the right to postpone our obedience to him as Lord as long as we want to!"[92] Willard then goes on to state that "Salvation apart from obedience is unknown in the sacred scriptures. This 'heresy' has created the impression that it is quite reasonable to be a 'Vampire Christian.' One in effect says to Jesus, 'I'd like a little of your blood, please, but I don't care to be your student or have your character. In fact, won't you just excuse me while I get on with my life and I'll see you in heaven?'"[93]

John MacArthur has also spoken out about what he believes is a misunderstanding regarding the relationship between salvation and obedience. He claims that some theologians have proposed a gospel wherein one can receive eternal life yet continue to live in rebellion against God.[94] He notes, "They've

---

[92] A. W. Tozer, *I Call It Heresy* (Harrisburg, Penn.: Christian Publications, 1974, p. 5, quoted by Dallas Willard, 2009-10-13, *The Great Omission,* HarperCollins. Kindle Edition), p. 229.
[93] Dallas Willard, *The Great Omission* (HarperCollins. Kindle Edition, 2009-10-13), pp. 13-14.
[94] John MacArthur, *The Gospel According to Jesus* ((Grand Rapids, Michigan, Zondervan Publishing House, 1988), p. 15.

been told that the only criterion for salvation is knowing and believing some basic facts about Christ. They hear from the beginning that obedience is optional."[95] MacArthur refutes this belief by asserting, "The gospel Jesus proclaimed was a call to discipleship, a call to follow Him in submissive obedience, not just a plea to make a decision or pray a prayer."[96]

Not Everyone Who Says to Me, "Lord, Lord," Will Enter the Kingdom of Heaven

Christ has a sobering warning for those who assume they are saved but are not. He proclaims this reality with some startling words, "Not everyone who says to me, '**Lord, Lord**,' will enter the kingdom of heaven, but the one who **does the will of my Father** who is in heaven" (Matt. 7:21). Christ warns that it's not those who call Him "Lord" who will be saved, but those who do the will of His Father. He asserts that it's not what a person says, but what they do that matters, and that it's possible to acknowledge Him as "Lord," but not be genuinely saved. This verse counters the argument of some who believe we can be saved yet not obey. Christ stresses that true faith is active and should include obedience to be saving faith. He claims that mere mental assent does not save, but must be accompanied by obedience to be genuine faith.

Notice also that Christ says, "On that day many will say to me, 'Lord, Lord, did we not prophesy in your name, and cast out demons in your name, and **do many mighty works in your name**?' And then will I declare to them, 'I never knew you; depart from me, you workers of lawlessness'" (Matt. 7:22–23).

Christ states that many will not enter the Kingdom of Heaven because they are basing their salvation on works, not faith. They believe their "mighty works" will save them, not their faith in

---

[95] Ibid., p. 17.
[96] Ibid., p. 21.

Christ alone. Christ warns us that salvation is not by works but by grace.

We find, then, two factors that can result in false salvation: (1) belief in God without obedience and (2) basing our salvation on works and not grace. Christ warns of both dangers in this passage.

The Role of Obedience in Expressing True Faith

Christ taught that genuine salvation should result in obedience: "Whoever **believes** in the Son has eternal life; whoever **does not obey** the Son shall not see life, but the wrath of God remains on him" (John 3:36). Interestingly, Christ uses the word "believe" as synonymous with "obey." According to Christ, believing is obeying, and obeying is believing. They are one and the same.

In this text, obedience to the Son is critical to receiving eternal life, and without it, we are not genuinely saved. Salvation is a free gift given by grace through faith in Christ, but the fruit, or evidence of salvation according to Christ, is obedience.

The Sermon on the Mount and Obedience

Another powerful example regarding the importance of obedience in relation to salvation is found at the end of the Sermon on the Mount:

> Everyone then who hears these words of mine and **does them** will be like a wise man who built his house on the rock. And the rain fell, and the floods came, and the winds blew and beat on that house, but it did not fall, because it had been founded on the rock. And everyone who hears these words of mine and **does not do them** will be like a foolish man who built his house on the sand. And the rain fell, and the floods came, and the winds blew and beat against that house, and it fell, and great was the fall of it (Matt. 7:24–27).

The difference between the salvation or destruction of each house (our lives) in the parable rested upon whether or not they obeyed Christ's words or just heard them.

Now the significance of this passage is weighty. The Sermon on the Mount is the longest sermon recorded in the Gospels that Christ preached. Some theologians have equated the Mount of Beatitudes (the location where Christ preached the Sermon on the Mount) with the Old Covenant given on Mt. Sinai. It's believed by some scholars that in the same way God gave the summation of the Old Covenant on Mt. Sinai, Christ gave the summation of the New Covenant on the Mount of Beatitudes.

If the summation of the New Covenant entails the importance of doing and obeying what Christ taught, then it would seem logical that the gospel message of salvation would include the same. Therefore, a gospel message that permits mental belief only in God, and excludes the need for obedience, would fall far short of what Christ proclaimed.

The Parable of the Sower

Christ also spoke about the marks of a genuine believer in the Parable of the Sower (Matt. 13:1–23). Christ sowed seed (His Word) upon four different kinds of soils (people's lives). The first soil rejected the seed (God's Word), and the next two soils showed life for a bit, but then died out and didn't produce fruit. It was only the soil (people) that produced fruit who were truly saved. According to Christ, the mark of a genuine believer is fruit, not just belief and faith in God.

The Rich Young Man

Christ engaged a rich young man who knew much of the Bible, believed in God, had much of Scripture memorized, and even kept many of the Ten Commandments, but wasn't saved. Jesus used this encounter to teach that salvation and obedience go hand in hand. Matthew 19 recounts the meeting:

> And behold, a man came up to him, saying, "Teacher, what good deed must I do **to have eternal life**?" And he said to him, "Why do you ask me about what is good? There is only one who is good. If you would enter life, keep the commandments." He said to him, "Which ones?" And Jesus said, "You shall not murder, You shall not commit adultery, You shall not steal, You shall not bear false witness, Honor your father and mother, and, You shall love your neighbor as yourself." The young man said to him, "All these I have kept. What do I still lack?" Jesus said to him, "If you would be perfect, go, sell what you possess and give to the poor, and you will have treasure in heaven; and come, follow me." When the young man heard this, he went away sorrowful, for he had great possessions (Matt. 19:16–22).

Interestingly, the rich young man knew he wasn't saved, and Jesus knew it as well. There was no debate about that. However, despite the rich young man's knowledge of God, belief in Him, and obedience to some of the Ten Commandments, he wasn't saved. He lacked one thing: he was unwilling to submit to, and follow Christ. This passage indicates that belief in God, and even some Christian activity, isn't enough to save us. Faith must be accompanied by obedience in order to be genuine, saving faith.

Defining Who Is in the Family of God

After a long session of teaching about the Parables of the Kingdom, in which Christ had emphasized the importance of putting His words into practice instead of just hearing them, Christ was told that His mother and brothers were seeking Him. His response to them was quite fascinating: "But he answered them, 'My mother and my brothers are those who **hear the word of God and do it**'" (Luke 8:21).

121

Christ states that it's those who do His words that are part of His family, not those who merely hear His words without doing them. He stresses the fact that salvation and obedience go hand in hand.

Hearing Without Obeying Brings Greater Condemnation

Christ continually warned that hearing without obeying brings greater condemnation because we know what to do but refuse to do it. The following passage speaks of those who heard Christ's words but chose not to obey them:

> Then he began to denounce the cities where most of his mighty works had been done, because they did not repent. "Woe to you, Chorazin! Woe to you, Bethsaida! For if the mighty works done in you had been done in Tyre and Sidon, they would have repented long ago in sackcloth and ashes. But I tell you, it will be more bearable on the day of judgment for Tyre and Sidon than for you. And you, Capernaum, will you be exalted to heaven? You will be brought down to Hades. For if the mighty works done in you had been done in Sodom, it would have remained until this day. But I tell you that it will be more tolerable on the day of judgment for the land of Sodom than for you" (Matt. 11:20–24).

We also see countless examples of punishment and condemnation in the Old Testament for those who heard God's words but chose not to obey them.

Conclusion

Despite the verses that teach salvation and obedience go hand in hand, some today are teaching that obedience is optional and that one can be saved without obeying and following Christ. I believe this misunderstanding is a significant factor leading to the neglect of discipleship among many.

12. The Belief in Salvation Without Works

The belief that we can be saved without bearing fruit or showing any evidence of our faith is also contributing to the lack of discipleship. Many think that as long as they believe and have faith in God, they are saved. They cling to their belief as sufficient for salvation and believe bearing fruit and being a follower of Christ are optional. Is it possible to be saved, yet have no works or expression of that faith in our lives? Is belief in God enough to save us, or must our faith be accompanied by works to be genuine, saving faith? Is salvation without works biblical?

Is Belief in God Without Fruit Genuine Faith?

The Book of James strives to define faith and works, otherwise known as belief and fruit. It attempts to clarify what genuine faith is and how it's expressed. It's not teaching that works save us, but that true faith should include fruit that provides evidence of salvation. Notice how James clarifies that belief in God and faith without works do not save:

> But someone will say, "You have faith and I have works. Show me your faith apart from your works, and I will show you my faith by my works. You believe that God is one; you do well. Even the demons believe — and shudder" (James 2:18-19).

Notice how James says that our faith (salvation) is shown by our works. Notice also that despite believing in God and shuddering, the demons are not saved. This proves that it's not our belief only that saves us, but our belief expressed through obedience. Belief is the necessary beginning point in salvation, but if it's not expressed through works (fruit), it's not true faith and doesn't produce genuine conversion.

123

James also clarifies another critical aspect of faith:

What good is it, my brothers, if someone says he has faith but does not have works? Can that faith save him? If a brother or sister is poorly clothed and lacking in daily food, and one of you says to them, "Go in peace, be warmed and filled," without giving them the things needed for the body, what good is that? **So also faith by itself, if it does not have works, is dead** (James 2:14–17).

James clarifies that genuine faith must be accompanied by works (fruit) to be true faith, and if not, it is dead. For those who claim that belief is enough to save them, John MacArthur boldly responds: "The faith they are relying on is only intellectual acquiescence to a set of facts. It will not save."[97]

Defining Biblical Faith

What is true faith according to Scripture? Is it only mental belief about certain facts or does it entail more?

In Hebrews 11, we find the longest and fullest treatise on the definition and example of biblical faith:

- By faith, Noah **built** an ark.
- By faith, Abraham **obeyed** and left his country to follow God to the Promised Land.
- By faith, Sarah **received** power to conceive.
- By faith, Abraham, when he was tested, **offered up** Isaac.
- By faith, Isaac **invoked** future blessings on Jacob and Esau.
- By faith, Jacob, when dying, **blessed** each of the sons of Joseph.
- By faith, Joseph, at the end of his life **made mention** of the exodus of the Israelites and **gave directions** concerning his

---

[97]John MacArthur, *The Gospel According to Jesus* (Grand Rapids, Michigan, Zondervan Publishing House, 1988), p. 170.

bones.

- By faith, Moses, when he was born, was **hidden** for three months by his parents.
- By faith, Moses, when he was grown up, **refused** to be called the son of Pharaoh's daughter, **choosing** rather to be mistreated with the people of God than to enjoy the fleeting pleasures of sin.
- By faith, Moses **kept** the Passover and sprinkled the blood so that the Destroyer of the firstborn might not touch them.
- By faith, the people **crossed** the Red Sea as on dry land.
- By faith, the walls of Jericho fell after the Israelites had **encircled** them for seven days.
- By faith, Rahab the prostitute did not perish with those who were disobedient because she had **given** a friendly welcome to the spies.
- By faith, Gideon, Barak, Samson, Jephthah, David, Samuel, and the prophets **conquered** kingdoms, **enforced** justice, **obtained** promises, **stopped** the mouths of lions, **quenched** the power of fire, **escaped** the edge of the sword, were **made** strong out of weakness, became **mighty** in war, and put foreign armies to **flight.**
- By faith, women **received** back their dead by resurrection; some were tortured, **refusing** to accept release, so that they might rise again to a better life.
- By faith, others suffered mocking and flogging, and even chains and imprisonment, they were stoned, they were sawn in two, they were killed with the sword, they **went about** in skins of sheep and goats, destitute, afflicted, and mistreated.

The fascinating truth about all these examples of faith is that they are characterized by an action. Their faith was followed by doing something, not mere static belief. Each example is followed by a verb, a verb of action, a verb of obedience. Each person displayed works that bore witness to their faith.

Now it's critical that we clarify the difference between works done to earn salvation and works done as the result of salvation. Works done to earn salvation is what Scripture calls a "false gospel." Works done as the result of salvation is what Scripture calls "fruit." Works, therefore, are the result of our salvation, not what earns it. However, if our faith does not have fruit, it is dead.

John the Baptist and Biblical Faith

John the Baptist strongly rebuked those in his day who thought they could just believe in God and not bear fruit: "But when he saw many of the Pharisees and Sadducees coming to his baptism, he said to them, 'You brood of vipers! Who warned you to flee from the wrath to come? **Bear fruit in keeping with repentance**. And do not presume to say to yourselves, 'We have Abraham as our father,' for I tell you, God is able from these stones to raise up children for Abraham. Even now the axe is laid to the root of the trees. Every tree therefore that **does not bear good fruit is cut down and thrown into the fire'**" (Matt. 3:7–10). This verse teaches that faith without fruit is not saving faith.

Christ and Biblical Faith

Christ's most used phrase in calling people to salvation was, "Follow Me." "And **calling the crowd** to him with his disciples, he said to them, 'If anyone would come after me, let him deny himself and take up his cross and **follow me'**" (Mark 8:34). The term "Follow Me" is a call to action. It's a verb and entails more than belief. In a practical sense, following Christ cannot be done without some kind of action on our part, either spiritually or physically.

Fruit Is the Evidence of Genuine Salvation

Christ spoke about true and false prophets and how we'd know the difference between them. He said, "Beware of false prophets, who come to you in sheep's clothing but inwardly are ravenous wolves. You will recognize them by their fruits. Are grapes gathered from thornbushes, or figs from thistles? So, every healthy tree bears good fruit, but the diseased tree bears bad fruit. A healthy tree cannot bear bad fruit, nor can a diseased tree bear good fruit. Every tree that does not bear good fruit is cut down and thrown into the fire. Thus, **you will recognize them by their fruits**" (Matt. 7:15–20).

Christ says the way we recognize genuine believers from false believers is by their fruits. He also said that the false believers would be cut down and thrown into the fire. Therefore, those who don't produce the fruit of genuine salvation are not true believers. According to Christ, it's the fruit of a person's life, not their belief in Him that distinguishes a true believer from a false believer.

Genuine Faith Is Expressed by Action

Genuine, saving faith should result in bearing fruit. It does not entail just mental assent and mere knowledge, but some action on our part that results in doing the will of our Master. It results in good works!

Throughout the whole of Scripture, we see biblical faith that is obedient always brings blessings from God, but mere mental assent without obedience always brings His judgment.

For example, the reason the nation of Israel was deported to Assyria and Babylon was because of their lack of obedience. Most Israelites believed in God; they just didn't obey Him. Their mere belief in God did not save them from being deported and escaping His judgment.

Good Works Is an Expression of Faith

The most quoted verses on the foundational doctrine that salvation is by grace through faith in Jesus Christ and not by works is Ephesians 2:8-9: "For by grace you have been saved through faith. And this is not your own doing; it is the gift of God, not a result of works, so that no one may boast."

However, most disassociate Ephesians 2:10 from Ephesians 2:8-9. Ephesians 2:10 reveals what the result or outflow of Ephesians 2:8-9 should be: "For we are his workmanship, created in Christ Jesus for **good works**, which God prepared beforehand, that we should walk in them." By seeing these verses together, we learn that salvation begins with faith in God, but does not end there. True faith should be evidenced by works in a believer's life if it is genuine, saving faith.

Conclusion

I believe that, according to Christ and the rest of Scripture, genuine salvation should result in fruit bearing. We should desire to follow, be obedient, and please our Master. True faith should produce fruit in our lives that bears witness to the fact that genuine salvation has occurred. The fruit produced doesn't save us, but is a by-product of salvation.

How does the belief that we can be saved without bearing any fruit affect discipleship? If we believe we can be saved without being a disciple and bearing any fruit, then we run the risk of being false believers. We'll also neglect discipleship as our focus will not be on serving God, but on a version of the gospel wherein we believe we can be saved, but live as we wish with little or no accountability before God.

Therefore, can a person be saved and not produce any fruit? I believe the answer is no. Genuine faith produces fruit, not the absence of it.

13. The Belief in Grace Without Effort

Another factor contributing to the neglect of discipleship today is the common belief that grace is opposed to effort in our spiritual growth. We talk a lot about God's grace, forgiveness of sin, and our freedom in Christ, but don't talk much about responsibility, discipline, and perseverance. We focus on God's role in granting us grace but neglect our role in exerting effort.

Is the belief that God's grace is opposed to human effort true, or do they work hand in hand? Is it okay to be lazy and casual in our Christian lives because God will love us no matter what, or is this dangerous water to enter? Is it okay to presume upon God's grace and forgiveness, or is this a treacherous road to walk?

Grace and Effort

I believe God's grace, that enables us to grow in Christ, be victorious over sin, and arrive at spiritual maturity, is not opposed to effort. Grace is opposed to earning salvation and God's love, but it's not opposed to the human agent's cooperation with God by exercising effort in spiritual growth. We see throughout Scripture that God is not opposed to effort in doing His will.

Hebrews chapter 11 outlines all the great heroes of the faith and exhibits how their efforts pleased God. Each expression of their faith was accompanied by effort.

We also see in the Apostle Paul's life how he cooperated with the grace of God by exercising effort: "But by the grace of God I am what I am, and his grace toward me was not in vain. On the contrary, **I worked harder** than any of them, though it was not I, but the grace of God that is with me" (1 Cor. 15:10). Paul notes how he worked harder than the rest of the Apostles with the grace of God, yet he credits God for everything. In this verse, we see a wonderful relationship between the grace of God and human effort. They work hand in hand, God granting grace and the human agent working and applying His grace to their life.

The well-known verses of Philippians 2:12–13 also speak of the role of effort in relation to salvation: "Therefore, my beloved, as you have always obeyed, so now, not only as in my presence but much more in my absence, **work out your own salvation** with fear and trembling, for it is God who works in you, both to will and to work for his good pleasure." Working out our salvation means working to bring it to completion, not working to earn it. It means living out and applying God's Word in our lives, not just knowing something and remaining unchanged.

Working out your own salvation with fear and trembling speaks of the seriousness we should take in our pursuit of spiritual maturity.

In these verses, God expects us to exercise our effort for spiritual growth in Christ. As Bill Hull states, "Grace, then, is God's continued gift of enabling us to do good works and to give great effort. These are as much a part of his grace as the act of salvation or conversion."[98]

God's Grace and Human Effort

I believe the Bible teaches that living by faith encompasses two aspects: (1) what God does and (2) what we do in response to what God does. Scripture clearly teaches that we are saved by grace through faith and not of works (Eph. 2:8–9). In addition, it also teaches that we grow in our relationship with Christ by grace as well (2 Pet. 3:18).

Therefore, every aspect of salvation and every aspect of growth in Christ involves God's grace helping us in the process.

---

[98] Bill Hull, *The Complete Book of Discipleship: On Being and Making Followers of Christ* (The Navigators Reference Library 1, 2014, NavPress. Kindle Edition), Kindle Locations 718-720.

Without God's grace, we would have no desire to receive Christ or grow in Him. It's all accomplished by God working in us and granting us the desire to do His will.

God clearly fulfills His role in granting us grace to grow in Christ. However, He doesn't do everything for us, though He enables and grants us grace for everything. He expects us to have a role in applying His grace. As mentioned, we are commanded to "Work out our salvation." This means we are to exert effort and work with God's enabling grace. God expects us to do our part in working with Him; if we don't, we'll fail to reach spiritual maturity and remain stunted in our growth in Christ.

It's important to understand the difference between effort exerted to earn salvation and effort exerted as the result of salvation. Effort exerted to earn salvation is what Scripture calls a "false gospel." Effort exerted as the result of salvation is what Scripture calls "working out our salvation." Effort, therefore, doesn't earn our salvation, but is what God expects of us as we work out our salvation to become spiritually mature.

For those who misunderstand the true meaning of grace, they'll tend to neglect discipleship as they'll see it as opposed to grace. They'll hold the common belief that God's grace means He'll overlook our lack of obedience, remove the consequences of laziness, and hold us unaccountable for how we live our lives and use the talents He gives us.

Abusing God's Grace

Today, we have a tendency to abuse God's grace. There's a lot of talk among Christians about our freedom in Christ and God's grace. For some, this means they can acquire salvation and then live as they wish. They boast about the grace of God and their freedom in Christ. They assume that because of God's grace He now just winks at and overlooks sin. This simply is not true.

The biblical definition of freedom and grace are very different from what many think today.

The biblical meaning of freedom is the ability Christ grants us to overcome sin, not the freedom to be engaged in it. It's freedom over sin, not freedom to sin. It's the freedom and power to do what we should, not freedom to do as we wish.

The biblical meaning of grace can be defined as God's supernatural enablement that helps us live in such a way as to please God — not the grace to disobey and be unaccountable to the consequences of sin. God's grace empowers us to obey; it doesn't grant us the liberty to disobey and escape God's judgment.

Presuming upon God's Grace

For those who presume upon God's grace and elevate forgiveness over obedience, they overlook a fatal flaw in the life of King Saul. He consistently presumed upon the grace and forgiveness of God by disobeying and assuming God would just overlook his sin. As a result, God removed him as king over Israel and said these harsh words to him through the Prophet Samuel:

> And Samuel said, "Has the Lord as great delight in burnt-offerings and sacrifices, as in **obeying** the voice of the Lord? Behold, to **obey** is better than sacrifice, and to listen than the fat of rams. For rebellion is as the sin of divination, and **presumption** is as iniquity and idolatry. Because you have rejected the word of the Lord, he has also rejected you from being king" (1 Sam. 15:22–23).

In God's eyes, obedience pleases Him far more than asking forgiveness and presuming upon His grace. For the believer who chooses to live casually in their obedience to God, and disobeys because they are counting on His grace and forgiveness, they should take great pause. To presume upon and abuse God's grace and forgiveness is a serious sin in God's eyes.

God's Grace Does Not Remove Sin's Consequences

Many Christians confuse God's grace and forgiveness of sin with the removal of the consequences. They are very different functions. God certainly forgives and removes our sins as far as the east is from the west, but He doesn't remove the consequences of them.

King David is a stark reminder of how sin affects our lives. After he committed adultery with Bathsheba and murdered her husband Uriah, his life was never the same. He lost fellowship with God for a time, lost the son he had from his adulterous encounter, lost his moral authority, ceased to speak out against sin in the lives of his family and nation, remained virtually impotent as a spiritual leader, and lost the respect of others. God loved and forgave him, but there were monumental consequences for his sin.

Dietrich Bonhoeffer reveals a weakness he sees in Christianity today that abuses and presumes upon God's grace. It's the belief that Christians can be saved and then do as they please because they are under grace. He counters this understanding by stating, "The word of cheap grace has been the ruin of more Christians than any commandment of works."[99] Bonhoeffer claims that true salvation will encompass discipleship and works. He warns against the idea that salvation can be attained apart from obedience and summarizes such a view as "cheap grace."[100] John MacArthur echoes this same concern when he says, "Grace does not grant permission to live in the flesh; it supplies power to live in the Spirit."[101]

---

[99] Dietrich Bonhoeffer, *The Cost of Discipleship* (SCM Classics, Hymns Ancient and Modern Ltd., Kindle Edition, 2011-08-16), Kindle Locations 770-771.
[100] Ibid., Kindle Locations 770-771.
[101] John MacArthur, *The Gospel According to Jesus* (Grand Rapids, Michigan, Zondervan Publishing House, 1988), p. 31.

Conclusion

Many Christians today are neglecting discipleship because they believe that exerting human effort is not that important or is opposed to God's grace. They believe they can just coast along, living as they please, because God will forgive and remove the consequences of their lazy choices. In so doing, they are abusing and presuming upon God's grace, believing discipleship is optional. As a result, few are seriously pursuing a life that leads to spiritual maturity.

Conclusion to Chapter 2

In this chapter, we looked at 13 key factors contributing to the neglect of discipleship and spiritual maturity. In the next chapter, we'll define biblical discipleship by examining key phrases Christ used in calling people to follow Him. In the process, we'll understand what discipleship was like in the time of Christ and see how it vastly differs from discipleship today.

Chapter 3

Defining Biblical Discipleship

In This Chapter

In chapter 1, we analyzed the state of discipleship and spiritual maturity today, concluding that they're in critical condition and being grossly neglected. In chapter 2, we investigated the key factors contributing to the neglect of discipleship and spiritual maturity.

In this chapter, we'll define biblical discipleship by examining key phrases Christ used in calling people to follow Him.

---

1. The Meaning of Biblical Discipleship

"To another he said, 'Follow me.' But he said, 'Lord, let me first go and bury my father.' And Jesus said to him, 'Leave the dead to bury their own dead. But as for you, go and proclaim the kingdom of God.' Yet another said, 'I will follow you, Lord, but let me first say farewell to those at my home.' Jesus said to him, 'No one who puts his hand to the plow and looks back is fit for the kingdom of God'" (Luke 9:59–62). These words reveal the depth of commitment Christ demands in order to be His disciple.

What is biblical discipleship and how is modern day discipleship starkly different from that of Christ's day?

What Is Biblical Discipleship?

Joseph Crockett, in his article "Is There Discipline in Our Discipleship," states that the term "disciple" is derived from the Latin term, *discipulus,* and refers to a pupil, student, and follower. Related ideas include: to learn, to take, or to accept.[102]

James Samra, in his article "A Biblical View of Discipleship," proposes that the word "discipleship" is used in a number of

---

[102] Joseph V. Crockett, *Is There Discipline in Our Discipleship?* (Source: Living Pulpit, Online, March 1, 2014, ATLA Religion Database with ATLASerials, Hunter Resource Library), p. 9, Accessed 11/5/2014.

different ways in the Bible.[103] Sometimes it's used to denote educational training, and sometimes it signifies life transformation or that of becoming like one's master.[104] Samra summarizes this concept by stating that discipleship can generally be understood to mean "the process of becoming like Christ."[105]

Greg Herrick says, "The Greek term *mathētēs* generally refers to any student, pupil, apprentice, or adherent, as opposed to a teacher. In the ancient world, it is most often associated with people who were devoted followers of a great religious leader or teacher of philosophy."[106] The Hebrew word for disciple is *talmidim*.

As mentioned in chapter 1, Dallas Willard makes an astute observation by revealing that the word "disciple" occurs 269 times in the New Testament, and the word "Christian" a scant three times.[107] Willard defines discipleship as the foundational aspect of what it means to be saved and a true follower of Christ.

Klaus Issler defines biblical discipleship as the responsibility to teach all believers to obey everything Christ commanded. Issler states that the Gospel of Matthew records five major discourses by Jesus, from which six broad themes are taken. A summary of these discourses is found in the Great Commission where Christ says, "Teaching them to obey everything I have commanded you."[108]

The word "disciple" is related to the word "discipline." A disciple, therefore, should be a highly disciplined person who is

---

[103] James G. Samra, *A Biblical View of Discipleship* (Bibliotheca Sacra: 219-34, Publication Type: Article, Database: ATLA Religion Database with ATLASerials, Hunter Resource Library), p. 219, Accessed 11/5/2014.
[104] Ibid., p. 219.
[105] Ibid., p. 220.
[106] Greg Herrick, *Understanding the Meaning of the Term "Disciple"*, 2004, Bible.org, https://bible.org/seriespage/2-understanding-meaning-term-disciple, Accessed 08/13/2015.
[107] Dallas Willard, *The Great Omission* (HarperCollins, Kindle Edition, 2009-10-13), p. 3.
[108] Klaus Issler, *Six Themes to Guide Spiritual Formation Ministry Based on Jesus' Sermon on the Mount* (Source: Christian Education, Journal Date: September 1, 2010. CEJ: Series 3, Vol. 7, No. 2. ATLA Religion Database with ATLASerials. Hunter Resource Library), pp. 367, 368, Accessed 11/5/2014.

focused on following and obeying all the commands of God (Matt. 28:20).

Discipleship in the Time of Christ

In order to understand biblical discipleship in its fullness, we must see how it functioned in the time of Christ. Ray Vander Laan provides rich understanding in this area. He notes, "Discipleship was a very common practice in Christ's day and especially in the Galilee area. The people of Galilee were the most religious Jews in the world in the time of Jesus. This is quite contrary to the common view that the Galileans were simple, uneducated peasants from an isolated area. This perspective is probably due to the comments made in the Bible, which appear to belittle people from this area."[109] Vander Laan continues, "The Galilean people were actually more educated in the Bible and its application than most Jews were. More famous Jewish teachers come from Galilee than anywhere else in the world. They were known for their great reverence for Scripture and their passionate desire to be faithful to it."[110]

Discipleship Training Began Early in Life

Training for discipleship, as we would know it today, actually started very young in the life of a Jewish child. They would enter grade school (called Beth Sefer) at around 4–5 years of age, which was generally held at the local synagogue. The teacher at the synagogue was called a rabbi. At this level, they would mainly be instructed in the Torah (first five books of the Old Testament), learning to read, write, and memorize it. The rest of the Old Testament was referred to as well. Much of the Torah

---

[109] Ray Vander Laan, *Rabbi and Talmidim,* That the World May Know, www.thattheworldmayknow.com/Rabbi-and-talmidim, Accessed 08/13/2015.
[110] Ibid., Accessed 08/13/2015.

was committed to memory, and it's likely that by the time this level of education was finished (age 13), they had much of it memorized.[111]

After grade school, the best students would then continue on to middle school (called Beth Midrash). They would continue to learn and memorize the Torah, but would branch out and learn the rest of the Old Testament as well, committing much of it to memory.

After the Beth Midrash level, those who wanted to continue in discipleship would then seek out a rabbi who would accept them as disciples. They would often leave home to travel with him for a lengthy period of time. These students were called talmidim (talmids) in Hebrew, which is translated, disciple.[112]

Memorization Was a Key Factor in Discipleship

Memorization was important during Jesus' day because most people didn't have their own copy of the Scriptures, so they either had to know it by heart or go to the synagogue to consult the local village scroll. As mentioned, by the time a child finished the Beth Midrash level of education, they had most of the Torah, and much of the Old Testament memorized.

The common memorization technique involved rote, constant repetition, a practice still used to this day.[113]

A Disciple Imitated His Rabbi

Discipleship in Christ's day involved a heavy dose of imitation. A talmid (disciple) emulated his rabbi in all facets of life. His goal was to be like his rabbi. Vander Laan adds, "There is much more to a talmid than simply calling one a student. A

---

[111] Ibid., Accessed 08/13/2015.
[112] Ibid., Accessed 08/13/2015.
[113] Ibid., Accessed 08/13/2015.

student wants to know what the teacher knows for the grade, to complete the class or the degree, or even out of respect for the teacher. A talmid wants to be like the teacher, that is, to become what the teacher is."[114] That meant that students were passionately devoted to their rabbi and noted everything he did or said.

Vander Laan continues, "The rabbi-talmid relationship was a very intense and personal system of education. As the rabbi lived and taught his understanding of the Scripture to his students, they listened, watched, and imitated him to become like him. Eventually, they would become teachers themselves, passing on a lifestyle to their own talmidim."[115]

Discipleship Entailed Learning Much Scripture

The very few talmids that reached the status of a rabbi were extremely respected and sought after. Those who became rabbis were incredibly knowledgeable in Scripture, and many had memorized much, if not all, of the Old Testament. As mentioned, during Christ's day, they didn't have their own personal Bibles like we do today, so they had to commit it to memory to be able to reference and discuss it. As a result of memorizing so much Scripture, the rabbis were extremely knowledgeable in God's Word.

Those who wanted to learn from a rabbi also committed much, if not all, of the Old Testament to memory as well. This was a requirement to be a disciple as their discussions about Scripture didn't mainly deal with what the Scriptures said, but what they meant. Rabbis in the time of Christ would be equivalent to theologians today who hold at least one Ph.D. in theology.

To reach the status of a rabbi was a great accomplishment. They were the ones who decided biblical doctrines, practices, and

---

[114] Ibid., Accessed 08/13/2015.
[115] Ibid., Accessed 08/13/2015.

customs of the country. Their words were exceptionally authoritative and valued. Doug Greenwold says, "In the world of Pharisaism, rabbis were the teachers who had been given the authoritative role to interpret God's Word for the living of a righteous life — defining what behavior would or would not please God."[116]

Rabbis were affiliated as well with many different groups such as the Pharisees, the Sadducees, the Essenes, and others. For example, John the Baptist was a rabbi who had his own disciples (Luke 5:33), and the Apostle Paul was a disciple of Gamaliel before eventually becoming a disciple of Christ at his conversion to Christianity. Some rabbis reached notable status and had a strong influence in religious and government affairs.

Strict Devotion Was Expected

The rabbis expected strict, complete devotion and adherence to their teachings. They expected loyalty and obedience even beyond that given to their families. Greenwold states, "If a rabbi ultimately agreed to a would-be disciple's request and allowed him to become a disciple, the disciple-to-be agreed to submit totally to the rabbi's authority in all areas of interpreting the Scriptures for his life. This was a cultural given for all observant Jewish young men — something each truly wanted to do. As a result, each disciple came to a rabbinic relationship with a desire and a willingness to do just that — surrender to the authority of God's Word as interpreted by his rabbi's view of Scripture."[117]

Different rabbis varied in their views of Scripture, so students would choose their rabbis according to their recognition in the country and their theological positions. It would be similar today as to which seminary a student might choose for their graduate

---

[116] Doug Greenwold, *Being a First-Century Disciple*, 2007, Bible.org, https://bible.org/article/being-first-century-disciple, Accessed 08/15/2015.
[117] Ibid., Access 08/15/2014.

level of theological training. These rabbis, on occasion, would take their students on training trips that could last from several days to several weeks. These were intense times of training where all distractions from the busyness of life were set aside, and the students would focus entirely on the teachings of their rabbi.

The rabbis also had favorite teaching places, one of which

 was on the Southern Steps that led up to the Temple Mount in Jerusalem. Tradition holds that even Christ taught His disciples

on these steps. I've been blessed to visit this site, and while there, imagined how it must have been.

Theological Discussions Were a Part of Discipleship

It was common for the rabbi and his disciples (a group called Yeshivas) to wrestle significantly with the Word of God. These yeshivas would intensely dialogue and debate over an aspect of life and what Scripture said about it.[118] "It was a standard part of rabbinic teaching methodology."[119] Greenwold adds, "Studying their rabbi's view of Scripture and wrestling with the text to comprehend God's way for the conduct of their life was the main priority of a disciple and the yeshiva experience. Since all disciples had memorized most, if not all, of their Hebrew Scriptures in preparation for their Bar Mitzvahs at age 13, the issue was not what God's Word said, rather what it meant and how it was to be lived out."[120] During their times of intense

---

[118] Ibid., Access 08/14/2014.
[119] Ibid., Access 08/14/2014.
[120] Ibid., Access 08/14/2014.

dialogue and debate, these yeshivas would arrive at their theological convictions and doctrinal positions.

Transparency and Accountability Was the Norm

There was amazing transparency in these groups of yeshivas as they spent much time together in their teaching sessions and discipleship training trips. Doug Greenwold says it well: "Unlike many of our contemporary discipleship programs, there was no curriculum or agenda for this multi-year discipling experience. Rather it was a continual daily relational living experience where either the rabbi would ask questions of the disciple as he closely observed the disciple's life, or the disciple would initiate a discussion by raising an issue or asking a question based on some aspect of his daily life."[121] In this discipleship format, not only was theology passed on, but character, attitudes, and behavior.

The Meaning of "Believe"

As a disciple learned from their rabbi, they were placing their entire trust and belief in him. This process was called, "believing." Unlike today, the term "believe" had a very different meaning in the Hebrew culture. Once again, Greenwold states it well: "The Semitic understanding of 'believe' was not based on an intellectual assent to a creed, doctrinal statement, or series of faith propositions. Rather, to a first-century disciple 'believe' is a verb in which you willingly submitted to your rabbi's interpretive authority regarding God's Word in every area of your life. Thus, to say you were a disciple in the name of Gamaliel, meant that you totally surrendered your life to Gamaliel's way of interpreting Scripture. As a result, you conformed all of your life's behavior to his interpretations."[122]

The word "believe" in the Hebrew culture meant taking some

---

[121] Ibid., Access 08/14/2014.
[122] Ibid., Access 08/14/2014.

action, applying knowledge to daily life, and changing some attitude or perspective on life, not just mentally knowing something and remaining unchanged. Today, the word "believe" is used more as a noun and slants toward mere intellectual agreement or mental assent, which is a very different meaning than the usage in Christ's day.

Discipleship Meant Commitment

Taking into account the historical meaning of discipleship, we can now better understand the discipleship process Christ employed with His disciples. He called them to follow Him, be with Him, learn from Him, practice what they learned, surrender completely to Him, and to love Him more than their families, friends, and culture. It meant even being willing to die for Him if needed.

Therefore, a disciple can be summed up as a disciplined learner or student who chooses to follow Christ, their rabbi, to such a degree that they submit their entire life, will, time, plans, desires, dreams, character, and efforts fully to Him and His teachings. They are willing to deny themself, take up their cross, and obey all His commands with total abandonment. A biblical disciple is a person who gives complete devotion and loyalty to Christ above any human relationship or influence. It's a person who is willing to die for the cause of Christ on a daily basis, and once and for all if needed.

We see in the discipleship process during the time of Christ that there was a strong emphasis on knowing God's Word, relational mentoring, character, discipline, commitment, and devotion.

Discipleship in Christ's Day Versus Discipleship Today

How are Christians and the church doing today in regards to biblical discipleship? The contrast is quite staggering between discipleship in Christ's time and discipleship today.

Unlike Christ's disciples who knew Scripture exceedingly well and had much of it memorized, 81% of Christians today don't read their Bibles regularly and are largely biblically illiterate. Unlike Christ's disciples who were fishers of men and took the gospel to the ends of the earth, 61% of Christians today haven't even shared their faith in the last six months. Unlike Christ's disciples who prayed extensively, the average Christian today prays somewhere between 1–7 minutes a day. And unlike Christ and the Apostles who made discipleship a core part of their ministries, 81% of pastors have no regular discipleship program for mentoring their people.

It's clear to see that the value Christ and the Apostles gave to discipleship versus the value the average Evangelical church and Christian give it today is vastly different.

2. The Meaning of Follow Me

"And calling the crowd to him with his disciples, he said to them, 'If anyone would come after me, let him deny himself and take up his cross and **follow me**'" (Mark 8:34). What does it mean to "follow Christ"?

The most common phrase Christ used in calling people to salvation and discipleship was "Follow Me." It's mentioned 23 times in the Gospels. If this was the key phrase Christ used to call people to be His disciples, then it's crucial we understand it in order to understand discipleship.

According to the Gospels, Jesus spent approximately 70% of His ministry time around the Sea of Galilee, with the northern shore being His most traversed area. In fact, He even set up His home base during His early ministry in the small town of Capernaum, which is right beside the Sea of Galilee on the northern shore (Matt. 4:13). Scripture records that Christ called all of His 12 disciples from the Galilee area (Acts 1:11).

I've had the privilege of walking the northern shore of the Sea

 of Galilee where Scripture records that Christ called four of the 12 disciples (Peter, Andrew, James, and John). I can see in my mind's eye this northern shore and can picture what it must have been like when Christ called His first disciples.

Picture a sunny day on the calm sea not far from the water's edge. Peter and his brother Andrew were fishing as they'd done

for many years. Not far down the shore were James and his brother John mending their nets. These two pairs of brothers were all fishing partners. What happened next would change their lives forever:

> While walking by the Sea of Galilee, he saw two brothers, Simon (who is called Peter) and Andrew his brother, casting a net into the sea, for they were fishermen. And he said to them, "Follow me, and I will make you fishers of men." Immediately they left their nets and followed him. And going on from there he saw two other brothers, James the son of Zebedee and John, his brother, in the boat with Zebedee, their father, mending their nets, and he called them. Immediately they left the boat and their father and followed him (Matt. 4:18–24).

Now from accounts in the other Gospels, these four disciples had previously had other encounters with Jesus. Each encounter served them in knowing Him just a little better. So in their decision to follow Christ, they knew what they were doing and what they were committing to. However, unlike their previous encounters with Christ, this time, He asked them to make a commitment. He called them to a decision. They chose to take the boldest step they had ever taken and decided to obey and follow Christ. They left their nets, renounced all, and chose to be disciples of Christ. Their lives would never be the same again.

David Platt articulates what this calling entailed: "When Jesus called the first disciples, He was also calling them away from other things. By calling these men to leave their boats, Jesus was calling them to abandon their careers. When He called them to leave their nets, He was calling them to abandon their possessions. When He called them to leave their father in the boat by himself, He was calling them to abandon their family and friends. Ultimately, Jesus was calling them to abandon themselves."[123]

A Big Decision and a New Life

Following Christ would mean a totally new life for these disciples. They would learn to know Christ better, to deny themselves, to take up their cross, and to lose their lives for the sake of Christ. But in so doing, they would actually find their lives. They would be changed by Christ, and then through Christ's Spirit, they would change the world.

Like the original disciples, have we left behind what hinders us in order to follow Christ? Is Christ more important than our careers, more important than our possessions, more important than our families, and more important than our own lives? Do we know what He wants us to do and become?

To follow Christ assumes that He is our Leader and that we obey our Leader's orders. It assumes we do what we're told, that we set aside our plans, and that we die to ourselves and live for Christ. By doing so, Christ will change us, and then through His Spirit, we will change the world.

Following Christ Means We Follow His Example

The word "Christian" was a name given to the followers of Christ in Acts 11:26 and referred to those who were like Him.

In following Christ, we need to ask ourselves, "How did He live His life, what were His values, and what did He do?" In the same way the original disciples learned from Christ and modeled His life, we should do the same.

First Peter 2:21 says, "For to this you have been called, because Christ also suffered for you, **leaving you an example**, so that you might follow in his steps." We are to follow in Christ's

---

[123] David Platt, *What It Means to Follow Christ*, LifeWay, http://www.lifeway.com/Article/christian-living-what-it-means-to-follow-christ, Accessed 07-22-2015).

steps and be like Him in our actions, attitudes, values, and purposes.

Following Christ Means We Seek Him

In order to follow someone, we need to get to know them and understand what they want us to do. It implies we have a responsibility to take action in following that person's will and plans for us.

Instead of following our own plans, we are to follow those of Christ. We are to seek Christ's will above ours: "But **seek first** the kingdom of God and his righteousness, and all these things will be added to you" (Matt. 6:33).

When we put following Christ first, everything else in life will fall into place. If we don't, then everything will be out of sync and messed up. We'll live frustrated lives without purpose, fruitfulness, and joy.

Following Christ Means We Listen and Obey

In the same way the original disciples listened and obeyed Christ's voice, we should do the same as well. How do we do this today? We do it primarily by knowing God's Word and obeying it. Christ said, "Whoever has my commandments and keeps them, he it is who loves me. And he who loves me will be loved by my Father, and I will love him and manifest myself to him" (John 14:21).

Following Christ Means We Spend Time with Him

In the same way the original disciples spent time with Jesus, we should do the same as well. We should have a daily quiet time where we pray, read His Word, learn from Him, and spend time with Him.

Following Christ Means We Walk with Him

Unlike the original disciples, we cannot walk with Christ physically as they did. How do we walk with Him today? We walk with Him spiritually. The Bible calls this "walking in the Spirit." "But I say, **walk by the Spirit**, and you will not gratify the desires of the flesh" (Gal. 5:16), and "If we live by the Spirit, let us also **walk by the Spirit**" (Gal. 5:25). Walking in the Spirit means that we are in tune with Christ throughout our waking hours. We are conscious of His presence, of what He wants us to do, what He wants us to say, and the attitudes He wants us to have.

Following Christ Means We Set Our Minds on Him

"If then you have been raised with Christ, seek the things that are above, where Christ is, seated at the right hand of God. **Set your minds** on things that are above, not on things that are on earth. For you have died, and your life is hidden with Christ in God" (Col. 3:1–3). Following Christ means we set our minds on Him and seek heavenly things. It means we store our riches in heaven and are more concerned about God's Kingdom than this life.

Christians Today and Following Christ

Unfortunately, the statistics reveal that many Christians today are not seriously following Christ. One of the first truths we should realize in our Christian lives is the need to die to ourselves and live for Christ. But if this is the case, why are we so slothful when it comes to following Christ? Why do we try to get by with doing the least we can in our walk with God? Why are we not serious about discipleship or making disciples? Why don't we care much about knowing God through knowing His Word? Why are many Christians biblically illiterate? Why are many still babes in Christ after years of being a Christian? It appears it's because we are still following our own will and plans instead of God's.

Many Christians live as if they are practical atheists. They don't pray much, they don't read their Bibles much, and they don't think about God much. They don't want to be inconvenienced, but just want to live their lives as they please and then go to heaven after they've checked off all the items on their bucket list.

Could it be that the reason there are so many weak and baby Christians today is that instead of following Christ and giving up our lives for Him, we are saving our lives and keeping them for ourselves? God states that when we receive Christ, we die to ourselves and are now alive in Him. Our wills are now yielded to His, and we're no longer the bosses of our lives.

Following Christ means we go where He leads, we do what He says, and we submit to His leadership. Like the original disciples, we make a commitment to set aside our own wills and plans and choose those of our Master. We choose to take a bold step and become fully devoted disciples of Christ. We allow Him to change us so we can change those around us. We choose to "lose" our lives and, in so doing, "find" them.

3. The Meaning of Deny Self

"And calling the crowd to him with his disciples, he said to them, 'If anyone would come after me, let him **deny himself** and take up his cross and follow me'" (Mark 8:34). What does it mean to deny self?

The Greek word for "deny self" is *arnéomai*. It means to refuse, disown, or repudiate.[124] In general, it means to say no to yourself and to yield your rights and decisions to another. It means choosing what pleases Christ instead of what pleases yourself. One scholar has noted, "Used within the context of the imagery of taking up the cross and following Jesus, 'denying yourself' conveys the sense of a person disassociating himself from his self-interest to serve a higher purpose."[125] Similarly, it means to die to self.

"Denying yourself" and "dying to yourself" are synonymous terms in the Bible. When Christ used these terms, He was referring to anyone who wanted to come after Him and be His disciple. In the same way Christ was going to deny Himself and die on the Cross, He was telling those who wanted to come after Him to do the same.

S. Michael Houdmann states, "Jesus spoke repeatedly to His disciples about taking up their cross (an instrument of death) and following Him. He made it clear that, if any would follow Him, they must deny themselves, which means giving up their lives spiritually, symbolically, and even physically if necessary."[126]

---

[124] Helpmewithbiblestudy.org, *What Did Jesus Mean "Deny Yourself and Take Up Your Cross"?*
http://helpmewithbiblestudy.org/9Salvation/SanctifyWhatDoesItMeanToCarryCross, Accessed 07/27/2015.
[125] Ibid., Accessed 07/27/2015.
[126] S. Michael Houdmann, *What Does the Bible Mean by "Dying to Self"?*
http://www.gotquestions.org/dying-to-self.html, Accessed 07/27/2015.

Denying self means that I am choosing Christ's will over mine. I am dying to my plans, desires, hopes, purposes, and pleasures, and choosing Christ's plans, desires, purposes, and will instead. It means I am no longer the boss of my life, but instead, Christ is.

The Example of Christ

Christ made the statement about denying self just after He had spoken to those present about how He was going to suffer, die, be buried, and rise from the dead (Luke 9:21–23). He was showing by example what it meant to deny self.

Denying Self Illustrated

Denying self or dying to self is a one-time event that should occur at the time we become saved, and then continue on a daily basis thereafter. Romans 6:3–4 speaks of how baptism symbolizes our death to self and adherence to Christ: "Do you not know that all of us who have been baptized into Christ Jesus were baptized into his death? We were buried therefore with him by baptism into death, in order that, just as Christ was raised from the dead by the glory of the Father, we too might walk in newness of life."

Dying to self is a one-time event, but it's also a daily event as well. Notice what Christ says, "If anyone would come after me, let him deny himself and take up his cross **daily** and follow me" (Luke 9:23).

The Apostle Paul illustrates this concept as well when he says, "I have been crucified with Christ. It is no longer I who live, but Christ who lives in me. And the life I now live in the flesh I live by faith in the Son of God, who loved me and gave himself for me" (Gal. 2:20). Here Paul reveals the lifestyle of a disciple. It is a person who has been crucified (dies to self-will) and now lives their life for Christ. It's now Christ who lives in them and runs the show; it's no longer they who are on the throne following their own will. They are denying themselves and allowing Christ to be in charge.

Denying Self Is Not Optional

S. Michael Houdmann states, "Dying to self is never portrayed in Scripture as something optional in the Christian life. It's the reality of the new birth. No one can come to Christ unless he is willing to see his old life crucified with Christ and begin to live anew in obedience to Him. Jesus describes lukewarm followers who try to live partly in the old life and partly in the new as those whom He will spit out (Rev. 3:15–16). That lukewarm condition characterized the church of Laodicea back then, but also many churches and Christians today."[127]

Some might think that denying self is purely symbolic. It's true it does involve a symbolic meaning, but it also has a completely literal meaning. History indicates that 11 of the 12 Apostles were martyred for their faith. Countless other believers have suffered death and severe persecution over the course of world history as well. It's even said that today there are more martyrs than at any other time in church history. When Christ spoke about dying to self, He was also talking about the possibility of physical death.

Jon Bloom conveys, "Not all who heard Christ's words to follow Him would necessarily die as martyrs, but all would have to die to themselves if they wanted to be His disciples. They would have to die to the desire for self-glory, die to the desire for worldly respect, die to the fear of man, die to the desire for an easy life, die to the desire for earthly wealth, and die a thousand other deaths as well to their earthly desires. Finally, they must die to their desire to save their earthly lives."[128]

---

[127] Ibid., Accessed 07/27/2015.
[128] Jon Bloom, *Let Him Deny Himself,* Desiring God.org., 2010, http://www.desiringgod.org/articles/let-him-deny-himself, Accessed 7/27/2015.

Denying Self Brings Life

The only things Jesus asks us to deny ourselves of are what will rob us of eternal joy. That's why the Holy Spirit said through Paul:

> For those who live according to the flesh set their minds on the things of the flesh, but those who live according to the Spirit set their minds on the things of the Spirit. For to set the mind on the flesh is death, **but to set the mind on the Spirit is life and peace**. For the mind that is set on the flesh is hostile to God, for it does not submit to God's law; indeed, it cannot. Those who are in the flesh cannot please God (Rom. 8:5-8).

Finding life and joy are found in saying no to our desires and yes to Christ's will for us. It's the opposite of what seems natural. It's the opposite of what most people do.

Christians Today and Denying Self

Today, many Christians are not denying self. When statistics show that 81% of Christians don't read their Bibles regularly, biblical illiteracy is at an all-time high, 61% of believers have not shared their faith in the last 6 months, and the average Christian prays around 1-7 minutes a day, it seems pretty obvious that many Christians are not denying themselves.

The reason numerous believers remain spiritual babies and are not growing in Christ as they should is because they are saving their lives instead of losing them. They are not denying themselves and saying yes to reading and studying their Bibles, praying, sharing Christ, serving, and storing up riches in heaven, but instead, are saying no to Christ and His will for them. For this reason, many Christians will fail to reach spiritual maturity and will have little or no rewards in heaven.

4. The Meaning of Take up Your Cross

"And he said to all, 'If anyone would come after me, let him deny himself and **take up his cross daily** and follow me'" (Luke 9:23). What does "take up your cross" mean?

Kurt Struckmeyer provides us insight: "Well, let's begin with what Jesus didn't mean. Many people interpret 'cross' as some burden they must carry in their lives: a strained relationship, a thankless job, or a physical illness. With self-pitying pride, they say, 'That's my cross I have to carry.' Such an interpretation is not what Jesus meant when He said, 'Take up your cross, and follow Me.'"[129]

Struckmeyer adds, "When Jesus carried His cross up Golgotha to be crucified, no one was thinking of the cross as symbolic of a burden to carry. To a person in the first-century, the cross meant one thing and one thing only: death by the most painful and humiliating means human beings could develop."[130] It was a one-way ticket to death.

Again, Struckmeyer states, "The cross was a particularly gruesome and humiliating device for brutally executing troublemakers. It was designed for people of the lower classes, for people who dared to challenge authority, and for people who threatened the status quo. It was intended to inflict prolonged pain and punishment. Bodies were left on the cross to rot and to be eaten by scavenger birds and dogs."[131] Moreover, they crucified those condemned to death in the most public places available so others would fear and submit to their authority.

Therefore, "take up your cross and follow me" means being

---

[129] Kurt Struckmeyer, *Take Up Your Cross*, http://followingjesus.org/changing/take_up_cross.htm, 2007, Accessed 08/03/2015.
[130] Ibid., Accessed 08/03/2015.
[131] Ibid., Accessed 08/03/2015.

willing to die in order to follow Jesus. This is called "dying to self." It's a call to absolute surrender.

Christ's Example

Christ made the statement to His followers that they must take up their cross daily and follow Him just after Peter's great confession that He was the Son of the living God. Then following these words, He added, "The Son of Man must suffer many things and be rejected by the elders and chief priests and scribes, and be killed, and on the third day be raised" (Luke 9:21–22).

Christ told all those present that He was going to Jerusalem to be crucified and die on a cross. He was leading by example! He would then tell His followers that if they wanted to come after Him and be His disciples, they must be willing to do the same. They must be willing to die on a daily basis to their wills and plans, and be willing to die physically, if needed, as well.

The disciple's cross demanded death to self-will, self-interest, and self-seeking. The term, "take up your cross," speaks of the cost of discipleship and the cost of following Christ.

Contrary to what many Christians today might think, Christ doesn't call disciples to Himself to make their lives easy and pleasant, but instead, holy and productive. Willingness to take up your cross, in the same way Christ took up His, is the mark of a true disciple. Unlike many Christians today, first-century believers understood that taking up your cross had a clear and distinct meaning. It didn't mean you gave to Christ what was convenient; it meant you gave Him your all.

Taking up Your Cross and the Cost of Discipleship

How does "taking up your cross" apply to us today? It would involve asking ourselves the following questions to see if we're truly willing to take up our cross. Are we willing to follow Jesus if it means:

- Giving up some of our time?
- Giving our finances to Him?
- Serving Him and others?
- Losing some of our closest friends?
- Alienation from our family?
- Losing our reputation?
- Losing our job?
- Suffering for Him?
- Being persecuted for Him?
- Standing against the new morality of our culture?
- Losing our life?

These sobering questions reveal, in a practical sense, what many Christians are unwilling to give up for Christ. They might claim to be devoted believers, but in real life, they hold on to their lives and refuse to sacrifice much. They don't give up much time for Christ to read their Bibles, to pray, to share Christ, to speak the truth, to serve Christ, to develop their spiritual gifts and abilities, to be biblical fathers and mothers, to have family devotions, and to be faithful in church attendance. Instead, it appears they are more occupied with their jobs, getting ahead, school, sports, entertainment, and pleasure.

Taking up Your Cross Means Commitment

When Christ talked about taking up your cross, He was stressing the depth of commitment that following Him would entail. He was underscoring the price it would take to be His disciple. Naturally, we shy away from commitments like this and prefer a low cost, non-committal form of Christianity that is high in blessings and low in cost. We want all the riches of Christ, all the blessings He has to offer in this life and the next, but with the least amount of effort as possible.

All the riches Christ has to offer are available, but there's a price to attain them. Christ explained this truth when He used the term, "take up your cross." This term highlights the cost of following Christ, which in turn, leads to His blessings. Simply put, we cannot have the full blessings of God without the willingness to pay the price for them.

God's Blessings Have a Cost

There are two basic principles in the Christian life when it comes to the concept of blessings: (1) blessings come from God and (2) most blessings require a sacrifice to obtain them. Blessings are what God gives us based upon our love for Him and the sacrifices we make to follow Him. They are called sacrifices because they are not what our natural desires would choose.

Our flesh loves pleasure, fun, ease, and entertainment. It naturally doesn't like pain, suffering, difficulty, discipline, and hard work. Therefore, when we choose what Christ would have us do instead of what we would normally choose, then we're sacrificing our desires to do God's will. Without sacrifice, there are few blessings. When we attempt to attain God's blessings without sacrificing our will to do His, then we are trying to obtain His blessings by violating one of His unmovable, universal laws:

> Do not be deceived: God is not mocked, for whatever one sows, that will he also reap. For the one who sows to his own flesh will from the flesh reap corruption, but the one who sows to the Spirit will from the Spirit reap eternal life. And let us not grow weary of doing good, for in due season we will reap, if we do not give up (Gal. 6:7-9).

Discipleship is a sacrifice we make to follow Christ on a daily basis. To the degree we engage in discipleship will be the degree to which we reap God's blessings. To the degree we neglect discipleship will be the degree to which we forfeit His blessings.

The belief that we can attain God's blessings without any cost is appealing, but it's just not true. It's a belief completely opposite of what Christ preached. It's a belief that wants something for nothing.

Taking up Your Cross Involves Sacrifice

Sacrifice values eternity, but non-sacrifice values the temporal pleasures of this fleeting life. Moses clearly understood this principle: "By faith Moses, when he was grown up, refused to be called the son of Pharaoh's daughter, choosing rather to be mistreated with the people of God than to enjoy the fleeting pleasures of sin. He considered the reproach of Christ greater wealth than the treasures of Egypt, for he was looking to the reward" (Heb. 11:24–26).

The call on our part to sacrifice is a major theme of Scripture. In fact, it's the pinnacle and crescendo of the message of Romans: "I appeal to you therefore, brothers, by the mercies of God, to present your bodies as a **living sacrifice**, holy and acceptable to God, which is your spiritual worship. Do not be conformed to this world, but be transformed by the renewal of your mind, that by testing you may discern what is the will of God, what is good and acceptable and perfect" (Rom. 12:1–2).

In Scripture, we see God's continual eagerness to develop within us an eternal perspective to life rather than a temporal one. He desires to see us laying up our treasures in heaven instead of on earth. However, it seems today there's more focus on enjoying this present life instead of sacrificing this life for the one to come.

Taking up Your Cross Values Eternal Riches

Discipleship has at its core a focus on eternity, whereas non-discipleship has at its core a focus on this momentary life. Taking up your cross is the willingness to sacrifice the temporal riches of this life in order to obey God and gain the eternal ones. As Jim Elliot so wisely stated, "He is no fool who gives what he cannot keep to gain what he cannot lose."

For this reason, Christ rebuked those who sought Him primarily for the temporal riches of this life and not the eternal riches of heaven. He scolded them for seeking only the material blessings He offered and not the spiritual ones.

Shortly after Christ fed the 5,000, those whom He fed came looking for Him. Christ knew they were mainly interested in the earthly blessings He provided them, so He said, "Truly, truly, I say to you, you are seeking me, not because you saw signs, but because you ate your fill of the loaves. **Do not work for the food that perishes, but for the food that endures to eternal life**, which the Son of Man will give to you" (Matt. 6:26–27).

Taking up Your Cross Illustrated

Abraham understood the cost of following God and was willing to make enormous sacrifices to do so. He is called, "Our Father of Faith," and was willing to leave his homeland, his father, mother, relatives, and friends to follow God. He was willing to sojourn in a foreign land, leaving everything without knowing what awaited him. Moreover, he was even willing to give up his son, Isaac, his most cherished possession, that for which he had waited for most of his entire life to have. His example is amazing!

Genesis 22 recounts this incredible story: "After these things God tested Abraham and said to him, 'Abraham!' And he said, 'Here I am.' He said, 'Take your son, your only son Isaac, whom you love, and go to the land of Moriah, and offer him there as a burnt-offering on one of the mountains of which I shall tell you'" (Gen. 22:1–2).

Scripture records that early the next morning Abraham saddled his donkey, took his son, and headed out on a three-day journey to Mount Moriah to sacrifice his son there. How many times do you think Abraham glanced at Isaac during those long, dusty, three days, thinking about what he was going to do? Yet, despite his inner struggle, he plodded on.

Upon arriving at Mount Moriah, he climbed the hill (which is the same Mount Moriah upon which the temple would later be built by King Solomon), bound his son, and then prepared himself to sacrifice Isaac upon the altar he had made. As the knife was on its way down, "The Lord called to him from heaven and said, 'Abraham, Abraham!' And he said, 'Here I am.' He said, 'Do not lay your hand on the boy or do anything to him, for now I know that you fear God, seeing you have not withheld your son, your only son, from me'" (Gen. 22:11–12).

Abraham displayed his faith and obedience to God by his willingness to sacrifice his "all" on the altar. As a result, he was blessed beyond measure and became a foundational figure in Scripture—so much so that he's called our "Father of Faith."

But notice that these blessings were given to him as a result of the cost he paid to follow God, not as a result of doing his own will and then expecting blessings for nothing. The belief that we can obtain the blessings of God without paying the cost for them has no support in Scripture.

God calls us to be like Abraham, our Father of Faith. He tests us in order to know how much we love Him and to see to what degree we're willing to pay the cost to follow Him. We show our love to God by our willingness to follow Him, regardless of the cost.

Taking up Your Cross Involves Obedience

Taking up your cross means that we obey God regardless of the price. It means that no matter how difficult it is to read our Bibles daily we should do it. In spite of how hard it is to pray, we should press on. Regardless of how painful it is to tithe, we should obey. No matter what our loved ones and friends think of us, we should stand firm to biblical truth. In spite of how costly it is to be faithful in church attendance, we should be loyal. No matter how inconvenient it is to have family devotions, we should persevere. Regardless of how unhappy it makes us feel, we should stand strong in the face of ridicule. No matter how boring it might be to read theological books that help us grow in Christ, we should endure. In spite of the cost to be a disciple, we should pay it.

Christians Today and Taking up Your Cross

If we want to be like Christ, Abraham, the prophets, and the Apostles, then we must be willing to follow God regardless of the cost. Unfortunately, many Christians today are not willing to pay the price. They prefer a non-committal kind of Christianity. They favor a path of happiness, pleasure, and ease instead of paying the cost of discipleship. In so doing, they choose temporal riches over eternal ones.

In modern Christianity, we have a strong focus on the blessings of God, but a weak focus on the cost for attaining them. We highlight the riches of Christ but neglect the price to obtain them. In a nutshell, we want something for nothing. We talk about God's blessings but avoid the reality of what taking up our cross means.

It's a form of Christianity that only wants half the truth. It could be labeled, "Entitlement Christianity." It's the belief that we're entitled to happiness, ease, blessings, health, wealth, and prosperity — and if God doesn't deliver, we'll take our business elsewhere! We fail to understand that God blesses us on His terms, not ours. Yes, God loves to bless us, but only as we take up our cross and are willing to follow Him despite the cost. God is continually trying to get us to lift our eyes off the fleeting treasures of this life and cast them upon the eternal ones.

How about us today, are we willing to take up our cross and follow Christ? We'll answer that question by the choices we make and the cost we're willing to pay to be disciples.

Billy Graham has wisely concluded, "You see, Jesus doesn't simply call us to believe that He existed, or even to believe that He can save us. He calls on us to commit our whole lives to Him — to trust Him alone for our salvation, and then to follow Him as His disciples."[132]

---

[132] Billy Graham, *What Did Jesus Mean When He Said We Have to Carry a Cross?* Billy Graham Evangelistic Association, 2006, http://billygraham.org/answer/what-did-jesus-mean-when-he-said-we-have-to-carry-a-cross, Accessed 08/17/2015.

5. The Meaning of Save Your Life and Lose Your Life

"And calling the crowd to him with his disciples, he said to them, 'If anyone would come after me, let him deny himself and take up his cross and follow me. For whoever would **save his life will lose it, but whoever loses his life** for my sake and the gospel's will save it. For what does it profit a man to gain the whole world and forfeit his soul?'" (Mark 8:34–35). What does it mean to save your life and lose your life?

Christ spoke numerous times about the theme of saving your life and losing your life. In fact, He mentions it six times in the Gospels (Matt. 10:39, 16:25; Mark 8:35; Luke 9:24, 17:33; and John 12:25).

What Does "Save Your Life" and "Lose Your Life Mean"?

What does it mean to save your life and lose your life? The word "save" in Greek is sozo and means to save, keep safe and sound, or to rescue from danger or destruction.[133] The word "save" in this context is referring to keeping control of your life and remaining the boss of it. Saving your life has two basic applications:

1. For the non-Christian, it refers to the rejection of Christ and the truth of the gospel. They want to remain the lord of their life and do as they please, so they refuse to yield their life to Christ and make Him Lord. It's all about control, and they refuse to relinquish it.

2. For the Christian, it refers to those who choose, in some areas

---

[133] Biblestudytools.com, *The NAS New Testament Greek Lexicon*, http://www.biblestudytools.com/lexicons/greek/nas/sozo.html, Accessed 08/05/2015.

of their life, to do their own will over that of Christ's. They can do this for two reasons: (1) they are unwilling to do what they should do even though they know what God wants them to do or (2) they don't fully know what Christ would have them do because they are still in the growing process and are learning how to yield to Christ in different areas of their life.

The word "lose" in Greek is *apolesē* and means to destroy, to put out of the way entirely, abolish, put an end to, ruin, render useless, to kill, to declare that one must be put to death, to devote or give over to eternal misery in hell, to perish, to be lost, ruined, to destroy, or to lose.[134]

The phrase "lose your life" is what God wants us to do. It's the positive side of discipleship. It speaks of the **willingness** to give up control of our lives in order to follow Christ.

The phrase "save your life" is the negative side of discipleship and is the opposite of what God wants us to do. It's opposed to discipleship and refers to the **refusal** to give up control in order to follow Christ.

Saving Your Life and Losing Your Life Illustrated

The concept of saving your life versus losing your life is a central and foundational truth to the salvation/discipleship message Christ taught. To impart this essential concept, He used four illustrations to convey its important meaning and purpose in life:

1. Matthew 10:34–39: Family Division

2. Matthew 16:24–28: Gaining the World and Losing Your Soul

3. Luke 17:32–33: The Example of Lot's Wife

4. John 12:23–25: A Grain of Seed That Dies

---

[134] Lumina.bible.org, https://lumina.bible.org/bible/Matthew+10, Accessed 08/05/2015.

Now let's look at each of these illustrations Christ used in order to better understand the meaning of saving your life and losing your life.

1. Matthew 10:34–39: Family Division

"Do not think that I have come to bring peace to the earth. I have not come to bring peace, but a sword. For I have come to set a man against his father, and a daughter against her mother, and a daughter-in-law against her mother-in-law. And a person's enemies will be those of his own household. Whoever loves father or mother more than me is not worthy of me, and whoever loves son or daughter more than me is not worthy of me. And whoever does not take his cross and follow me is not worthy of me. Whoever **finds his life will lose it, and whoever loses his life** for my sake will find it."

Here Christ uses the illustration of family division to communicate His message of saving your life and losing your life. He says that choosing to follow Him will likely bring division and strife into our family relationships, and unless we're willing to follow Him instead of keeping our family relationships in peace, then we cannot be His disciple. He speaks of allegiance to Him rather than loyalty to our families.

Currently, in many countries choosing to follow Christ can mean total separation between family members and even death. I remember visiting Israel some years ago, and while there, my wife and I met a converted Christian from Islam. He told us that if his family knew of his recent conversion, they would most likely totally disown him and possibly have him turned over to be severely punished or killed. In his case, following Christ was costing him his relationship with his family. He had to choose between Christ or his family, and He wisely was choosing Christ.

In most Christian's lives, it won't cost them their life to follow Christ, but it might cost them family peace, their friendships, and their reputation. Choosing to follow Christ can be costly, but it's the price we must pay to be His disciple.

2. Matthew 16:24–28: Gaining the World and Losing Your Soul

"Then Jesus told his disciples, 'If anyone would come after me, let him deny himself and take up his cross and follow me. For whoever would **save his life will lose it, but whoever loses his life** for my sake will find it. For what will it profit a man if he gains the whole world and forfeits his soul? Or what shall a man give in return for his soul?'"

In this illustration, Christ talks about those who give their lives to acquiring wealth, power, popularity, prestige, pleasure, and all the luxuries this present world has to offer. They value the riches of this life rather than eternal ones. They store up their treasures on earth instead of heaven, and in the process, save their lives and lose their souls.

3. Luke 17:32–33: The Example of Lot's Wife

"Christ said, 'Remember Lot's wife. Whoever seeks to **preserve his life will lose it, but whoever loses his life** will keep it.'" What about Lot's wife? What did she do that would cause Christ to use her as an example of saving your life instead of losing your life?

Genesis 13:10 says, "Lot lifted up his eyes and saw that the Jordan Valley was well watered everywhere like the garden of the Lord, like the land of Egypt, in the direction of Zoar." While Sodom and Gomorrah were wicked cities during his time, Lot still chose to live close-by: "Now the men of Sodom were wicked, great sinners against the Lord" (Gen. 1:13).

Maybe Lot's wife influenced him to live close-by because she loved the bright lights and pleasures of Sodom, even though it was a wicked city. Later on, Lot chose to move into the city of Sodom, even though Scripture says his heart was vexed within him (2 Pet. 2:7). Later, God sent two angels to rescue Lot. They told him to get out of the city because God was going to destroy it. Even so, Lot lingered: "As morning dawned, the angels urged Lot, saying, 'Up! Take your wife and your two daughters who are here, lest you be swept away in the punishment of the city.'" But Lot continued to linger, so the men seized him, his wife, and his two daughters by the hand and brought them outside the city. "And as they brought them out, one said, 'Escape for your life. Do not look back or stop anywhere in the valley. Escape to the hills, lest you be swept away'" (Gen. 19:15–17).

The angels warned them not to look back at Sodom. The best meaning of this phrase is to "not look back to desire anything within it—none of its pleasures, values, activities, sins, and customs." Nonetheless, Lot's wife loved Sodom and all the pleasures it had to offer. So, as they were fleeing the burning city of Sodom, Lot's wife looked back: "But Lot's wife, behind him, looked back, and she became a pillar of salt" (Gen. 19:26).

By all appearances, Lot's wife had built her life upon earthly pleasures. She chose to save her life and ended up losing it. She had little desire to live for God and paid an immense price, of which, I assume, she still regrets to this day. For the person who is unwilling to submit to Christ and attempts to save their life, they'll pay the same price as Lot's wife.

4. John 12:23–25: A Grain of Seed That Dies

"And Jesus answered them, 'The hour has come for the Son of Man to be glorified. Truly, truly, I say to you, **unless a grain of wheat falls into the earth and dies**, it remains alone; but if it dies, it bears much fruit. Whoever **loves his life loses it, and whoever hates his life** in this world will keep it for eternal life'" (John 12:23–25).

In this passage, Christ uses a grain of wheat to illustrate the principle that the only way a Christian can bear fruit is by dying to themselves and living for Him. The words "truly, truly" mean: listen up, this is critically important, don't let this get by you! Christ implied that there will be no fruit in our lives unless we die to ourselves and live for Him. Therefore, those who wish to save their lives will lose them, but those who are willing to lose their lives will find their lives and bear much fruit.

They will be like the grain of wheat that dies and brings forth many more grains than just itself. If we live for ourselves, we'll just be one grain that will eventually be lost in the end, but if we'll die to ourselves and live for Christ, we'll produce much fruit and enjoy that fruit for all eternity.

These four illustrations show what Christ meant by saving your life and losing your life. Rarely does Christ illustrate a truth with so many examples, so this certainly was a key point He wanted to make clear.

Church Attendance and Saving Your Life

Regarding church attendance, Richard Krejcir quotes some disheartening stats done by the Institute of Church Leadership Development (FASICLD). Krejcir reports that:

- 20.5% of Americans frequently attended church in 1995
- 19% of Americans frequently attended church in 1999
- 18% of Americans frequently attended church in 2002[135]

Krejcir adds, "Now, by extrapolating the data and doing some statistical evaluation and adding some hope for revival, we can see the figures drop to 15% of Americans in church attendance in 2025, and a further drop to 11% or 12% by 2050. Soon, we will catch up with Europe, which currently is 'enjoying' two to four

---

[135] Richard J. Krejcir, *Statistics and Reasons for Church Decline*, 2007, www.churchleadership.org/apps/articles/default.asp?articleid=42346&columnid=4545, Accessed 08/07/2015.

percent of its population in regular church attendance. By the time these predictions come to pass, Europe may have no significant church presence at all."[136]

Church Leaders and Saving Your Life

Even many pastors are adopting a version of Christianity that embraces saving your life. Research done by Richard Krejcir reveals that almost 40% of pastors polled said they have had an extra-marital affair since beginning their ministry, and 70% said the only time they spend studying the Bible is when they are preparing their sermons.[137] Krejcir adds, "Focus on the Family reports that Christians in the United States lose a pastor a day because he seeks an immoral path instead of God's, seeking intimacy where it must not be found."[138] Moreover, LifeWay Research shows that 39% of Protestant pastors believe it's okay to get a divorce if a couple no longer loves one another.[139] And additional studies reveal that the average pastor only prays five minutes a day.[140]

The lifestyles and choices of some in leadership are undoubtedly contributing to the mentality that saving your life is more important than losing your life for Christ.

Christians Today and Saving Your Life

How are we doing today in this critical area of saving your life versus losing your life? Not so well according to the statistics!

---

[136] Ibid., Accessed 08/07/2015.

[137] Richard J. Krejcir, *Statistics on Pastors: What is Going on with the Pastors in America?* 2007, www.churchleadership.org/apps/articles/default.asp?articleid=42347&columnid=4545, Accessed 08/06/2015.

[138] Ibid., Accessed 08/07/2015.

[139] LifeWay Research, *Views on Divorce Divide Americans*, 2015, LifeWayResearch.com, http://www.lifewayresearch.com/2015/08/12/views-on-divorce-divide-americans, Accessed 08/19/2015.

[140] Deborah Beeksma, *The Average Christian Prays a Minute a Day; Prayer by the Faithful Helps Their Relationships*, GodDiscussion.com, 2013, Accessed 07/27/2015.

Could it be we've set aside Christ's foundational teaching on discipleship, and we're now living a form of Christianity that's very different from what Christ and the Apostles taught?

Today, many Christians are living a brand of Christianity where they are unwilling to give up much control of their lives. They value their time, money, friends, families, activities, lifestyles, dreams, entertainment, and sinful choices too much to let them go. They are choosing to save their lives instead of losing them. They are refusing to give up control of their lives to Christ.

6. The Meaning of Hate Your Father, Mother, Wife, and Family

"If anyone comes to me and **does not hate his own father and mother and wife and children and brothers and sisters**, yes, and even his own life, he cannot be my disciple" (Luke 14:26). What does it mean to hate father, mother, wife, and family?

The Role of Family During the Time of Christ

The importance of family in the Jewish culture played a much higher role than it does today in the Western world. Since the time of Abraham, the Jewish culture was family oriented. During their 400 years in Egypt, they lived as a very close-knit unit, bonded together by their unique circumstances in a foreign land.

Afterward, when they wandered in the Sinai Desert for 40 years, they lived within an even closer proximity, all learning the same lessons and sharing the same experiences.

Upon settling the Promised Land, they divided the land, and each tribe received a portion to inhabit. Then, each tribe divided their allotment of land among the family units within its tribe. The land given to each family unit would then normally have remained in their possession for hundreds upon hundreds of consecutive years.

Therefore, for example, a family living in Nazareth during the time of Christ would have had their ancestors living there for countless years before them. Each family would live in family units with parents, grandparents, great-grandparents, children, brothers, sisters, aunts, and uncles, all living in the same family complex or close-by. Unlike today, where people change locations regularly and move half way across the country, the Jews were not mobile, but instead, lived in the same town for generation after generation.

For this reason, it was virtually impossible to exist outside the family structure during the time of Christ. The family was everything. It was their support system, job provider, relationship center, and emotional stability structure. So when Christ said, "Unless you hate your father and mother, wife, children, and brothers and sisters you cannot be my disciple," His words would have sent shockwaves up and down the spines of His hearers.

What Does It Mean to Hate Family Members?

What was Christ saying by stating that we need to hate our father, mother, and so on, and how would His Jewish audience have interpreted it? Unlike us today, who don't quite understand these seemingly severe and harsh words, to the Jews, it was a common way of expressing a contrast between two concepts or loyalties. It was used in a comparative sense to describe such terms like "more than" or "less than," "first" and "second," and extremes such as "first" and "last." The terms love and hate, while appearing as opposites, is expressed in English by terms such as "love more" and "love less."[141]

Kyle Butt provides help on the meaning of the word "hate" by stating, "Numerous Greek scholars have added their combined years of study to the discussion to conclude that the word 'hate' (*miseo*) in Luke 14:26 does not mean 'an active abhorrence,' but means 'to love less.'"[142] Moreover, A. B. Bruce, in *The Expositor's Greek Testament*, states that the practical meaning of the word "hate" in this verse is "love less."[143]

The use of the Greek word *miseo* is also used many other times in Scripture to illustrate the concept of "loving more" or

[141] Biblicalhebrew.com, *Hate your Parents: Hate your Father, Matthew 10:37, Luke 14:26*, www.biblicalhebrew.com/nt/lovehate.htm, Accessed 08/08/2015.
[142] Kyle Butt, *Hate Your Parents—or Love Them?* Apologeticspress.org, 2004, apologeticspress.org/AllegedDiscrepancies.aspx?article=781, Accessed 08/08/2015.
[143] Ibid., Accessed 08/08/2015.

"loving less." In fact, Christ uses the terms "love more" and "love less" in a similar passage when speaking of discipleship in Matthew 10:37: "Whoever loves father or mother **more than** me is not worthy of me, and whoever loves son or daughter **more than** me is not worthy of me."

Therefore, a correct interpretation of "hating your father, mother, wife . . ." would be to love them less in contrast to our love for Christ. So, Christ wasn't telling his audience to literally hate their father, mother, wife, and so on. Instead, He was telling them that in comparison to their love and devotion to Him, the gap should be so wide and the distance so great between their love for Him and their most cherished family members that their love for family would appear as hate in comparison.

Choosing Christ over Family

Christ was using this contrasting terminology to drive home the truth that to be His disciple there cannot be any competing relationship that would come close to having the same place of loyalty and affection in our hearts as Him. Our love and devotion to Christ should be light-years away from that of the closest people in our lives on earth.

In order to be Christ's disciple, we must be willing to put Him above all earthly relationships. Therefore, if our family members or close friends will not follow Jesus, or even if they disown us for being Christians, we must still choose Christ over them.

Christ's Example

Christ not only spoke about the need to love Him more than anyone on earth, but He lived out and experienced what He taught. He was rejected by most of His paternal brothers, He was rejected by those in His hometown of Nazareth, He was rejected by Judas — one of His disciples — and He was rejected and crucified by His own people. He knew firsthand what it meant to love and obey God more than any person on earth.

When Christ faced the reality of the Cross, His commitment to the Father over His own will was lived out when He said, "Not My will be done, but Yours be done" (Matt. 26:39). That should be our life motto as well.

Christ's command that we love Him more than father, mother, wife, brother, or sister is not just limited to those in our close family circles, but also applies to any relationship in our lives that we might love and be influenced by more than Him.

Christians Today and Close Relationships

How are Christians today doing in the area of loving Christ more than any personal relationship on earth? For many, putting Christ and His commands above their family and friends is a deep struggle. Loving Christ more than anyone else is the ultimate test.

It's the same test God put before Abraham when He asked him to sacrifice his "all" (Isaac) on an altar to Him. It's the same test for us today. Therefore, if we have anyone in our lives who is hindering us from being fully devoted to Christ, we need to make a choice, once and for all, to choose Christ over them.

If we're going to follow Christ, we must not fear being ridiculed or marginalized for standing with Him and His Word. We must "hate" all others in comparison to our love for Christ.

7. The Meaning of Hate Your Life

"If anyone comes to me and does not hate his own father and mother and wife and children and brothers and sisters, yes, **and even his own life**, he cannot be my disciple"(Luke 14:26). What does it mean to hate your life?

Jesus taught this same truth with slight variations in Matthew 10:37–39, 16:24–27, Mark 8:34–38, and Luke 9:23–26, and 17:33.

What Does "Hate Your Life" Mean?

As noted in the previous section about what it means to hate father, mother, wife, and other family members, Christ was not telling His audience to literally hate their own lives, but was telling them that, in comparison to their love and devotion to Him, the gap would be so wide and the distance so great between their love for Him and their own lives that it would appear as hate.

Why is it important to "hate your life"? First of all, it's the only way to save it.

Jesus' words apply to everyone who wants to follow Him. He assumes that we all want to save our lives, but tells us that the only way to save them is to lose them for His sake and the gospel's. There's no other option! If we want true joy, meaning, purpose, fulfillment, and eternal rewards in heaven, then the only way to get them is through hating our lives.

What does it mean to hate your life, and how can we hate our life in order to find it? We find some excellent illustrations in the life of Christ and Scripture.

Christ's Example

Christ provides the perfect example of hating your life by laying down His life and being crucified for our sins. By giving

His life on the Cross, Jesus bore much fruit: "Truly, truly, I say to you, unless a grain of wheat falls into the earth and dies, it remains alone; but if it dies, it bears much fruit" (John 12:24). Christ used the example of a grain of wheat falling to the ground as an illustration of how a single grain of wheat, if it is planted and dies, will produce much fruit. In farming, it's quite normal for an average kernel of wheat to reproduce and multiply itself a hundred percent.

When Christ laid down His life and died, He produced countless fruit for all eternity. In the same way, when we lay down our lives, we bear much fruit as well.

How to Bear Fruit

If we save our lives and do what we want with them, then we'll be unfruitful, but if we lay them down, we'll bear much fruit. To the degree we die to ourselves, our plans, our wills, our desires, and yield them to Christ instead, is the degree to which we will be fruitful.

The way to measure whether or not we are dying to ourselves and hating our lives is by looking at how much fruit we're producing. If there's little fruit in our lives, it means we are saving our lives and not hating them. It means we are not doing what Christ wants, but what we want. God wants us to bear fruit, and the only way to do it is by dying to ourselves.

What Is Biblical Fruit?

What does the Bible refer to as fruit? It can be defined as the evidence in a person's life that reflects the result of actions and choices made. The following is referred to as biblical fruit:

- **Galatians 5:22–23 and 2 Peter 1:5–8:** The Bible refers to the development of Christian character as fruit.

- **Colossians 1:10:** Our knowledge of God's Word that results in good deeds is referred to as fruit.

- **Philippians 1:22:** Our labor and work for Christ are counted as fruit.

- **Romans 1:13 and 1 Corinthians 16:15:** Evangelism is considered fruit.

- **Hebrews 13:5:** We bear fruit with our lips when we praise God and glorify Him in our hearts, before non-believers, and with fellow Christians.

- **Romans 15:28 and Philippians 4:17:** Giving to the Lord's work is spoken of as fruit.

- **Matthew 3:8–10 and 7:15–20:** Repentance from sin and turning to the Lord is referred to as fruit as indicated in the ministries of John the Baptist and Christ.

Why We Love Our Lives

While Christians have been given a new nature at salvation, we do, however, retain our old nature. This old nature—called the sinful nature or the flesh—desires that which is contrary to Christ and our new nature.

When the Bible refers to our old nature as the "flesh," it doesn't mean that our physical bodies are sinful, but that our sinful nature, referred to as "flesh," is sinful.

Our flesh doesn't care about anything but feeling good and gorging itself on pleasure. If we allow it to dictate our choices in life, then we'll never align with God's will. We'll never submit to His authority, and we'll end up suffering enormous loss if we're Christians or wind up in hell if we're non-believers. But if we recognize that our fleshly desires are fatal to the soul and choose to live for God instead, then we'll end up with eternal rewards and joy.

When Christ says we must hate our lives, He is describing how we must hate our fleshly desires and refuse to let them control our priorities in life.

How to Lose Your Life in Order to Find It

We must realize that our fleshly nature is at war with the Holy Spirit and the new nature God has given us. This is why we continually have a battle going on inside of us. In order to win the battle, we need to walk in the Spirit: "But I say, walk by the Spirit, and you will **not gratify** the **desires of the flesh**. For the **desires of the flesh are against the Spirit**, and the **desires of the Spirit are against the flesh**, for these **are opposed to each other**, to keep you from doing the things you want to do" (Gal. 5:16–17).

We must put to death the desires of our flesh with God's enabling help: "For if you live according to the flesh you will die, but if **by the Spirit you put to death the deeds of the body**, you will live" (Rom. 8:13). If we walk in the Spirit and put to death the desires of our flesh, then we will find life and peace. We will, in essence, "find our lives." If not, we'll find pain and sorrow and "lose our lives."

In summary, hating your life means that instead of loving your life and living for the present, you give up your fleshly desires and live for Christ and your future life in heaven.

8. The Meaning of Gain the World and Lose Your Soul

"For whoever desires to save his life will lose it, but whoever loses his life for My sake and the gospel's will save it. For what will it profit a man if he **gains the whole world, and loses his own soul?** Or what will a man give in exchange for his soul?" (Mark 8:36–37, NKJV).

What does it profit to gain the whole world and lose your soul? This statement by Christ is really a "no-brainer" question and a simple one to answer. It was a question posed by Christ to show the stupidity of even asking such a ridiculous question.

But to make matters worse, Christ showed the absurdity of our rationale in that, while no sane person would be willing to lose their soul at the expense of gaining the whole world, they are willing to lose it for the hope of gaining just a fraction of it. How amazing! Who would be willing to lose their soul for just gaining a little bit of the "good life"? Of course, no one would, right? That's the point of the question. Who in their right mind would choose to lose their soul at the expense of a few fleeting years of pleasure? No one, right? Wrong! That's exactly what most do.

Is Gaining the World Smart?

Gaining the world for Christians means that they give a higher priority to their earthly affairs than seeking God and pursuing spiritual maturity. It means they choose to store up the majority of their riches on earth rather than in heaven.

Our souls are who we are, the part of us that's eternal. The term "world" represents materialism, pleasure, and prestige (1 John 2:15). No logical person would reason that a few years of wealth, pleasure, and prestige would be worth the cost of losing their eternal soul. The math is simple: a few years of pleasure versus endless years of torment in hell? Even a 5-year-old can figure that one out.

Tragically, though, many surgeons, scientists, professionals, adults, and students can't do the simple math. With all their brilliance, they can't even do a simple math equation that a 5-year-old can do. They value a few fleeting years of pleasure above all the eternal glories of heaven and choose hell instead. Humbly said, that is the height of stupidity and foolishness. It's completely off the radar, incomprehensible, ridiculous, absurd, and ludicrous! Yet, it's what most people choose in this life. What a tragedy!

Gaining the World and Christians Today

How about us Christians? Can we do the math? Are we any smarter than the vast majority of people in this world who cannot? Can we figure out that a few fleeting years of pleasure in this life aren't worth the loss of eternal rewards in heaven? Unfortunately, according to recent statistics, many Christians can't do the simple math either. They are caught up in materialism, pleasure, and prestige, and are sacrificing their eternal rewards on the altar of a few vanishing years of gratification. They are deaf to the call of discipleship; and instead, are gaining the world but losing their eternal rewards in the process. How foolish! God warns us of this deadly trap in John 2:15–17:

Do not love the world or the things in the world. If anyone loves the world, the love of the Father is not in him. For all that is in the world — **the desires of the flesh and the desires of the eyes and pride of life** — is not from the Father but is from the world. And the world is passing away along with its desires, but whoever does the will of God abides forever.

What hinders many Christians from putting discipleship as their highest priority in life? God says it's the desires of the flesh (materialism), the desires of the eyes (pleasure), and the pride of life (prestige) — all of which are enemies of discipleship. They are choosing the pleasures of the world that are passing away and ignoring the eternal riches and rewards of heaven.

Many Christians today choose to give priority to their nice homes, nice cars, retirement accounts, vacations, electronic devices, pleasure, and entertainment rather than being disciples of Christ and storing their riches in heaven. They are living for the here and now, not eternity! This is called saving, loving, and finding your life instead of losing and hating your life. For the person who chooses this life over the next one, all their pleasures will end when they die. They will have spent their years enjoying this life and will suffer the consequences in the one to come.

Gaining the World and Losing Your Soul for the Non-Believer

For the non-Christian, the clear meaning of gaining the world and losing your soul is simple to understand. Losing your soul speaks of the reality of hell, a topic that's very uncomfortable, yet spoken of repeatedly in Scripture. Christ spoke more about hell and the judgments of God than about heaven. He described hell as:

- A fiery lake of burning sulfur that is unquenchable and never goes out (Matt. 25:46; Mark 9:43–44; Rev. 21:8).
- Everlasting destruction away from the presence of the Lord (2 Thess. 1:9).
- Where people will gnash their teeth in pain (Matt. 13:50).
- Where the devil and his angels suffer (Matt. 25:41).
- A gloomy dungeon (2 Pet. 2:4).
- Where the worm never dies (Mark 9:48).
- A fiery furnace (Matt. 13:42).

- Where people will be salted with fire (Mark 9:49).
- A place of weeping (Matt. 13:50).
- A place of utter darkness (Jude 1:13).

Hell is a real place, and many will choose to go there as a result of rejecting Christ and attempting to gain the world's treasures. They'll choose materialism, pleasure, and the pride of life over the salvation of their souls and the eternal riches of Christ.

Although God defines success in life as being spiritually mature, most people define success in life as being wealthy, enjoying pleasure, and being well liked.

9. The Meaning of Being Ashamed of Christ and His Words

"For whoever is **ashamed of me and of my words** in this adulterous and sinful generation, of him will the Son of Man also be ashamed when he comes in the glory of his Father with the holy angels" (Mark 8:38). What does it mean to be ashamed of Christ and His words?

What Does "Ashamed" Mean?

The word "ashamed" comes from the Greek word *epaischunomai* and means apologetic, bashful, embarrassed, shy, timid, and hesitant. It's the sense in which we can be silent, fearful, reluctant, and ashamed by identifying and standing up for Christ and His words. It's the same word Paul uses in Romans 1:16 when he boldly proclaims, "For I am not **ashamed** of the gospel, for it is the power of God for salvation to everyone who believes, to the Jew first and also to the Greek."

The Apostle Paul and Not Being Ashamed of Christ

Paul paid a heavy price for not being ashamed of Christ and recounts it in 2 Corinthians 11:23–28:

> With far greater labors, far more imprisonments, with countless beatings, and often near death. Five times I received at the hands of the Jews the forty lashes less one. Three times I was beaten with rods. Once I was stoned. Three times I was shipwrecked; a night and a day I was adrift at sea; on frequent journeys, in danger from rivers, danger from robbers, danger from my own people, danger from Gentiles, danger in the city, danger in the wilderness, danger at sea, danger from false brothers; in toil and hardship,

through many a sleepless night, in hunger and thirst, often without food, in cold and exposure. And, apart from other things, there is the daily pressure on me of my anxiety for all the churches.

Paul also proudly stated when writing from prison in Rome for preaching Christ and the gospel:

For I know that through your prayers and the help of the Spirit of Jesus Christ this will turn out for my deliverance, as it is my eager expectation and hope that I will not be at all **ashamed**, but that with full courage now as always Christ will be honored in my body, whether by life or by death. For to me to live is Christ, and to die is gain (Phil. 1:19–21).

Paul was certainly not ashamed of Christ and His words, and tradition holds that he was martyred as a result.

The Example of Others and Not Being Ashamed of Christ

The 12 Apostles also paid a high price for not being ashamed of Christ and His words. History records that 11 of them were martyred for not being ashamed of Christ, and John, while uncertain as to whether or not he died for Christ, was thrown into boiling oil and severely tortured.

Hebrews 11 recounts many of the Old Testament saints who suffered severely because they were not ashamed of God:

Some were tortured, refusing to accept release, so that they might rise again to a better life. Others suffered mocking and flogging, and even chains and imprisonment. They were stoned, they were sawn in two, they were killed with the sword. They went about in skins of sheep and goats, destitute, afflicted, mistreated — of whom the world was not worthy — wandering about in deserts and mountains, and in

186

dens and caves of the earth (Heb. 11:35–38).

Today, in some parts of the world, many Christians are being martyred and persecuted at unprecedented rates. Why is this so? It's because they are not ashamed of Christ and His words. In fact, it's believed there are more martyrs for Christ today per year than at any other time in the history of the church. Estimates range from between 8,000–100,000 Christians who are now being martyred yearly for Christ.[144]

Moreover, it's estimated that from the birth of the early church to the present, 70 million Christians have been martyred for Christ.[145] All these chose to die for Christ rather than being ashamed of Him and His words.

Christians Today and Being Ashamed of Christ

The contrast between those who have chosen to be martyred for Christ instead of being ashamed of Him and His words, and many Christians today is staggering.

As mentioned, statistics show a whopping 61% of Christians have not shared their faith in the last six months, and nearly half (48%) of Christians have never even invited a friend to church. Many are also silent on key moral issues of our day and are choosing a path of peace and conformity rather than confrontation—a very different strategy than what Christ and the Apostles chose.

Many Christians today don't want to stir the waters, cause problems, or hurt people's feelings, so they idly stand by watching the moral decay and destruction from the sidelines. To them, it's not worth the friction. They are ashamed of Christ and

---

[144] Cath Martin, *70 Million Christians' Martyred for their Faith Since Jesus Walked the Earth*, 2014, ChristianityToday.com, http://www.christiantoday.com/article/70.million.christians.martyred.faith.since.jesus.walked.earth/38403.htm, Accessed 08/28/2015.
[145] Ibid., Accessed 08/28/2015.

His words and choose silence over engagement.

Many Christians today fear their friends, family, and culture more than God. Countless don't speak up for Christ because they are afraid of violating the new cardinal sins of political correctness, and fear being labeled judgmental, intolerant, dogmatic, or hateful.

Some Christians, however, don't speak up because they are simply ignorant of the truths of God's Word and don't know what to say. And sadly, some Christians are vocal about what they believe, but what they stand for is contrary to God's Word, so they wind up promoting what our culture says rather than what God says. They are babes in Christ tossed to and fro by the winds of false teachers and false philosophies circulating in our culture.

Conclusion to Chapter 3

In this chapter, we defined discipleship using key phrases Christ used in calling people to follow Him. In the next chapter, we'll discover the 14 essential components of discipleship that must be understood and practiced in order to be a disciple of Christ and attain spiritual maturity?

We're now coming to the heart of the book, so get ready to be challenged as we delve into the 14 essential components needed for growing in Christ!

Chapter 4

The Essential Components of Discipleship

In This Chapter

1. Knowledge of God and Discipleship

2. Self-Discipline and Discipleship

3. Obedience and Discipleship

4. Abiding in Christ and Discipleship

5. Prayer and Discipleship

6. Mentoring and Discipleship

7. Church Involvement and Discipleship

8. Evangelism and Discipleship

9. The Inner Life and Discipleship

10. Spiritual Gifts and Discipleship

11. Serving and Discipleship

12. Spiritual Attitudes and Discipleship

13. Character and Discipleship

14. Stewardship and Discipleship

In chapter 1, we analyzed the state of discipleship and spiritual maturity today, concluding that they're in critical condition and being grossly neglected. In chapter 2, we investigated the key factors contributing to the neglect of discipleship and spiritual maturity. In chapter 3, we defined biblical discipleship by examining key phrases Christ used in calling people to follow Him.

In this chapter, we'll discover the essential components for the discipleship-making process that must be understood and obeyed in order to fulfill the Great Commission Mandate and attain spiritual maturity.

What Are the Essential Components of Discipleship?

I'm a long-term missionary in Mexico, and on one occasion, five churches asked me to provide leadership training for their pastors and leaders. The central theme was discipleship. However, as I began to ponder and pray about what I was going to include in this training, my own lack of understanding surfaced. I then began to research other notable theologians and pastors to discover what they would see as essential aspects of discipleship.

What I discovered was many different angles and approaches to the discipleship-making process. Some stressed knowledge as the key, some focused on evangelism, others on spiritual disciplines, and the list continued. Each one underscored their approach as the best and most biblical.

How about you as a reader? If a newer believer approached you out of respect for your maturity in Christ and asked you to disciple or mentor them, what would you include in the discipleship-making process? I think if we're honest, we'd say we're probably not certain. However, other than the essence of the gospel, is there a topic more important to understand?

First Things First

The essential components of discipleship function as vehicles which combine the grace of God and human effort for attaining spiritual maturity. They are not an end in and of themselves, but rather, provide a structure for attaining spiritual maturity. They are biblical, not mere inventions or ideas of people, and they exist to transform us into the image of Christ. These same essential components were used by Christ and the Apostles, and should be used by us as well.

If we practice these essential components with the intent of achieving spiritual maturity, then they will serve the purpose for which God intended. However, if we think that through mere ritualistic conformity to them that we will grow to maturity, then we are greatly mistaken. Christianity is a relationship with God, not mere conformity to a set of rules. Spiritual maturity, therefore, is impossible without the development of our relationship with God.

What Is Spiritual Maturity?

Spiritual maturity is not perfection, but the attainment of fullness, completeness, adulthood, or excellence in each of the essential components of the discipleship-making process.

Christ highlighted obedience as an overarching aspect of spiritual maturity in the Great Commission Mandate: "Teaching them to **observe all that I have commanded you.** And behold, I am with you always, to the end of the age" (Matt. 28:20). Spiritual maturity, according to Christ, is summed up by complete obedience to all of Scripture.

The Apostle Peter focused on knowledge, attitudes, and character as essential to spiritual maturity: "For this very reason, make every effort to supplement your faith with virtue, and virtue with knowledge, and knowledge with self-control, and self-control with steadfastness, and steadfastness with godliness, and

191

godliness with brotherly affection, and brotherly affection with love" (2 Pet. 1:5–7).

In addition to Christ's and Peter's definition of spiritual maturity, the Apostle Paul defines spiritual maturity as:

1. A person who can understand and receive the wisdom of God from Scripture: "Yet among the **mature** we do impart wisdom, although it is not a wisdom of this age or of the rulers of this age, who are doomed to pass away" (1 Cor. 2:6).

2. A person who is mature in their thinking capabilities: "Brothers, do not be children in your thinking. Be infants in evil, but in **your thinking be mature**" (1 Cor. 14:20).

3. A person who has arrived at the measure of the full stature of Christ: "Until we all attain to the unity of the faith and of the knowledge of the Son of God, to **mature** manhood, to the measure of the stature of the **fullness** of Christ" (Eph. 4:13).

4. A person who can discern good from evil through the constant practice of using God's Word, and can understand and feed on the solid food (deep things) of Scripture: "But solid food is for the **mature**, for those who have their powers of discernment trained by constant practice to distinguish good from evil" (Heb. 5:14).

5. A person with a transformed mind: "Do not be conformed to this world, but be transformed by the renewal of your mind, that by testing you may discern what is the will of God, what is good and acceptable and **perfect**" (Rom. 12:2). This verse presents two options for each person: (1) be conformed to this world or (2) be transformed by Scripture to God's perfect will. Spiritual maturity is the process of moving from the conformity of this world to the conformity of God's will.

A spiritually mature person thinks as God thinks, acts like God acts, and values what God values. They have the same characteristics, attitudes, beliefs, and perspective of life that God does. They are led by the Spirit and submit to Him in all things. They love the Lord their God with all their heart, soul, mind, and strength, and they love their neighbor as themselves.

In summary, a spiritually mature person is someone who has arrived at fullness, excellence, and completeness in all of the 14 areas of the discipleship-making process outlined in this chapter.

Spiritual Maturity Is God's Purpose for Us

As mentioned, it's important to note that spiritual maturity is not the same as perfection. We will never reach that level in this life. However, it's a state of maturity that reflects, by and large, the image of Christ and His values. It's not like a popular bumper sticker that reads, "Not perfect, only forgiven." While this slogan contains truth, it overlooks the majority of our Christian growth to maturity after forgiveness and makes an excuse for bad behavior in the meantime.

Between being forgiven for our sins at salvation, and spiritual maturity, lies a wide gap. This gap is where we labor with the grace of God to attain spiritual maturity. We all begin as spiritual infants at salvation but should not stay there. We are called to much more than forgiveness; we are called to attain spiritual maturity. This is our goal and purpose in life: "Until we all attain to the unity of the faith and of the knowledge of the Son of God, to **mature manhood**, to the measure of the stature of **the fullness of Christ**" (Eph. 4:13).

God's deepest desire is that we would attain spiritual maturity. In fact, He sharply rebukes those who are slow or fail to attain it as seen in Hebrews 5:11–14:

About this we have much to say, and it is hard to explain, since you have become **dull of hearing**. For though **by this time** you ought to be teachers, you need someone to teach you again the **basic principles** of the oracles of God. You **need milk**, not solid food, for everyone who lives on milk is **unskilled** in the word of righteousness, since he is a **child**. But solid food is for the mature, for those who have their powers of discernment trained by constant practice to distinguish good from evil.

God was angry and rebuked these Hebrew believers because they were slothful in attaining spiritual maturity. God feels the same about us today! He expects us to become spiritually mature within a reasonable length of time and is grieved when we fail to do so.

God was also grieved with the nation of Israel for the same reasons: "But they obeyed not, neither inclined their ear, but made their neck stiff, that they might not hear, nor receive instruction" (Jer. 17:23).

The Importance of Understanding and Practicing the Essential Components of Discipleship

If the Great Commission Mandate and summation of Christ's ministry was discipleship (Matt. 28:19–20), and if the summation of the Apostles' ministry was the same (Col. 1:28–29), then understanding the essential components of the discipleship-making process is paramount for fulfilling these commands.

God has designed discipleship as the vehicle to bring us to spiritual maturity. That's why it was the summation of Christ's and the Apostles' ministries. The essential components in this chapter are servants of discipleship. They are the nuts and bolts, the specifics, the structure, the application of discipleship for attaining spiritual maturity. They are principles Christ and the Apostles used and work for all people for all time.

1. Knowledge of God and Discipleship

Of all the essential components for discipleship, none is as important as the knowledge of God. While the others are critical, I believe this component rises above them all. Donald Whitney states, "No spiritual discipline is more important than the intake of God's Word. Nothing can substitute for it. There is simply no healthy Christian life apart from a diet of the milk and meat of Scripture."[146]

Why Is God's Word So Vital to Discipleship?

God's Word forms the foundation upon which all the other essential components rest. It's the main component God uses in the transformation of our mind, which in turn, leads to spiritual maturity. Alister McGrath, in his article "The Passionate Intellect: Christian Faith and the Discipleship of the Mind," centers his focus of discipleship on the importance of knowledge.[147] He claims that theology was once the "queen of the sciences" and held in the highest esteem, but is no longer the case. It has declined in recent decades, and this should give us pause.[148]

McGrath believes knowledge serves believers in both their own personal understanding of God and in providing greater effectiveness in sharing this understanding with others. McGrath adds, "Christians need to realize that there is an intellectual core to the Christian faith which requires a discipleship of the mind in

---

[146] Donald Whitney, *Spiritual Disciplines for the Christian Life* (Colorado Springs: NavPress, 1991), p. 24.

[147] Alister McGrath, "The Passionate Intellect; Christian Faith and the Discipleship of the Mind" (Source: Pro Ecclesia, 22 no 1 Winter 2013, pp. 118-121. Publication Type: Review ATLA Religion Database with ATLASerials. Hunter Resource Library), Accessed 11/5/2014.

[148] Ibid., p. 118.

order to understand."[149] He further states, "Christians should be guided by a rational faith which provides the foundation for all their understanding of God and life."[150]

We Are Commanded to Love the Lord with Our Minds

The greatest command is to "Love the Lord your God with all your heart and with all your soul and **with all your mind** and with all your strength" (Mark 12:30). God wants us to love Him, not only with our heart, soul, and strength, but with our mind as well. A strong case can be made that loving God begins with loving Him with our minds because it's through our knowledge of Him that we understand how to love Him with our hearts. However, many are ignorant of this truth and are biblically illiterate.

We've noted that the latest Bible reading statistics of Christians, according to LifeWay Publishing, are dismal at best. Only 19% of Christians read their Bibles regularly. That leaves 81% of Christians who are basically biblically illiterate. These believers are certainly not loving God with their minds.

Christians Today and Biblical Illiteracy

Albert Mohler shares his concern about the state of evangelicalism and biblical illiteracy by asserting: "While America's Evangelical Christians are rightly concerned about the secular worldview's rejection of biblical Christianity, we ought to give some urgent attention to a problem much closer to home — biblical illiteracy in the church. This scandalous problem is our own, and it's up to us to fix it."[151]

---

[149] Ibid., p. 119.
[150] Ibid., p. 119.
[151] Albert Mohler, *The Scandal of Biblical Illiteracy: It's Our Problem*, Christianity.com, http://www.christianity.com/1270946, Accessed 08/18/2015.

Researchers George Gallup and Jim Castelli state the problem bluntly, "Americans revere the Bible — but, by and large, they don't read it. And because they don't read it, they have become a nation of biblical illiterates. How bad is it? Researchers tell us that it's worse than most could imagine."[152]

The fact that the majority of so-called "Evangelical believers" rarely or never read their Bibles is staggering. It's no wonder many Christians today are "throwing in" with the new progressive morals of our culture and are spiritually immature.

Christians Today and Theological Illiteracy

Not only are many believers biblically illiterate, but they are theologically illiterate as well. They don't read theological books that would significantly deepen their knowledge of God and give them a correct worldview.

God has given gifted men and women to the church who have spent countless hours studying and writing books to aid us in becoming spiritually mature. However, only about 3% of believers read theological books and only about 10% read Christian, non-fiction books. Unfortunately, most Christians are indifferent and disregard these precious gifts of God, and as a result, choose to remain spiritually immature.

All the Components of Discipleship Rest upon God's Word

Every aspect of discipleship is linked to the knowledge of God's Word. Without it, we wouldn't know who God is, who we are, who others are, the purpose for our existence, the purpose for creation, where we have come from, where we are going, what God desires from us, and how we should behave. Some downplay the importance of the knowledge of Scripture, but in so doing, contradict the value Christ gives it.

---

[152] Ibid., Accessed 08/18/2015.

During Christ's day, discipleship had a heavy focus on the knowledge of the Bible. Most disciples had much, if not the majority, of the Old Testament, memorized. They would go on discipleship training trips to get away from the distractions of life and focus on learning Scripture from their rabbi.

Christ placed enormous weight upon knowing Scripture and emphasized it throughout His ministry. In fact, Scripture is so important to God that He calls Christ the "Word." "In the beginning was the Word, and the Word was with God, and the Word was God . . . And the Word was made flesh, and dwelt among us" (John 1:1, 14). Christ is the Living Word! To say that the knowledge of Scripture is not important is to say that Christ is not important.

Klaus Issler, in his article "Six Themes to Guide Spiritual Formation Ministry Based on Jesus' Sermon on the Mount," makes the knowledge of God's Word one of his six major themes of discipleship. He states that it was important for Jesus' disciples to know Scripture, and interpret it correctly, to be able to follow its genuine teaching.[153] He goes on to say, "Jesus' own life was bathed in Scripture since the phrase 'It is written' or some variation occurs 23 times on his lips."[154]

How Can We Know God?

There are two basic ways to know God: (1) by observing His creation and (2) by knowing His Word. Theologically, we call the field of knowing God through His creation "General Revelation." All rational humans can know general things about God through contemplating His creation: "For what can be **known about God** is plain to them, because God has shown it to them. For his

---

[153] Klaus Issler, "Six Themes to Guide Spiritual Formation Ministry Based on Jesus' Sermon on the Mount" (Source: Christian Education, Journal Date: September 1, 2010. CEJ: Series 3, Vol. 7, No. 2. ATLA Religion Database with ATLASerials. Hunter Resource Library), p. 372, Accessed 11/5/2014.
[154] Ibid., p. 372.

invisible attributes, namely, **his eternal power** and **divine nature**, have been **clearly perceived**, ever since the creation of the world, in the things that have been made. So they are without excuse" (Rom. 1:19–20).

Through creation, every person knows certain truths about God. They know He is all-powerful, eternal, and all-knowing. Scripture also records in Psalm 19 that "The heavens declare the glory of God, and the sky above proclaims his handiwork. Day to day pours out speech, and night to night reveals knowledge. There is no speech, nor are there words, whose voice is not heard. Their voice goes out through all the earth, and their words to the end of the world" (Ps. 19:1–4). We see, then, that through creation all mankind has been blessed to know certain things about God.

While what we can know about God through His creation is amazing, it is nonetheless, limited. We don't know the details about God, just the big picture. How can we know the details? Through learning and applying God's Word to our lives. Theologically, we call the field of knowing God through His Word, "Special Revelation."

It's special because it's unique and allows us to know God in His fullness. It also gives us understanding about who we are, the purpose for life, the plan of God for His creation, and our surroundings—all extremely important things to know.

In the remainder of this section, we'll look at why knowing and applying God's Word to our lives is so essential to the discipleship-making process.

The Bible Is Unique and Unlike Any Other Writing Known to Mankind

- **The Bible claims to be inspired and to contain the very words of God:** 2 Timothy 3:16–17 states, "All Scripture is breathed out by God and profitable for teaching, for reproof, for correction, and for training in righteousness, that the man of God may be competent, equipped for every good work." Also, 2 Peter 1:20–21 affirms, "Knowing this first of all, that no prophecy of Scripture comes from someone's own interpretation. For no prophecy was ever produced by the will of man, but men spoke from God as they were carried along by the Holy Spirit." Unlike any other writing known to mankind, Scripture claims to be the very words of God.

- **The Bible claims to be living:** Hebrews 4:12 asserts, "For the word of God is living and active, sharper than any two-edged sword, piercing to the division of soul and of spirit, of joints and of marrow, and discerning the thoughts and intentions of the heart." Scripture is living and active because God inhabits His Word and speaks through it. No other writing is like it.

- **Christ affirmed the Bible to be the very Word of God:** Christ continually made statements concerning Scripture, such as "It is written," "So that the Scripture might be fulfilled," and "Have you not read?" He also used it continuously in His ministry and teaching. "And he said to them, 'O foolish ones, and slow of heart to believe all that the prophets have spoken! Was it not necessary that the Christ should suffer these things and enter into his glory?' And beginning with Moses and all the Prophets, he interpreted to them in all the Scriptures the things concerning himself" (Luke 24:25–27).

- **Christ claimed to be the very Word of God:** John 1:1 boldly states, "In the beginning was the Word, and the Word was with God, and the Word was God." Then John clarifies Who the Word is: "The **Word became flesh and dwelt among us**, and we have seen his glory, glory as of the only Son from the Father, full of grace and truth" (John 1:14). Not only do we have the written Word of God that claims to be living, but this living Word also is a Person called Jesus Christ.

- **The Apostles affirmed the Bible as the very Word of God**: The Apostles asserted that Scripture was inspired and used it continually. For example, Peter quoted large passages of Scripture in his sermon on the day of Pentecost, as found in Acts 2:14–42; quoting Joel 2:28–32, Psalm 16:8–11, and Psalm 110:1. The other Apostles also used a heavy dose of Scripture in their ministries.

- **The New Testament writers affirmed the Bible as the very Word of God:** God fashioned the New Testament to rest upon the foundation of the Old Testament. Therefore, God inspired the human writers of the New Testament to quote the Old Testament an amazing 855 times.[155] Many of these quotes were by Christ Himself, which gives further validation that Scripture is inspired and is the very Word of God.

- **History supports the Bible as being the Word of God:** The Bible has been the most important writing in the history of mankind. From its inception until the present, it has been the most read, the most valued, the most copied, the most discussed, the most quoted, and the most sold piece of literature ever. It has ranked far above all other writings. Moreover, countless millions of people claim it has changed their lives and have been willing to die for it.

- **The Bible claims to be eternal:** The Prophet Isaiah wrote, "The grass withers, the flower fades, but the word of our God will stand forever" (Isa. 40:8). The Apostle Peter penned, "But the word of the Lord remains forever. And this word is the good news that was preached to you" (1 Pet. 1:25). Moreover, Christ proclaimed, "Heaven and earth will pass away, but my words will not pass away" (Matt. 24:35).

---

[155] Blue Letter Bible, BlueLetterBible.org, *Study Resources: Charts and Quotes,* www.blueletterbible.org/study/pnt/pnt08.cfm, Accessed 10/14/2015.

We Follow Christ by Following His Word

When Christ says, "Follow Me," He is telling us to follow Him and His commands. The original disciples entered into 3 ½ years of intense discipleship training with Christ, and then, after His death, His Spirit was with them as they continued as His disciples. Today, Christ primarily teaches us through His Word. However, the average believer spends little time learning from Christ through His Word. Therefore, they are unable to follow Christ.

Here's the latest Bible reading statistics of Christians according to LifeWay Publishing:[156]

- 19% read their Bibles daily or regularly
- 26% read their Bibles a few times a week
- 14% read their Bibles once a week
- 22% read their Bibles once a month
- 18% rarely or never read their Bibles

According to these stats, 81% of Christians don't read their Bibles regularly. That's unbelievable! And of the 19% who do read their Bibles regularly, many don't study or read it in-depth. Moreover, most don't read all of the Bible, but just parts of it as devotional reading.

In general, most Christians are eons away from being the kind of disciples who know and handle God's Word with precision and clarity as commanded in 2 Timothy 2:15. As a result, most Christians are babies or adolescents in their spiritual maturity, and are not serious about discipleship and becoming like Christ (Heb. 5:11–14). This is a severe indictment on the state of Christianity and discipleship today.

If the main avenue Christ used to teach His disciples was His

---

[156] Russ Rankin, *Study: Bible Engagement in Churchgoer's Hearts, Not Always Practiced,* Nashville, 2012, http://www.lifeway.com/Article/research-survey-bible-engagement-churchgoers, Accessed 07/23/2015.

words, and if the main avenue today is His words as found in Scripture, then most Christians today are extremely deficient in their ability to be disciples because their knowledge of Scripture is so desperately lacking. Unlike the original disciples who had much of Scripture committed to memory, many Christians today are biblically illiterate. Discipleship without a high dose of God's Word is impossible, as it's the main way Christ teaches us.

Following Christ means following His commands in Scripture. However, if we don't know His Word, we won't know His commands, so we'll be weak, ineffective disciples. We'll be disciples who grieve Christ instead of please Him.

God Expects Us to Know His Word

God instructs us in 2 Timothy 2:15 (NASB) to "Be **diligent** to present yourself **approved** to God as a workman who does not need to be ashamed, **accurately handling the word of truth**." God expects us to exert diligent effort in understanding and handling His Word, not to be indifferent and mediocre with it. 2 Peter 1:5 adds, "For this very reason, **make every effort** to supplement your faith with virtue, and virtue with **knowledge**." God commands us to know His Word, handle it correctly, and grow in it. In order to do this, we must be diligent and make every effort to know it.

The Importance of God's Word in Discipleship

As mentioned, Scripture is the most important component in the discipleship-making process because God supernaturally uses His inspired, living words to transform us into His image and bring us to full maturity in Christ.

The following are vital functions God's Word plays in discipleship and our growth in Christ:

- **It's food for our souls:** Matthew 4:2–4 asserts, "And after fasting forty days and forty nights, he was hungry. And the tempter came and said to him, 'If you are the Son of God, command these stones to become loaves of bread.' But he answered, 'It is written, Man shall not live by bread alone, but by every word that comes from the mouth of God.'" Scripture is the food that feeds our souls. In the same way our body hungers, the soul of a born-again believer hungers as well. Unfortunately, according to the Bible reading stats, 81% of believers are starving their souls, and by doing so, will never reach spiritual maturity.

- **It causes us to grow in Christ:** "But grow in the grace and knowledge of our Lord and Savior Jesus Christ" (2 Pet. 3:18). 1 Peter 2:2 adds, "Like newborn infants, long for the pure spiritual milk, that by it you may grow up into salvation — if indeed you have tasted that the Lord is good." Newborn infants have nothing on their mind except milk. We too, like newborn infants, should crave the Word of God so we can grow to spiritual maturity.

- **It renews our minds and changes our thinking:** Unlike any other writing known to mankind, Scripture transforms and renews our mind, which in turn, changes our behavior and brings us to spiritual maturity. Romans 12:2 declares, "Do not be conformed to this world, but be transformed by the renewal of your mind, that by testing you may discern what is the will of God, what is good and acceptable and perfect."

- **It strengthens our faith:** "So faith comes from hearing, and hearing through the word of Christ" (Rom. 10:17).

- **It gives us life:** "It is the Spirit who gives life; the flesh is no help at all. The words that I have spoken to you are spirit and life" (John 6:63). Also, Psalm 19:8 beautifully adds, "The precepts of the Lord are right, rejoicing the heart; the commandment of the Lord is pure, enlightening the eyes."

- **It instructs us in all matters:** "All Scripture is breathed out by God and profitable for teaching, for reproof, for correction, and for training in righteousness, that the man of God may be complete, equipped for every good work" (2 Tim. 3:16–17). Moreover, Psalm 119:105 states, "Your word is a lamp to my feet and a light to my path."

- **It protects us from sin and destruction:** King David attested, "I have stored up your word in my heart, that I might not sin against you" (Psalm 119:11).

- **It brings success in life:** God commanded Joshua to keep Scripture in the forefront of his life and meditate on it always so he would be successful: "This Book of the Law shall not depart from your mouth, but you shall meditate on it day and night, so that you may be careful to do according to all that is written in it. For then you will make **your way prosperous**, and then you will have **good success**" (Josh. 1:8).

Bible Intake

The role of Scripture in the life of a believer cannot be overemphasized. There are four key methods for acquiring it: (1) through reading, (2) through hearing, (3) through study, and (4) through memorization. The first three methods are the most common, and the last method, the least.

It's debatable as to whether or not Scripture memorization should be a separate and distinct essential component of the discipleship-making process as it has strong biblical and historical support. However, because it's part of the way we obtain the knowledge of God, I've included it in this category instead.

Personally, I've made Scripture memorization a part of my life and have experienced amazing benefits and blessings as a result. Not only has it sharpened my mental capabilities, but most of all, it has embedded the Word of God in my heart. I can say from experience that there's nothing like memorizing and meditating on God's Word. It's so rich, so powerful, so sweet, and so very life changing.

Conclusion

Bible intake is critical for attaining spiritual maturity and should not be neglected. To the degree we allow it to dwell in us richly and transform us will be the degree to which we will reach spiritual maturity. To the degree we neglect it will be the degree to which we will remain stunted and retarded in our spiritual growth.

2. Self-Discipline and Discipleship

Why is self-discipline so important that it's listed as an essential component of the discipleship-making process? Because it provides the structure, motivation, and perseverance necessary for attaining spiritual maturity, and the lack of it has been the downfall of countless Christians.

A strong case can be made that self-discipline is the most important factor needed for discipleship, and for that matter, life in general. Without it, none of the essential components of discipleship will be implemented and put into practice. Therefore, it can be argued that everything rests on discipline and without it, little else matters!

Donald Whitney boldly states, "I can say that I've never known a man or woman who came to spiritual maturity except through discipline. Godliness comes through discipline."[157] I believe Whitney is right. However, statistics today reveal that the average Christian has a definite lack of self-discipline. Due to this lack, many Christians are stuck in their journey toward spiritual maturity, and some will never arrive.

Discipleship Requires Self-Discipline

The word "disciple" is related to the word "discipline." A disciple, therefore, should be a highly-disciplined person in following Christ. Without it, they will struggle.

As a pastor and missionary, I've seen firsthand the consequences the lack of self-discipline produces. I've seen people destroy their marriages, families, jobs, finances, health, bodies, and lives. I've seen countless people, who have wonderful hearts,

---

[157] Donald Whitney, *Spiritual Disciplines for the Christian Life,* (Colorado Springs: NavPress, 1991), p. 15.

live in pain and sorrow. Moreover, I've seen many Christians fail to reach spiritual maturity because they lack the self-discipline to attain it.

Self-Discipline Is a Key Purpose of the Book of Proverbs

Discipline is stated as a major theme of the Book of Proverbs: "For attaining wisdom and **discipline**; for understanding words of insight" (Prov. 1:2, NIV 1984).

A variant of the word "discipline" is mentioned 12 times throughout Proverbs, and the lack of discipline is mentioned numerous times: "And at the end of your life you groan, when your flesh and body are consumed, and you say, 'How I hated **discipline**, and my heart despised reproof!'" (Prov. 5:11–12).

Self-Discipline Is One of the Fruits of the Spirit

Galatians 5:23 states that self-control is a fruit that the Holy Spirit produces in the life of a believer. Self-control is synonymous with self-discipline. A self-controlled person is a disciplined person who makes themself do what they ought to do, not what they want to do.

Self-Discipline Is Related to Training

1 Timothy 4:6–8 uses the theme of training to convey the need for discipline in the Christian life: "If you put these things before the brothers, you will be a good servant of Christ Jesus, being **trained** in the words of the faith and of the good doctrine that you have followed. Have nothing to do with irreverent, silly myths. Rather **train yourself for godliness**; for while bodily training is of some value, godliness is of value in every way, as it holds promise for the present life and also for the life to come."

Here we see the value of discipline in training ourselves in godliness. However, most of us shy away from it. Bill Hull notes our tendency by stating, "Let's face it — discipline isn't something most of us like. We avoid discipline if we can, because it disrupts the normal and comfortable pattern of our life."[158]

Self-Discipline Is Related to Military Terminology

The Apostle Paul uses military vocabulary with Timothy in communicating the importance of self-discipline, enduring hardships, and being a tough soldier for Christ. He asserts, "Share in suffering as a good **soldier** of Christ Jesus" (2 Tim. 2:3). And again, "No **soldier** gets entangled in civilian pursuits, since his aim is to please the one who enlisted him" (2 Tim. 2:4).

According to the statistics of Christians today, self-discipline is lacking and needs to be built into our character if we're going to be deliberate disciples of Christ and reach spiritual maturity.

Self-Discipline Is Related to Sports Terminology

In 1 Corinthians 9:24–27, God uses sports language to convey the need for self-discipline:

> Do you not know that in a race all the runners run, but only one gets the prize? Run in such a way as to get the prize. Everyone who competes in the games goes into **strict training**. They do it to get a crown that will not last, but we do it to get a crown that will last forever. Therefore, I do not run like someone running aimlessly; I do not fight like a boxer beating the air. No, I strike a blow to my body and make it my slave so that after I have preached to others; I myself will not be disqualified for the prize.

The Apostle Paul uses the Olympic Games as a metaphor for the importance of discipline in our Christian lives. In the same

---

[158] Bill Hull, *The Complete Book of Discipleship: On Being and Making Followers of Christ* (The Navigators Reference Library 1, 2014, NavPress. Kindle Edition), Kindle Locations 445-447.

way athletes competing in these games would undergo strict training, we too must submit ourselves to spiritual training in godliness in order to be faithful disciples.

The Role of Self-Discipline in Discipleship

In Joseph V. Crockett's article "Is There Discipline in Our Discipleship?" he stresses that discipline is the major theme of discipleship. Crockett attests that "Even if you are an athlete, the term 'discipline' may not invoke warm and fuzzy feelings of excitement, yet discipline is necessary, even though it may not be welcomed."[159] Crockett challenges, "Where is the discipline in discipleship?"[160] Crockett even goes one step further and states that "It is difficult, if not impossible, to follow Jesus, to be His disciple, without accepting, embracing, and embodying spiritual disciplines for Christian formation."[161]

Raymond Edman also has strong words for us today: "We need the rugged strength of Christian character that can come only from discipline: the discipline of spirit, of mind, of body, of society."[162] Today, we are a soft, indulgent society! All our modern conveniences and luxuries have eaten away at our strength and discipline, and we're paying a high price for it.

Edman goes on to boldly state, "Discipleship means 'discipline!' The disciple is that one who has been taught or trained by the Master, who has come with his ignorance, superstition, and sin, to find learning, truth, and forgiveness from the Savior. Without discipline, we are not disciples, even though we profess his name and pass for a follower of the lowly

---

[159] Joseph V. Crockett, "Is There Discipline in Our Discipleship?" (Source: Living Pulpit, Online, March 1, 2014, ATLA Religion Database with ATLASerials, Hunter Resource Library), p. 9, Accessed 11/5/2014.
[160] Ibid., p. 10.
[161] Ibid., p. 10.
[162] Raymond Edman, *The Disciplines of Life* (Minneapolis, Minnesota: World Wide Publications, 1948), preface.

Nazarene."[163] Edman is so bold as to state that an undisciplined person is unable to be a disciple. These are strong words, words worth pondering and absorbing, words worth putting into practice!

Bill Hull sums up the thinking of many when he says, "Most of us want to reap the harvest of discipline while living a life of relative sloth."[164] Without self-discipline, we won't attain spiritual maturity or accomplish much for the Kingdom of God, and we'll arrive in heaven with few or no rewards.

The Importance of Spiritual Discipline

Developing spiritual discipline should be a high priority in our lives because it's the gasoline that powers spiritual growth. Without it, we'll stagnate and run aground. Therefore, we should purposefully make spiritual commitments despite how tough they might be. For example, every believer should establish the spiritual discipline to at least pray and read Scripture daily. Additional commitments can be made such as Bible memorization, journaling, spiritual gift development, reading, and fasting.

Establishing spiritual disciplines are biblical and have been used for millenniums. They take the theoretical and make it practical. They put "feet" on discipleship, applying it to where the rubber meets the road. We can say, "We should," or "It would be great if," but that gets us nowhere. Discipline is what moves us.

Spiritual disciplines establish clear, measurable, biblical steps that lead us to spiritual maturity. Christ practiced them, and they are found throughout Scripture. Donald Whitney states, "The

---

[163] Ibid., p. 9.
[164] Bill Hull, *The Complete Book of Discipleship: On Being and Making Followers of Christ* (The Navigators Reference Library 1, 2014, NavPress. Kindle Edition), Kindle Locations 451-452.

Spiritual Disciplines are those personal and corporate disciplines that promote spiritual growth. They are the habits of devotion and experiential Christianity that have been practiced by the people of God since biblical times."[165] Whitney continues, "I will maintain that the only road to Christian maturity and godliness passes through the practice of the Spiritual Disciplines."[166]

Conclusion

Through self-discipline, we put into practice the principles that carry us to spiritual maturity. Without it, we remain spiritually immature. It provides the structure, motivation, and perseverance necessary for attaining spiritual maturity, and the lack of it has been the downfall of countless Christians.

A strong case can be made that self-discipline is the most important factor needed for discipleship, and for that matter, life in general. Without it, none of the essential components of discipleship will be implemented and put into practice. For this reason, it can be argued that everything rests on self-discipline and without it, little else matters!

---

[165] Donald Whitney, *Spiritual Disciplines for the Christian Life*, (Colorado Springs, NavPress, 1991), p. 15.
[166] Ibid., p. 14.

3. Obedience and Discipleship

The role of obedience is another vital component of discipleship. Without it, we go nowhere; with it, we go everywhere. The lack of obedience in the Christian life is one of the biggest roadblocks in our growth to spiritual maturity. Our choices are real and bring consequences in this life and the one to come. By obedience, we obtain God's richest blessings, and without it, we bring upon ourselves His discipline, displeasure, and judgment.

Christ's most used phrase, "Follow Me," calls for obedience, and it's impossible to follow Him without it. However, when 81% of Christians do not read their Bibles regularly, a whopping 61% of believers have not shared their faith in the last six months, 75% of church members do not attend a Bible study or small group, and the average Christian only prays somewhere between 1–7 minutes a day, it appears obvious that most Christians today are not obeying Christ as they should.

Discipleship and Obedience

Discipleship in the time of Christ called for strict adherence and obedience to a disciple's rabbi. No rabbi would even consider a candidate who was unwilling to pledge to him their total allegiance and obedience.

Christ employed this same concept in His call to discipleship: "And calling the crowd to him with his disciples, he said to them, 'If anyone would come after me, let him deny himself and take up his cross and follow me. For whoever would save his life will lose it, but whoever loses his life for my sake and the gospel's will save it'" (Mark 8:34–35). These verses call for obedience in the strictest manner. Christ knows that in order to follow Him, and be His disciple, we must have no other allegiance above Him. He calls for completely devoted followers.

Obedience and Legalism

Obedience is often viewed by many Christians as cold and opposed to God's love and grace. Some react to a focus on obedience as a form of legalism (the belief that our efforts earn salvation and God's love). It's true that obedience to a set of rules does not earn salvation or God's love, but it does please Him and is vitally necessary for growth in Christ. Without obedience, we displease God and grieve His Spirit (Eph. 4:30).

If we truly believe that the wages of sin is death, then we must acknowledge that obedience saves us from sin's destruction.

Interestingly, when God gave the Ten Commandments and the Mosaic Covenant on Mt. Sinai, obedience was the cornerstone component God required: "Now, therefore, if you will indeed **obey my voice and keep my covenant**, you shall be my treasured possession among all peoples, for all the earth is mine" (Ex. 19:5).

As mentioned, some within Christianity are uncomfortable with a focus on obedience as they see it as a form of legalism. However, what does Scripture teach? Is obedience opposed to God's love and grace? Interestingly, God says they are not. Consider the following verses:

- **John 14:15:** "If you love me, you will keep my commandments."

- **John 14:21:** "Whoever has my commandments and keeps them, he it is who loves me. And he who loves me will be loved by my Father, and I will love him and manifest myself to him."

- **John 15:10:** "If you keep my commandments, you will abide in my love, just as I have kept my Father's commandments and abide in his love."

- **John 15:14:** "You are my friends if you do what I command you."

- **1 John 2:3–4:** "And by this we know that we have come to know him, if we keep his commandments. Whoever says 'I know him' but does not keep his commandments is a liar, and the truth is not in him."

- **1 John 3:24:** "Whoever keeps his commandments abides in God, and God in him. And by this we know that he abides in us, by the Spirit whom he has given us."

- **Matthew 5:19:** "Therefore, whoever **relaxes one of the least of these commandments** and teaches others to do the same will be called least in the kingdom of heaven, but whoever does them and teaches them will be called great in the kingdom of heaven."

God makes it overwhelmingly clear that our love for Him (which is the greatest commandment) is expressed by our obedience. To not obey God is not to love Him! He asks for our obedience because He loves us and it's the best for us. Keeping His commandments is the greatest way we can love ourselves as they bring us life and blessings. God does not see obedience as legalism that is opposed to His love and grace, but as the fulfillment and greatest expression of our love to Him.

Obedience and Knowing God

God says that the measuring stick for determining whether or not we actually "know" Him is through our obedience (1 John 2:3–4). Moreover, He says that obedience is the determining factor as to whether or not we are abiding in Him (1 John 3:24).

God expresses His love to us through His commands; we express our love to Him by obeying them.

Conclusion

The role of obedience is a critical component of discipleship. Without it, we go nowhere; with it, we go everywhere. The lack of obedience in the Christian life is one of the biggest roadblocks in our growth to spiritual maturity. God expects us to obey Him and is grieved when we don't. We show God how much we love Him through our obedience; we show Him our lack of love through our disobedience.

Obedience is a key factor in the discipleship process, and we'll get stuck in our spiritual growth if we don't take it seriously. If we presume upon God's love and grace, we greatly displease Him and damage ourselves in the process.

4. Abiding in Christ and Discipleship

What does abiding in Christ mean and how does it play such a key role as one of the essential components of discipleship?

Christ gave a vivid illustration of what "abide" means and its importance in John 15:1–6:

> I am the true vine, and my Father is the vinedresser. Every branch in me that does not bear fruit he takes away, and every branch that does bear fruit he prunes, that it may bear more fruit. Already you are clean because of the word that I have spoken to you. **Abide** in me, and I in you. As the branch cannot bear fruit by itself, unless it **abides** in the vine, neither can you, unless you **abide** in me. I am the vine; you are the branches. Whoever **abides** in me and I in him, he it is that bears much fruit, for apart from me you can do nothing. If anyone does not **abide** in me he is thrown away like a branch and withers; and the branches are gathered, thrown into the fire, and burned.

Christ uses the word "abide" five times in this passage. The word "abide" means to remain in, or stay connected to something. One author has noted, "To abide is to live, continue, or remain— so to abide in Christ is to live in Him or remain in Him."[167]

John MacArthur defines abiding in Christ as "Remaining inseparably linked to Christ in all areas of life. We depend on Him for grace and power to obey. We look obediently to His Word for instruction on how to live. We offer Him our deepest adoration and praise, and we submit ourselves to His authority over our lives. In short, Christians should gratefully know that Jesus Christ

---

[167] Gotquestions.org, *What Does It Mean to Abide in Christ?* http://www.gotquestions.org/abide-in-Christ.html, Accessed 10/20/2015.

is the source and sustainer of their lives."[168]

Grapevines and Abiding in Christ

The illustration of the vine and the branches in John 15 provides an incredible picture of what abiding means. A branch is completely dependent upon the vine for its nutrients and life. The moment it's detached, it quickly withers and dies.

Many years ago, I managed a vineyard and saw this firsthand. Often, due to the wind, a tractor, or other reasons, a branch would get disconnected from its vine. Within minutes, the branch would begin withering and dying. Grapevines are very different from other plants and are more susceptible to withering than most. That's why Christ used this illustration. He knew the Jewish culture was familiar with grapevines and would instantly understand His point.

Therefore, in the same way a grape branch withers and dies if it is not connected to its vine, we as well, will wither and die spiritually if we don't stay connected to Christ and abide in Him.

Walking in the Spirit and Abiding in Christ

Abiding in Christ can also be defined as walking in the Spirit or being led by the Spirit. "But I say, walk by the Spirit, and you will not gratify the desires of the flesh. For the desires of the flesh are against the Spirit, and the desires of the Spirit are against the flesh, for these are opposed to each other, to keep you from doing the things you want to do. But if you are led by the Spirit, you are not under the law" (Gal. 5:16–18).

Setting Our Minds on Christ and Abiding in Christ

Abiding in Christ means we are constantly setting our minds

---

[168] John MacArthur, *What Does It Mean to "Abide" in Christ?* Gty.org, www.gty.org/resources/Questions/QA161/What-does-it-mean-to-abide-in-Christ, Accessed 10/20/2015.

upon Him and His Word throughout our waking hours and seeking to obey Him. We take into consideration what He thinks, we pray for His help and guidance often, and we are in tune with His Spirit within us.

We don't wander far from Him throughout the day, are constantly checking in with Him, and are bringing every thought into obedience to Him and His Word (2 Cor. 10:4–5). We, in essence, live in the presence of God and pray without ceasing (1 Thess. 5:17). Praying without ceasing doesn't mean we do nothing else during the day but bow our heads in prayer; but rather, it carries the idea of living in the presence of God and attempting to please and obey Him in all things.

Seeking the Things Above and Abiding in Christ

Colossians 3:1–2 also helps us understand what the word "abide" means: "If then you have been raised with Christ, seek the things that are above, where Christ is, seated at the right hand of God. Set your minds on things that are above, not on things that are on earth." Abiding means we set our minds on God, on His Word, and on seeking His Kingdom. It values the things of God over the things of earth and continually makes adjustments that reflect this priority.

Conclusion

As alluded to earlier, John 15:5 says, "Whoever abides in me and I in him, he it is that bears much fruit, for **apart from me you can do nothing**." Without abiding in Christ, we can do nothing. We cannot be disciples, we cannot have right attitudes, we cannot grow in Christ, we cannot attain spiritual maturity, and we are absolutely helpless and dead. This is why abiding in Christ is so important to discipleship and should be one of its essential components.

5. Prayer and Discipleship

As we noted earlier, according to recent stats, the average Evangelical Christian prays between 1–7 minutes a day. In addition, Daniel Henderson did some recent research and discovered the following stats regarding Christians and prayer. He states the average person lives 77 years. That equates to 28,000 days, 670,000 hours, or 40 million minutes, and during their lifetime, they spend this time doing the following things:[169]

- The average person spends 24 minutes a day getting dressed. That equals 13 hours a month, 7 days a year, or 1 year in a lifetime.
- The average person spends 40 minutes a day on the phone. That factors out to 20 hours a month, 10 days a year, or 2 years in a lifetime.
- The average person spends 1 hour a day in the bathroom. That amounts to 30 hours a month, 15 days a year, and 3 years in a lifetime.
- The average person spends 3 hours a day watching television. That is 90 hours a month, 45 days a year, and 9 years in a lifetime.
- The average Christian spends less than 10 minutes a day in prayer. That equates to less than 6 hours a month, 3 days a year, and 7 months in a lifetime.[170]

What a tragedy that prayer, which should be our most important priority, receives the least amount of time and attention. Christians have time to talk on the phone 40 minutes a

[169] Daniel Henderson, *No Time to Pray,* Praying Pastor Blog, PrayingPastorBlog.blogspot, http://prayingpastorblog.blogspot.mx/2009/02/no-time-to-pray-no-time-to-pray.html, Accessed 10/16/2015.
[170] Ibid., Accessed 10/16/2015.

day and watch TV 3 hours a day, but can only pray less than 10 minutes a day. What's the problem? The only reasonable explanation is that it's not very important, and therefore, not a priority. Can you imagine how God feels about that? He's worth less than TV, phone time, the Internet, and almost every other activity!

Another recent survey shows even more disturbing news. It reveals that the average Christian prays just a minute a day: "It appears Christian prayers have apparently morphed into tweets to God."[171] Deborah Beeksma quotes the Rev. Nathan Shutes as saying, "My fear is that this generation has missed out on [being] prayer warriors. We have become an instant gratification generation. We tweet in 140 characters, and prayer can be just as short. Here are some numbers that ought to make you cringe; on the Baptist Board website, they say the average Christian prays a minute a day, and the average pastor prays five minutes a day. God have mercy on us for such little devotion to the Sovereign One of the universe. No wonder our nation is falling away from God."[172]

What Is Prayer?

Mary Fairchild suggests, "Prayer is not a mysterious practice reserved only for clergy and the religiously devout. Prayer is simply communicating with God — listening and talking to him. Believers can pray from the heart, freely, spontaneously, and in their own words."[173] Andrew Murray also enhances our understanding of prayer when he says, "Prayer is not monologue, but dialogue; God's voice is its most essential part. Listening to

---

[171] Deborah Beeksma, *The Average Christian Prays a Minute a Day; Prayer by the Faithful Helps Their Relationships,* GodDiscussion.com, 2013, Accessed 07/27/2015.
[172] Ibid., Accessed 07/27/2015.
[173] Mary Fairchild, *Basics to Prayer,* Christianity.About.com, http://christianity.about.com/od/prayersverses/a/basicstoprayer.htm, Accessed 10/16/2016.

God's voice is the secret of the assurance that He will listen to mine."[174]

Through prayer, we can be honest, open, express our frustrations, problems, joys, and sorrows. Prayer is simple, yet its effects are powerful. Prayer connects us to the ultimate power of the universe because it connects us with the Sovereign, Almighty God, Ruler, Owner, and King of it. No time spent in prayer is wasted; on the contrary, there is nothing more important we could do.

The Importance of Prayer in Discipleship

We see the importance of prayer all throughout the Bible. It's mentioned around 316 times and was a key characteristic of all godly men and women. Richard Foster, in his book *Celebration of Discipline,* claims that prayer is one of the most important aspects of discipleship: "Of all the Spiritual Disciplines, prayer is the most central because it ushers us into perpetual communion with the Father."[175] Moreover, Foster says, "All who have walked with God have viewed prayer as the main business of their lives."[176]

Jesus and Prayer

Unlike the average Christian, who prays around 1–7 minutes a day, prayer throughout the Bible is seen as a central focus of life. Christ set an impeccable example in His prayer life despite being, in very essence, God:

- He prayed regularly and on many occasions got away by Himself to spend time with the Father.

- After feeding the 5,000 and dismissing the crowd, Scripture

[174] Andrew Murray, Power to Change, Great Quotes on Prayer, http://powertochange.com/experience/spiritual-growth/prayerquotes, Accessed 11/16/2015.
[175] Richard Foster, *Celebration of Discipline* (HarperCollins, Kindle Edition, 2009), p. 33.
[176] Ibid., p. 34.

records, "He went up on the mountain by himself to pray. When evening came, he was there alone" (Matt. 14:23).

- Despite His busyness, He made time for prayer: "And rising very early in the morning, while it was still dark, he departed and went out to a desolate place, and there he prayed" (Mark 1:35).

- Before making the immeasurable decision to choose the twelve disciples, He spent a whole night in prayer to seek His Father's will: "In these days he went out to the mountain to pray, and all night he continued in prayer to God. And when day came, he called his disciples and chose from them twelve, whom he named apostles" (Luke 6:12–13).

- He stressed the importance of prayer to His disciples: "And he told them a parable to the effect that they ought always to pray and not lose heart" (Luke 18:1).

- Christ also overcame temptation and taught His disciples to do the same through prayer: "Watch and pray that you may not enter into temptation. The spirit indeed is willing, but the flesh is weak" (Matt. 26:41).

- We also find in John 17, the better part of an entire chapter, wherein Christ devoted Himself to prayer for His disciples and all who would follow Him afterward.

The Apostles and Prayer

Following Christ's example and teaching on the importance of prayer, the Apostles, and the early church also prayed constantly.

- Shortly after Christ's resurrection, the disciples continued in prayer: "All these with one accord were devoting themselves to prayer, together with the women and Mary the mother of

Jesus, and his brothers" (Acts 1:14).

- After the church was born on Pentecost, the early church devoted themselves to prayer: "And they devoted themselves to the apostles' teaching and the fellowship, to the breaking of bread and the prayers" (Acts 2:42).

- The lame man that Peter and John healed at the temple was a result of going to the temple to pray (Acts 3:1).

- After being persecuted for preaching the Word, the disciples, and the early church prayed for boldness to keep pressing on: "And when they had prayed, the place in which they were gathered together was shaken, and they were all filled with the Holy Spirit and continued to speak the word of God with boldness" (Acts 4:31).

- When faced with busyness and administrative challenges, prayer became a priority of the elders of the early church: "But we will devote ourselves to prayer and to the ministry of the word" (Acts 6:4).

- Prayer also accompanied each missionary journey by Paul and his companions: "Then after fasting and praying they laid their hands on them and sent them off" (Acts 13:3).

Christians Today and Prayer

The Bible is replete with examples of godly men and women praying. Yet today, the average Christian prays between 1–7 minutes a day. What a contrast! Samuel Chadwick states, "The one concern of the devil is to keep Christians from praying. He fears nothing from prayerless studies, prayerless work, and prayerless religion. He laughs at our toil, mocks at our wisdom, but he trembles when we pray."[177] It appears Satan is rejoicing

---

[177] Christian Prayer Quotes, *Prayer Quotations*, http://www.christian-prayer-quotes.christian-attorney.net, Accessed 10/20/2015.

over the lack of prayer in the lives of many Christians today.

Why should we pray, and why does it play such a large role in discipleship and our transformation towards spiritual maturity? Scripture provides, at least, six essential reasons:

1. By Prayer, We Have a Relationship with God

Having a relationship with the living God is the essence of the Christian life and our purpose for existing. It's what God sought to regain with mankind after their fall in the Garden of Eden and is a determining factor in whether a person is saved or not. The simple fact is that we cannot have a relationship with God without prayer. It's how we communicate and talk to Him.

Dan Hayes says it well, "I am first called to prayer because it is a key vehicle to building my love relationship with Jesus Christ. Hear me now — this is important. Christianity is not primarily rules. It is relationship."[178]

We are to love the Lord our God with all our heart, soul, mind, and strength. Christ exemplified this truth in His prayer life with the Father. He continually was in communion with the Father and walked every step while listening to His voice.

If we want to have a relationship with God, then we must pray. Samuel Chadwick states, "Prayer is the acid test of devotion."[179] It's in our obedience and commitment to commune with our Father that we show Him our true love.

2. By Prayer, God Gives Us the Power to Overcome Temptation

Christ provides compelling instruction, and an example, on how to overcome temptation. In Luke 22:39–46, Christ is facing His last hours on earth before being crucified. He is in the Garden

---

[178] Dan Hayes, *Motivating Reasons to Pray,* StartingWithGod.com, www.startingwithgod.com/knowing-god/motivating, Accessed 10/20/2015.
[179] Christian Prayer Quotes, *Prayer Quotations,* http://www.christian-prayer-quotes.christian-attorney.net, Accessed 10/20/2015.

of Gethsemane, embracing the reality of paying for the sins of mankind for all time and eternity. He begins this time by teaching His disciples how to overcome temptation: "And he came out and went, as was his custom, to the Mount of Olives, and the disciples followed him. When he came to the place, he said to them, '**Pray that you may not enter into temptation.**'" Then Christ practiced what He taught: "And he withdrew from them about a stone's throw, and knelt down and prayed, saying, 'Father, if you are willing, remove this cup from me. Nevertheless, not my will, but yours, be done.'"

Christ's temptation to avoid the pain of the Cross was so intense that His sweat became bloody: "And being in an agony he prayed more earnestly; and his sweat became like great drops of blood falling down to the ground." Despite His temptation, He remained in prayer, yielded to God's will, and was victorious over the Cross and death.

Afterward, He returned to His disciples to find them half-asleep. He then told them again about prayer and its role in temptation: "And when he rose from prayer, he came to the disciples and found them sleeping for sorrow, and he said to them, 'Why are you sleeping? Rise and pray that you may not enter into temptation.'"

Interestingly, Christ began His instruction on how to overcome temptation by telling the disciples about prayer, then showing by example how to do it, and then repeating His instruction again.

If we're going to be victorious over temptation, we need to follow Christ's example. Unfortunately, much of the time, prayer is not the first thing we do when confronting temptation, so we succumb and fall as a result. How much better we would be if it were our first line of defense. Dan Hays asserts, "What about seeing prayer as our first option so that God can give us courage and strength prior to our temptations? Certainly, if we would pray more, we would yield less to sin!"[180]

3. By Prayer, God Leads and Directs Our Paths

There are two general areas in life where we need God's direction: (1) in fully understanding truth and morals already revealed in the Bible and (2) in the practical areas of life that Scripture does not address.

God has already revealed much of His will to us through Scripture. For example, His will is that we become saved, are transformed into the image of Christ, attain spiritual maturity, and that we love God and others. However, in matters not directly revealed in Scripture, it gets trickier. Areas like whom we should marry, what job we should take, or what college we should attend, become harder to discern.

If we obey God in the areas already revealed in Scripture, then the areas not revealed will become much simpler to perceive. However, if we are disobedient to God's clear, revealed will in Scripture, then we'll struggle to find His will in other matters as well.

It's also important to note that Scripture provides wisdom and direction for finding His will by directing us to others. Proverbs 11:14 speaks of the role of counselors, Proverbs 1:8 shows the role of our parents, and James 1:5 speaks of directly receiving wisdom from God through prayer.

Through prayer, God will miraculously open and close doors in our lives. He loves us dearly, and when He sees His children seeking His Kingdom first and desiring above all else to please Him, He goes out of His way to supernaturally guide and direct their paths.

---

[180] Dan Hays, *Motivating Reasons to Pray,* StartingWithGod.com, www.startingwithgod.com/knowing-god/motivating, Accessed 10/20/2015.

4. By Prayer, We Accomplish God's Work

Charles Spurgeon declared, "I would rather teach one man to pray than ten men to preach."[181] Moreover, Andrew Murray claimed, "The man who mobilizes the Christian church to pray will make the greatest contribution to world evangelization in history."[182]

Prayer rallies the power of the Almighty and involves Him in our efforts. With Him, we are everything, but without Him, we are nothing. Christ said, "I am the vine; you are the branches. Whoever abides in me and I in him, he it is that bears much fruit, for **apart from me you can do nothing**" (John 15:5).

A careful look at Scripture reveals that everything accomplished for God happens through prayer. The births of Isaac, the Prophet Samuel, and John the Baptist all came through prayer. The wisdom of Solomon, the dedication of the temple, and the countless deliverances of Israel from her enemies came through prayer. The work of Christ, the works of the early church, and the spread of the gospel all came through prayer. Likewise, if we want God's blessing in our lives and ministries, it will only come through prayer as well.

5. By Prayer, We Are Victorious in Spiritual Warfare

The battle between good and evil and the reality of spiritual warfare is clear in Scripture. We see it in the life and ministry of Christ, the Apostles, and the early church. It is also specifically addressed in Ephesians 6:12: "For we do not wrestle against flesh and blood, but against the rulers, against the authorities, against the cosmic powers over this present darkness, against the spiritual forces of evil in the heavenly places."

It's through prayer that we tap into God's power and become

---

[181] Christian Prayer Quotes, *Prayer Quotations,* http://www.christian-prayer-quotes.christian-attorney.net, Accessed 10/20/2015.
[182] Ibid., Accessed 10/20/2015.

victorious over Satan and his evil forces. We are no match for them on our own, but we are more than conquerors over them through Christ.

Prayer is also the overarching armor in our spiritual warfare: "Praying at all times in the Spirit, with all prayer and supplication. To that end keep alert with all perseverance, making supplication for all the saints" (Eph. 6:17–18).

6. By Prayer, God Grants Us Peace

We find peace through prayer: "Casting all your anxieties on him, because he cares for you" (1 Pet. 5:7).

Additionally, "Do not be anxious about anything, but in everything by prayer and supplication with thanksgiving let your requests be made known to God. And the peace of God, which surpasses all understanding, will guard your hearts and your minds in Christ Jesus" (Phil. 4:6–7).

Prayer is what alleviates our worries and stress. It ushers God's peace into our hearts by taking our burdens, and concerns, and placing them on God.

Conclusion

By prayer, we have a relationship with God, overcome temptation, find God's will, accomplish much for God's Kingdom, are victorious in spiritual warfare, and receive God's peace. As the great prayer warrior E. M. Bounds says, "Prayer should not be regarded as a duty which must be performed, but rather as a privilege to be enjoyed, a rare delight that is always revealing some new beauty."[183]

Prayer is an essential component of discipleship, and without it, spiritual maturity is unattainable. We cannot grow in our relationship with God without communicating with Him.

---

[183] Ibid., Accessed 10/20/2015.

6. Mentoring and Discipleship

One of the central themes of discipleship during the time of Christ was that of relationships and mentoring. It was normal for a rabbi to take his disciples on trips that lasted from several days to several weeks in order to train them. They would dedicate this time for intense mentoring, teaching, practicing, and learning. All the distractions of life would be set aside for the purpose of interaction between the rabbi and his students. Teaching was highly relational and modeled, and the disciples would learn how to apply Scripture, in large part, by observing the conduct and practices of their rabbi.

What Is Mentoring?

Biblical mentoring is an informal relationship wherein a more spiritually mature person teaches and models godly, life-skills to others who are generally less spiritually mature. It can be formal, informal, take place in a group setting, take place in an individual setting, can be regular, or somewhat sporadic.

Examples of mentoring include small group Bible studies, Sunday School classes, youth group, one on one discipleship studies, accountability partners, and so forth.

The most effective mentoring takes place in a one on one setting, or in a small group where specific truths and life-skills are intentionally passed on.

Mentoring Provides an Example

Christ was a rabbi who modeled what He taught to His disciples. This was done as they spent time together, took trips together, lived together for periods of time, and served together. After learning from Christ, His disciples would then practice what they learned.

We see mentoring as a central focus for teaching and training in other examples from Scripture as well: Moses mentored Joshua, Naomi mentored Ruth, Elijah mentored Elisha, and Paul mentored Timothy. After Paul had mentored Timothy, he encouraged Timothy to mentor others: "You then, my child, be strengthened by the grace that is in Christ Jesus, and what you have heard from me in the presence of many witnesses entrust to faithful men who will be able to teach others also" (2 Tim. 2:1).

Modern-Day Discipleship

Discipleship in our day is very different from what it was in the time of Christ. Today, we primarily focus on teaching certain truths and think that after several classes on discipleship training we're finished. Normally, this is because we're focusing primarily on imparting knowledge and not on all the essential components of discipleship like character, attitudes, spiritual gift development, self-discipline, and so on.

Discipleship is much more than taking a class for several weeks and thinking we're done. Instead, it must be engaged in throughout our lifetime. We are never finished and must always be looking for new opportunities to grow in all the essential components of the discipleship-making process.

Mentoring in the Church

A number of recent scholars and theologians have highlighted the importance of mentoring in discipleship. Voddie Baucham Jr., in his article "Equipping the Generations: A Three-Pronged Approach to Discipleship," shows that Paul clearly instructs Titus to make disciples using a mentoring model.[184]

---

[184] Voddie Baucham Jr, "Equipping the Generations: A Three-Pronged Approach to Discipleship" (Source: Journal of Family Ministry, 2 no 1 Fall-Winter 2011, Publication. ATLA Religion Database with ATLASerials. Hunter Resource Library), pp. 74-79, Accessed 11/5/2014.

There are three key themes Baucham draws out from the Book of Titus that underscores what successful discipleship should entail:

1. Godly, mature men and women in the church
2. Godly, manly pastors and elders
3. Biblically functioning homes

Baucham stresses that each of these three themes represents one leg of a three-legged stool, and each leg is vital in the discipleship-making process.[185] His reasoning is as follows:

1. Godly, mature men and women in the church are those whom Scripture charges with teaching the younger men and women the truths of God.
2. Godly, manly elders provide the example to the flock and leadership within the church.
3. Godly homes are the best place for discipleship to take place as this is where most of life is lived.[186]

Each of these themes uses mentorship as the vehicle through which discipleship is carried out.

Relationships and Discipleship

James G. Samra, in his article "A Biblical View of Discipleship," stresses the importance of relationships in discipleship. He indicates that in the Gospels discipleship literally meant following Christ where He went and learning from Him in a personal setting. It involved learning to suffer with Christ, leaving all behind, seeing what Christ did, hearing what He said, being corrected by Him, and following His example.[187] Samara

---

[185] Ibid., p. 75.
[186] Ibid., pp. 76–77.
[187] James G. Samra, "A Biblical View of Discipleship" (Bibliotheca Sacra: 219-34. Publication Type: Article, Database: ATLA Religion Database with ATLASerials. Hunter Resource Library), p. 222, Accessed 11/5/2014.

affirms, "In the rest of the New Testament, because Christ is no longer physically present, discipleship involved imitation of other mature believers rather than literally following Christ (1 Thess. 1:6; 1 Cor. 11:1)."[188]

Samra also says that in the Old Testament there are some examples of what discipleship looked like as carried out in the likes of Moses and Joshua as well as Elijah and Elisha.[189] In all these examples, relationships and mentoring provide the environment wherein discipleship takes place.

Avery Willis, in his article "MasterLife: Discipleship Training for Leaders," stresses the role of relationships in the process of discipleship. Willis states, "Discipleship is accomplished through the practice of basic Christian disciplines under the guidance of mature, practicing disciplers . . . and is carried out in the context of a small group of approximately eight persons."[190] Willis' model uses mentoring as a key component of effective discipleship.

Conclusion

The example of Christ and other mentoring relationships in Scripture highlight the importance mentoring plays in discipleship. For this reason, it's one of the essential components needed in the discipleship-making process. Many affirm that we learn more by observing than by hearing. The mentoring relationship puts this truth into practice as it allows us to see the truth of Scripture lived out and applied to real life.

---

[188] Ibid., p. 224.
[189] Ibid., pp. 226–227.
[190] Avery T. Willis Jr, "MasterLife: Discipleship Training for Leaders" (Source: Theological Educator, no 28 Spr 1984, p 3-5. Publication Type: Article. Subjects: Baptists--Education; Christian life ATLA Religion Database with ATLASerials. Hunter Resource Library), p. 3, Accessed 11/5/2014.

7. Church Involvement and Discipleship

Why is church involvement one of the essential components of the discipleship-making process, and how does God use it to transform our lives and bring us to spiritual maturity?

The Church Is God's Invention

The church is not a new fad or invention of man. God birthed it on the Day of Pentecost, and it plays a unique role in His plan for believers. It consists of both the universal and the local church.

The universal church consists of all those who have a genuine, personal relationship with Jesus Christ: "For in one Spirit we were all baptized into one body — Jews or Greeks, slaves or free — and all were made to drink of one Spirit" (1 Cor. 12:13). The local church can be defined as found in Galatians 1:1–2: "Paul, an apostle . . . and all the brothers who are with me, to the churches in Galatia."

The church is God's caring community where believers find instruction, encouragement, correction, inspiration, and fellowship. Faithful involvement in church helps all believers attain spiritual maturity while a lack of it will stunt a believer's growth.

Church Involvement Develops Spiritual Maturity

"And he [Christ] gave the apostles, the prophets, the evangelists, the shepherds and teachers, to equip the saints for the work of ministry, for building up the body of Christ, until we all attain to the unity of the faith and of the knowledge of the Son of God, to mature manhood, to the measure of the stature of the fullness of Christ" (Eph. 4:11–13). Christ has given the church gifted men and women for the equipping of believers so that we might all attain spiritual maturity. Therefore, without their influence in our lives, spiritual maturity is unattainable.

Church Involvement Provides Sound Doctrine to Protect Us

In church, we find God's instruction for combatting the lies of Satan and our culture: "So that we may no longer be children, tossed to and fro by the waves and carried about by every wind of doctrine, by human cunning, by craftiness in deceitful schemes" (Eph. 4:14).

Church Involvement Provides Encouragement and Fellowship

Within the church, we find inspiration and encouragement in our Christian lives. As a famous illustration reveals, "A piece of coal removed from other burning coals will soon go out, but a coal left with other burning coals will keep on burning."

Dale Robbins asserts, "Receiving the preaching and teaching of the Word of God increases our faith and builds us up spiritually. Every believer knows what it is to face spiritual conflicts to their faith, and must realize the importance of being fed spiritually so that they can overcome the challenges."[191]

Church Involvement Provides a Unique Visitation of the Lord's Presence

Even though Christ resides in the heart of every believer, there's a special visitation of His presence when believers are gathered together. Consider the following verses:

1. The glory of the Lord filled the Tabernacle Moses built when the people of God were gathered together (Ex. 40:34).

2. The glory of the Lord filled the Temple Solomon built when the people of God were gathered together (1 Kings 8:11).

---

[191] Dale Robbins, *Why Christians Should Attend Church*, Victorious.org, www.victorious.org/pub/why-church-169, Accessed 10/21/2015.

3. The church was born on Pentecost as believers were gathered together (Acts 2).

4. When persecution faced the early church, they prayed, and the place shook with God's presence (Acts 4).

5. The missionary journeys of Paul and his companions were commissioned by the Lord when the church was gathered together (Acts 13).

6. Doctrinal decisions were made when the church was gathered together (Acts 15).

7. Many of the spiritual gifts are intended to be exercised when the church is gathered together (1 Cor. 12–14).

8. Prayer for healing is encouraged by calling together the elders of the church (James 5).

God moves in a unique way when believers gather, and we experience His special visitation when we're a part of it.

Church Involvement Is an Expression of Our Love for God

Dale Robbins says, "Going to church is a visible, tangible expression of our love and worship to God. It is where we can gather with other believers to publicly bear witness of our faith and trust in God, something that is required of all Christians (Matt. 10:32–33), and where we can bring Him offerings of praise, thanks, and honor, which are pleasing to Him."[192] King David wrote, "I will declare Your name to My brethren; In the midst of the assembly I will praise You" (Ps. 22:22).

Being involved in what God loves reveals our love for Him, and God certainly loves the church: "Husbands, love your wives, as **Christ loved the church** and gave himself up for her, that he might sanctify her, having cleansed her by the washing of water

---

[192] Ibid., Accessed 10/21/2015.

with the word, so that he might present the church to himself in splendor, without spot or wrinkle or any such thing, that she might be holy and without blemish" (Eph. 5:25–27).

God Commands Church Involvement

Because God loves us and knows what we need, He commands us to be involved in church for our own good: "And let us consider how to stir up one another to love and good works, not neglecting to meet together, as is the habit of some, but encouraging one another, and all the more as you see the Day drawing near" (Heb. 10:24–25).

Conclusion

In church, we receive from God and others critical components we need for discipleship, and we, in turn, give to others what they need for discipleship. We express our love to God and have the privilege and responsibility to minister to others with our gifts. Moreover, as we engage in this wonderful process, we move toward spiritual maturity.

8. Evangelism and Discipleship

Evangelism is one of the essential components of the discipleship-making process because it's part of the Great Commission Mandate. It's not just for missionaries in a distant land or those with the gift of evangelism, but for all. Everyone should participate in evangelism in some way or another.

Christ's Focus on Evangelism

The Great Commission Mandate includes evangelism: "Go therefore, and make disciples of all nations, baptizing them in the name of the Father and of the Son and of the Holy Spirit," (Matt. 28:19). Moreover, the corresponding text of Mark 16:15 tells us to "Proclaim the gospel to all creation."

We also see in the life and work of Christ His concentrated focus on evangelism. He was continually calling people to follow Him, revealing the passion of His heart: "For the Son of Man came to seek and to save the lost" (Luke 19:10). If we want to be like Christ, then we must have a passion for evangelism like He does.

We can measure, in part, our spiritual maturity by the level of passion we have for evangelism. If one of Christ's main purposes on earth was to seek and save the lost, it certainly should be one of ours as well.

Unfortunately, the majority of Christians don't share their faith or invite their friends to church. For this reason, Christ would sadly say to many Christians today the same thing He said to those during His day: "The harvest is plentiful, but the laborers are few; therefore, pray earnestly to the Lord of the harvest to send out laborers into his harvest" (Matt. 9:37–38).

Christ Called His Disciples to Be Fishers of Men

"And he said to them, 'Follow me, and I will make you

fishers of men'" (Matt. 4:19). The same message applies to us today. We are called to be fishers of men. A "fisher of men" symbolizes a person who evangelizes. They have a passion for reaching people with the good news of Christ, seeing them saved, reunited with their Maker, and rescued from sin's destructive domain.

For the person who neglects evangelism, it should give them great pause. How can they claim to love God and others, and care so little about God's passion for reaching the lost? How can they idly stand by as others destroy their lives, head for hell, and not warn them?

Most Christians Are Not Fishers of Men

In research done by Jon D. Wilke, the statistics regarding Evangelical Christians today who share their faith are troublesome. Wilke reveals, "When it comes to discipleship, churchgoers struggle most with sharing Christ with non-Christians according to a recent study of church-going American Protestants. The study conducted by LifeWay Research found 80% of those who attend church one or more times a month believe they have a personal responsibility to share their faith, yet 61% have not told another person about how to become a Christian in the previous six months."[193] Wilke continues, "The survey also asked how many times they have personally invited an unchurched person to attend a church service or some other program at their church. Nearly half (48%) of church attendees responded, 'zero.'"[194]

Many so-called Evangelical Christians are not only extremely negligent in sharing the gospel, but many don't even invite their unsaved friends to church. Christ said He would make His

---

[193] Jon D. Wilke, *Churchgoers Believe in Sharing Faith, Most Never Do,* LifeWay.com, http://www.lifeway.com/article/research-survey-sharing-christ-2012, Accessed 08/04/2015.
[194] Ibid., Accessed 08/04/2015.

disciples fishers of men. However, for many so-called modern day disciples, evangelism isn't even on their radar screen.

Christ Calls Every Believer to Be His Witness

Moments before Christ's ascension to heaven, as recorded in Acts 1:8, He repeated the Great Commission Mandate using slightly different words, "But you will receive power when the Holy Spirit has come upon you and you will be my witnesses in Jerusalem and in all Judea and Samaria, and to the end of the earth."

Notice carefully what Christ said, "You will be my witnesses in **Jerusalem** and in all **Judea** and **Samaria**, and to the **end of the earth**" (Acts 1:8). Another term for "witness" is "evangelize." Christ said some would be witnesses in Jerusalem (their hometown), some would be witnesses in Judea (a little larger circle), some would be witnesses in Samaria (their country), and some would be witnesses to the ends of the earth (foreign missions). Even though they were to be witnesses in different places, all had the privilege and responsibility to evangelize.

Paul instructed Timothy, who apparently was somewhat shy and timid, to fulfill his responsibility in evangelism: "As for you, always be sober-minded, endure suffering, **do the work of an evangelist**, fulfill your ministry" (2 Tim. 4:5). Even though it was uncomfortable for Timothy, he still needed to do the work of an evangelist.

God has given all of us the ministry of reconciliation: "All this is from God, who through Christ reconciled us to himself and gave us the **ministry of reconciliation**; that is, in Christ God was reconciling the world to himself, not counting their trespasses against them, and entrusting to us the **message of reconciliation**" (2 Cor. 5:18–19). In the same way Christ had the ministry of reconciliation (reuniting God with sinners), we have the same ministry as well.

Some feel evangelism is primarily for missionaries or others who have the gift of evangelism. While it's true some might have this gift, it does not alleviate others from participating in evangelism.

We Need to Speak, Not Just Show

A common belief today is that we should let our lives do the talking for us and evangelize primarily by "letting our light shine" before others. This belief does contain truth and is what gives us the right to share our faith, yet if we omit the balancing responsibility of evangelizing through speaking, we are misguided.

If letting our light shine was enough, then Christ, being perfect, would have just shown up, not said a word, and let His "light shine." However, Christ is referred to as the "Word" in Scripture who became flesh and dwelt among us (John 1:14). The spoken word is so important that Christ is called, the "Word." He spent His life speaking and did so much that John concluded his Gospel by stating, "Now there are also many other things that Jesus did. Were every one of them to be written, I suppose that the world itself could not contain the books that would be written" (John 21:25).

Virtually every example we see in Scripture where God wants to communicate something, He uses both a clean vessel (letting our light shine) and the spoken word. We need to be careful we don't allow the fear of evangelism scare us away from sharing the gospel through the spoken word and use the excuse of "letting our light shine" as a reason for not speaking and being bold for Christ.

Conclusion

Believers who are not involved in evangelism are believers who don't share Christ's passion for winning the lost. They are failing to obey Christ in fulfilling the Great Commission Mandate and display indifference to the fact that unbelievers are going to hell. If the purpose of Christ was to spread the gospel, then His disciples today should do the same. Nevertheless, the majority of Christians today are not fishers of men as Christ and His disciples were, and seem to loathe evangelism.

There's a huge disconnect today in the lives of many Christians between what they should do and what they do. The fact that the vast majority of Christians don't share their faith or invite their friends to church speaks volumes about their level of spiritual maturity and devotion to Christ.

9. The Inner Life and Discipleship

Why is attention to our inner life one of the essential components of the discipleship-making process? Because what takes place in our inner life is the truest expression of our life in Christ. It's where we apply and live out true spirituality.

According to Christ, an outward focus on keeping His commands with the intent to impress others has no value. He calls it hypocritical and vain: "You hypocrites! Well did Isaiah prophesy of you, when he said: 'This people honors me with their lips, but their heart is far from me; in vain do they worship me, teaching as doctrines the commandments of men'" (Matt. 15:5-9).

Our Inner Life Is the True Mark of Our Spirituality

In the Sermon on the Mount, Christ addresses the issue of the inner life as the mark of true spirituality. He speaks of anger, lust, divorce, oaths, bitterness, retaliation, loving our enemies, giving to the needy, prayer, and fasting, all from the perspective of the inner life before God versus mere external acts done before others to impress them. He warns that merely obeying His commands with the intention of impressing others does not please Him.

Lying deep within our hearts is the tendency to be more concerned about what others think of us than what God thinks. We often strive to impress others by appearing good on the outside, but are inwardly different. Many of the spiritual leaders of Christ's day were guilty of this snare as they did much of their service to God solely to impress others, with little concern for what God thought. They were full of pride and selfish ambition.

Unfortunately, we can be the same. Christ recognized this tendency within our hearts and addressed it with a strong rebuke: "Woe to you, scribes and Pharisees, hypocrites! For you are like whitewashed tombs, which outwardly appear beautiful, but within are full of dead people's bones and all uncleanness. So you also outwardly appear righteous to others, but within you are full of hypocrisy and lawlessness" (Matt. 23:27–28). We must take great care to serve with pure hearts that seek to impress God, not others!

The Importance of the Inner Life

Klaus Issler, in his article "Six Themes to Guide Spiritual Formation Ministry Based on Jesus' Sermon on the Mount," emphasizes that the key theme of the Sermon on the Mount is inner heart formation.[195] We can observe that virtually every theme Christ cites from the Old Testament is a clarification of the importance of the inner heart for the New Covenant. Issler sees the segment on the Beatitudes as a further verification of the importance of the inner life in the discipleship process.[196]

Dietrich Bonhoeffer devotes three chapters of his classic book, *The Cost of Discipleship,* to the topic of the inner life.[197] The inner life is where we live, where God knows our thoughts, motives, desires, and goals. When we bypass the inner life and attempt to "go through the motions" or "fake" our spirituality before others, we displease God and worship Him in vain.

Attention to Our Inner Life Protects Us from Legalism

When we neglect the inner life and pursue obeying God's commandments primarily to impress others, we risk the danger of falling into legalism and hypocrisy. For example, some Christians are boastful of their knowledge of Scripture and think they are

---

[195] Klaus Issler, "Six Themes to Guide Spiritual Formation Ministry Based on Jesus' Sermon on the Mount" (Source: Christian Education, Journal Date: September 1, 2010. CEJ: Series 3, Vol. 7, No. 2. ATLA Religion Database with ATLASerials. Hunter Resource Library), p. 370, Accessed 11/5/2014.

[196] Ibid., p. 371.

[197] Dietrich Bonhoeffer, *The Cost of Discipleship* (SCM Classics, Hymns Ancient and Modern Ltd. Kindle Edition, 2011-08-16), Kindle Locations 2163-2398.

more spiritual as a result. However, the problem is not that they are knowledgeable in Scripture, but that they have a desire to impress others with their knowledge.

It's the same with all God's commandments. If we do them to impress others, then we have completely missed the mark. This is why a focus on the inner life is so important. Without it, much of what we do can be vain and displease God.

Christ is certainly not telling us we shouldn't obey His commands, but stresses that if we obey them merely to impress others, then we have missed the point entirely. It all begins with pleasing God inwardly, and then we will live our external lives correctly.

The Inner Life and How We Live at Home

Interestingly, how a person lives in the privacy of their home, and how they treat others within it, is also viewed as an extension of the inner life by God. For this reason, God requires those aspiring to be elders or deacons to display their spirituality in their homes before being qualified to be leaders in the church: "He must manage his own household well, with all dignity keeping his children submissive, for if someone does not know how to manage his own household, how will he care for God's church?" (1 Tim. 3:4–5).

The Inner Life and the Lack of Spiritual Growth

God also indicates that if we neglect our inner life with Him, it will inhibit or block our ability to understand His Word and grow. This was a problem with the Israelites and applies to us today as well: "You hypocrites! Well did Isaiah prophesy of you, when he said: 'This people honors me with their lips, but their heart is far from me; in vain do they worship me, teaching as doctrines the commandments of men'" (Matt. 15:5–9).

Similarly, in the Book of Isaiah, God makes a connection

between the Israelite's inability to understand Scripture and their lack of attention to the inner life: "And the vision of all this has become to you like the words of a book that is sealed. When men give it to one who can read, saying, 'Read this,' he says, 'I cannot, for it is sealed.' And the Lord said: 'Because this people draw near with their mouth and honor me with their lips, while their hearts are far from me, and their fear of me is a commandment taught by men'" (Isa. 29:11, 13).

This same principle is confirmed again in Christ's ministry:

Then the disciples came and said to him, "Why do you speak to them in parables?" And he answered them, "To you it has been given to know the secrets of the kingdom of heaven, but to them it has not been given. For to the one who has, more will be given, and he will have an abundance, but from the one who has not, even what he has will be taken away. This is why I speak to them in parables, because seeing they do not see, and hearing they do not hear, nor do they understand. Indeed, in their case the prophecy of Isaiah is fulfilled that says: **'You will indeed hear but never understand, and you will indeed see but never perceive**.' For this people's heart has **grown dull**, and with their ears **they can barely hear**, and **their eyes they have closed**, lest they should see with their eyes and hear with their ears and understand with their heart and turn, and I would heal them.'" (Matt. 13:10–15).

Conclusion

If we honor God with our lips, but our hearts are far from Him, we too will struggle to understand Scripture and can even lose the knowledge and understanding of it we once had, thus, becoming spiritually blind. What a severe judgment from God! Moreover, we can displease God and worship Him in vain. This is why attention to our inner life is so important.

10. Spiritual Gifts and Discipleship

Understanding and practicing our spiritual gifts is another essential component of discipleship. Interestingly, they are not included as an essential component in other lists I researched. Why have I included them in this book? Because Scripture reveals their importance, not only in our own lives, but also in the life of others in the church.

What Are Spiritual Gifts?

Spiritual gifts are special abilities God gives to each believer for their own personal benefit and for the benefit of others. They are endowments that come in the form of grace and special help. They are supernatural enablements given by the Holy Spirit primarily for building up the body of Christ so that all may attain spiritual maturity.

Spiritual Gifts Have Been Given to All Believers

God has given every believer spiritual gifts. These gifts become part of who we are and how we serve God and others. Without understanding and practicing our spiritual gifts, we seriously hinder our own growth and the growth of others in the body of Christ. Ephesians 4:8–15 affirms this truth:

> When he [Christ] ascended on high, he led a host of captives, and he gave **gifts to men**. *These spiritual gifts have been given by God to* "Equip the saints for the work of ministry, for building up the body of Christ, until we all attain to the unity of the faith and of the knowledge of the Son of God, to **mature manhood**, to the measure of the stature of the **fullness of Christ**." *And* "Speaking the truth in love, we are to grow up in every way into him who is the head, into Christ, from

whom the whole body, joined and held together by every joint with which it is equipped, **when each part is working properly, makes the body grow** so that it **builds itself** up in love" (Eph. 4:8, 12–13, 15).

God has given each person spiritual gifts for attaining the measure of the fullness of Christ, which is synonymous with spiritual maturity.

A spiritually mature person is one who knows their spiritual gifts, and has honed and sharpened them for maximum usage in God's Kingdom. They use their gifts not only for their own personal discipleship development, but in making disciples as well. Spiritual gifts are God's special abilities for these purposes.

No spiritually mature person, therefore, would reject God's supernatural enablement for becoming and making disciples. After all, if the Great Commission Mandate to make disciples is taken seriously, then by default, we must take seriously God's gifts that help us fulfill His mandate. It is, therefore, impossible to be spiritually mature without understanding and practicing our spiritual gifts. For this reason, they are included as one of the essential components of the discipleship-making process.

What Are the Spiritual Gifts?

There are four main passages in Scripture that speak of the spiritual gifts: Romans 12:6–8, 1 Corinthians 12:7–10 and 12:28, and Ephesians 4:11–12. The following gifts are mentioned in these passages:

- **Romans 12:6–8:** "Having gifts that differ according to the grace given to us, let us use them: if **prophecy**, in proportion to our faith; if **service**, in our serving; the one who **teaches**, in his teaching; the one who **exhorts**, in his exhortation; the one who **contributes**, in generosity; the one who **leads**, with zeal; the one who does **acts of mercy**, with cheerfulness." Seven gifts are mentioned here.

- **1 Corinthians 12:7–10:** "To each is given the manifestation of the Spirit for the common good. For to one is given through the Spirit the utterance of **wisdom**, and to another the utterance of **knowledge** according to the same Spirit, to another **faith** by the same Spirit, to another gifts of **healing** by the one Spirit, to another the working of **miracles**, to another **prophecy**, to another the ability to **distinguish between spirits**, to another **various kinds of tongues**, to another the **interpretation of tongues**. All these are empowered by one and the same Spirit, who apportions to each one individually as he wills." Nine gifts are mentioned here.

- **1 Corinthians 12:28**: "And God has appointed in the church first **apostles**, second **prophets**, third **teachers**, then **miracles**, then gifts of **healing**, **helping**, **administrating**, and various kinds of **tongues**." Eight gifts are mentioned here.

- **Ephesians 4:11–12**: "And he gave the **apostles**, the **prophets**, the **evangelists**, the **shepherds** and **teachers**, to equip the saints for the work of ministry, for building up the body of Christ." Five gifts are mentioned here.

In total, there are 29 gifts mentioned. However, some are mentioned more than once. Considering this, there are 21 different spiritual gifts mentioned in these four passages.

- **Five Gifts Are Mentioned Indirectly in Scripture:** (1) celibacy (1 Cor. 7), (2) hospitality (Heb. 13:2), (3) missions (Paul's journeys), (4) intercession (Luke 18:1; James 5:17–18; 1 Thess. 5:17), and (5) casting out demons (Matt. 17:18; Mark 16:17; Acts 16:16–18, 19:11–16).

Adding the 21 gifts from the verses mentioned directly in Scripture to those mentioned indirectly, we arrive at 26 spiritual gifts mentioned in these passages.

Are All the Spiritual Gifts for Today?

My intention is not to deal with this question in this book, as time and space don't permit. Instead, my purpose is to simply mention the gifts found in Scripture in order to provide the most comprehensive, extensive information as possible. However, I will provide some clarification that might be helpful.

Those who believe all the gifts are for the whole period of the church are called "Continuationists" (from the word "continue"). Those who believe many of the gifts, but not all, are for today are called, "Cessationists" (from the word "cease").

What Are the Purposes of the Spiritual Gifts?

- **To bring us to spiritual maturity:** Ephesians 4:8–15 states that as each member of Christ ministers to one another using their spiritual gifts, believers are built up and move toward spiritual maturity.

- **To manifest God's presence:** Wayne Grudem articulates, "One of his [Holy Spirit's] primary purposes in the new covenant age is to manifest the presence of God — to give indications that make the presence of God known. And when the Holy Spirit works in various ways that can be perceived by believers and unbelievers, this encourages people's faith that God is near and that He is working to fulfill His purposes in the church and to bring blessing to His people."[198]

- **To build unity within the church:** In his letter to the Ephesians, the Apostle Paul encourages believers to be "Eager to maintain the unity of the Spirit in the bond of peace

---

[198] Wayne Grudem, *Systematic Theology: An Introduction to Biblical Doctrine* (Zondervan Publishing House, Grand Rapids, Michigan, 1994), p. 641.

until we all attain to the unity of the faith and of the knowledge of the Son of God, to mature manhood" (Eph. 4:12–13).

- **To reveal our interdependence upon one another:** The gifts are for the building up of the Body of Christ as each member understands and exercises their gifts. We are intertwined and dependent on one another. If one member suffers, we all suffer. If one member is weak, we all are affected (1 Cor. 12:21–26). This can also mean that if one member does not understand and practice their spiritual gifts, then the rest of the body suffers and can be hindered from attaining spiritual maturity.

- **To bring glory to God:** As each member understands and practices their spiritual gifts, the Body of Christ grows, and God is glorified. However, when believers are ignorant of their gifts or do not practice them, then God's glory is diminished in the church, and the Body of Christ suffers.

For these reasons, understanding and practicing our spiritual gifts is one of the essential components of the discipleship-making process.

The Need to Develop and Sharpen Our Spiritual Gifts

Not only should we know what our spiritual gifts are, but we should also develop and sharpen them so that we become masters at using them. The Apostle Paul said he was a master builder: "According to the grace of God given to me, like a **skilled master builder** I laid a foundation, and someone else is building upon it. Let each one take care how he builds upon it. For no one can lay a foundation other than that which is laid, which is Jesus Christ" (1 Cor. 3:10–11).

Paul was a skilled master builder. He had honed and sharpened his gifts and abilities in order to be the most effective tool as possible in the hands of God. He was extremely knowledgeable in God's Word, had impeccable character, was self-disciplined, hardworking, willing to suffer, persevered, and was completely devoted to the Kingdom of God and its advancement. We too should strive to be like Paul and become skilled master builders who know our gifts and use them with precision and excellence.

Conclusion

God has given each person spiritual gifts for attaining the measure of the fullness of Christ, which is synonymous with spiritual maturity.

A spiritually mature person is one who knows their spiritual gifts, and has honed and sharpened them for maximum usage in God's Kingdom. They use their gifts not only for their own personal discipleship development, but in making disciples as well. Spiritual gifts are God's special abilities for these purposes.

No spiritually mature person, therefore, would reject God's supernatural enablement for becoming and making disciples. After all, if the Great Commission Mandate to make disciples is taken seriously, then by default, we must take seriously God's gifts that help us fulfill His mandate. It is, therefore, impossible to be spiritually mature without understanding and practicing our spiritual gifts.

11. Serving and Discipleship

Why is serving one of the essential components of the discipleship-making process, and how does it help us attain spiritual maturity? Serving is essential as it fulfills several key purposes for our lives and existence.

God Created Us to Serve

"For we are his workmanship, created in Christ Jesus for **good works**, which God prepared beforehand, that we should walk in them" (Eph. 2:10). The very purpose for which God created us is to serve Him and others. For this reason, serving is one of the essential components of discipleship.

1 Peter 4:10–11 adds, "As each has received a gift, use it to **serve** one another, as good stewards of God's varied grace: whoever speaks, as one who speaks oracles of God; whoever **serves**, as one who **serves** by the strength that God supplies — in order that in everything God may be glorified through Jesus Christ. To him belong glory and dominion forever and ever. Amen."

When we fulfill the reason for which we were created, we find the greatest joy, meaning, and purpose in life. We also bring glory to God, bless others, and bless ourselves.

Christ Came to Serve

After a dispute among the disciples about who would be the greatest among them, Christ taught them a significant purpose for His earthly life and ours as well:

But Jesus called them to him and said, "You know that the rulers of the Gentiles lord it over them, and their great ones exercise authority over them. It shall not be so among you.

But whoever would be great among you must be your **servant**, and whoever would be first among you must be your **slave**, even as the Son of Man came not to be served but to **serve**, and to give his life as a ransom for many'" (Matt. 20:25–28).

Christ came to serve … and did so to such a degree that He died on a cross in His service to us.

Christ also illustrated the example of serving when He, being the Creator of the universe, humbled Himself and washed the feet of the disciples:

> When he had washed their feet and put on his outer garments and resumed his place, he said to them, "Do you understand what I have done to you? You call me Teacher and Lord, and you are right, for so I am. If I then, your Lord and Teacher, have washed your feet, you also ought to wash one another's feet. For I have given you an example, that you also should do just as I have done to you. Truly, truly, I say to you, a servant is not greater than his master, nor is a messenger greater than the one who sent him. If you know these things, blessed are you if you do them" (John 13:12–17).

If the purpose of God is that we would be transformed to become like Christ, then serving would rank as essential as it's who Christ is in His nature. If we want to be like Christ, then we must learn to serve as He does.

Laziness and Pride: the Enemies of Serving

God has nothing positive to say about laziness and pride as they kill a serving spirit. Key themes in the Book of Proverbs are warnings about the negative effects of laziness and pride. Both attitudes are self-seeking and end in ruin. Instead, God commands that we develop a servant's heart like Christ: "Do nothing from selfish ambition or conceit, but in humility count others more significant than yourselves. Let each of you look not only to his own interests, but also to the interests of others" (Phil. 2:3-4). He then gives us an example in Christ:

> Have this mind among yourselves, which is yours in Christ Jesus, who, though he was in the form of God, did not count equality with God a thing to be grasped, but emptied himself, by taking the form of a servant, being born in the likeness of men. And being found in human form, he humbled himself by becoming obedient to the point of death, even death on a cross (Phil. 2:5-8).

Christ was a servant, and He calls us to be one too. Laziness and pride must be resisted, and in their place, a servant's spirit developed.

Those who serve God and others will be honored: "If anyone **serves** me, he must follow me; and where I am, there will my servant be also. If anyone **serves** me, the Father will honor him" (John 12:26). What greater honor could one attain than that of the Father?

Conclusion

In the same way Christ is a servant, God created us to serve as well. When we fulfill the purpose for which we were created, we find the greatest joy, meaning, and purpose in life. We bring glory to God, bless others, and bless ourselves. However, the world says just the opposite. It says fulfillment is found in being served. It says power, prestige, and pride define greatness, not humility and servanthood.

Instead of following the world's self-serving attitude, we need to follow Christ's other-serving attitude. Spiritual maturity is other-serving; spiritual immaturity is self-serving.

We must take to heart God's will for us: "Do not be **slothful in zeal**, be **fervent** in spirit, **serve** the Lord" (Rom. 12:11).

12. Spiritual Attitudes and Discipleship

Spiritual attitudes have largely been overlooked in discipleship today. Why are they so important that they would be included as an essential component of discipleship?

Many years ago, I was involved in a children's ministry program in the church I attended and was continually puzzled by the leader's poor attitudes. She had been a believer for many years, was knowledgeable in Scripture, and appeared to be spiritually mature. Yet, she was grumpy, rude, harsh, and unpleasant. I wrestled with how this could be. As a young believer, it was all so conflictive to me. How could she overlook a major theme of Scripture, and why would her church put her in a leadership position having such great deficiencies in her attitudes?

Defining Attitudes

Attitudes can be defined as a mental state of mind, a way of thinking, a feeling, a way of behaving, a disposition, a demeanor, or an emotional state of being. Attitudes can be both positive and negative. They are the expression of our inner thoughts, feelings, emotions, beliefs, and values. Without exception, we always have some kind of an attitude.

Attitudes are the living outflow of our lives and always manifest themselves in a certain action or behavior. We will act a certain way depending on what kind of attitude we have at that time. Our attitudes are the reason we do what we do, obey or disobey, or feel what we feel. They are the servants of our will and affect how we interact and treat others.

Biblical Attitudes in Scripture

We see both positive and negative attitudes all throughout

Scripture. Galatians 5:22–23 lists several positive attitudes: "But the fruit of the Spirit is love, joy, peace, patience, kindness, goodness, faithfulness, gentleness, self-control."

Despite the likelihood of being in a cold prison cell in Rome, the Apostle Paul's main theme of the Book of Philippians is joy. Not only was Paul joyful, but he saw it as an essential part of our Christian life: "Convinced of this, I know that I will remain and continue with you all, for your progress and **joy** in the faith" (Phil. 1:25).

Philippians 2:5–8 (NASB) tells us to have the same attitude of humility as Christ: "Have this **attitude** in yourselves which was also in Christ Jesus, who, although He existed in the form of God, did not regard equality with God a thing to be grasped, but emptied Himself, taking the form of a bond-servant, and being made in the likeness of men. Being found in appearance as a man, He humbled Himself by becoming obedient to the point of death, even death on a cross."

Jesus also demonstrated the role of spiritual attitudes in His life. One author has noted, "He maintained a perfect attitude in every situation because He prayed about everything and worried about nothing. Jesus' attitude was never to become defensive, discouraged, or depressed, because His goal was to please the Father rather than to achieve His own agenda. In the midst of trials, Jesus was patient. In the midst of suffering, He was hopeful. In the midst of blessing, He was humble. Even in the midst of ridicule, abuse, and hostility, He 'made no threats … and did not retaliate. Instead, He entrusted Himself to Him who judges justly.'"[199]

In the Sermon on the Mount, Christ speaks of key attitudes He wants us to possess such as being poor in spirit, mournful, meek, righteous, merciful, pure, peacemakers, and having a

[199] Gotquestions.org, *What Does the Bible Say About Attitude?* www.gotquestions.org/Bible-attitude.html, Accessed 10/23/2015.

willing attitude towards persecution.

Negative Attitudes

There are also many negative attitudes mentioned in
Scripture that God commands us to avoid. 2 Timothy 2:3 states,
"But understand this, that in the last days there will come times of
difficulty. For people will be lovers of self, lovers of money,
proud, arrogant, abusive, disobedient to their parents, ungrateful,
unholy, heartless, unappeasable, slanderous, without self-control,
brutal, not loving good."

Galatians 5:19–21 also mention several negative attitudes:
"Now the works of the flesh are evident: sexual immorality,
impurity, sensuality, idolatry, sorcery, enmity, strife, jealousy, fits
of anger, rivalries, dissensions, divisions, envy, drunkenness,
orgies, and things like these."

Attitudes Are a Choice

We have a choice in what kind of attitude we have at any
given point in time, and the attitude we choose affects all factors
of life.

Chuck Swindoll highlights the value of choosing the right
attitudes: "This may shock you, but I believe the single most
significant decision I can make on a day-to-day basis is my choice
of attitude. It is more important than my past, my education, my
bankroll, my successes or failures, fame or pain, what other
people think of me or say about me, my circumstances, or my
position. Attitude is that 'single string' that keeps me going or
cripples my progress. It alone fuels my fire or assaults my hope.
When my attitudes are right, there's no barrier too high, no valley
too deep, no dream too extreme, no challenge too great for me."[200]

---

[200] Chuck Swindoll, *Strengthening Your Grip* (Word Books, Waco, TX, 1982), pp. 205-206.

Conclusion

Spiritual attitudes have largely been overlooked in discipleship today. Our attitudes are the visible expression of our inner thoughts, feelings, emotions, beliefs, and values. They directly affect how we interact and treat both God and others, either positively or negatively.

All the essential components of the discipleship-making process are linked to our attitudes. We can reach the highest level possible in each essential component of discipleship, but if we lack the right attitudes in each category, we will still be spiritually immature. This truth is strongly emphasized in 1 Corinthians 13:1–3: "If I speak in the tongues of men and of angels, but have not love, I am a noisy gong or a clanging cymbal. And if I have prophetic powers, and understand all mysteries and all knowledge, and if I have all faith, so as to remove mountains, but have not love, **I am nothing**. If I give away all I have, and if I deliver up my body to be burned, but have not love, **I gain nothing**."

All the essential components of discipleship must be carried along and bathed in godly attitudes, or they mean little, or nothing.

13. Character and Discipleship

Character is another essential component in the discipleship-making process that has been largely overlooked today, but is foundational to discipleship and extremely important.

Character Is Foundational

In biblical times, knowledge was built upon the foundation of Scripture and godly character. Critical character traits like honesty, respect, self-discipline, diligence, hard work, loyalty, responsibility, etc., formed the foundation upon which knowledge rested.

One of the ways character was taught was by using the Book of Proverbs. It was employed in Israel's educational system, and the study of it was a required subject.

The overall theme of Proverbs deals with character development. Its opening introduction states its purpose: "To know wisdom and instruction, to discern the sayings of understanding, to receive instruction in **wise behavior**, **righteousness**, **justice** and **equity**; to give **prudence** to the naive, to the youth knowledge and discretion" (Prov. 1:2–4, NASB). In these verses, wise behavior, righteousness, justice, equity, and prudence are foundational character traits.

I have come to the firm conclusion that character is more important than skills, giftedness, knowledge, social skills, and other important traits. Character is what determines how all our abilities are used, for either good or bad, and is the structure upon which abilities hang.

For example, a person could be extremely gifted musically, but if they don't have the character of self-discipline to practice, the conviction to produce wholesome music, integrity in their financial dealings, and a commitment to humility amidst success, they will be a total failure, causing severe damage to themself and others. With good character, abilities and knowledge can be acquired, but without it, all of life comes crumbling down.

The Importance of Character in Discipleship

Dallas Willard, in his book *The Great Omission,* speaks of the importance of character in discipleship when he claims, "God is greatly concerned with the quality of character we are building. The future He has planned for us will be built on the strength of character we forge by His grace."[201]

Beverly Vos, in her article "The Spiritual Disciplines and Christian Ministry," refers to the role of character in discipleship: "Through spiritual disciplines one builds great character, and therefore, the disciplines go hand in hand with the power of God demonstrated in one's life."[202]

What Is Character?

Character can be defined as inner traits we possess, aspects of our nature, our moral fiber, and our foundational makeup and essence. It's who we are and what we do in secret when no one is watching. Furthermore, our convictions and decisions are controlled by it.

In Scripture, several Greek words are used interchangeably in reference to character. The following are their usages:

1. *Dokimēn*: meaning approved, tried character.
2. *Ethē*: referring to morals.
3. *Aretēn*: meaning a virtuous course of thought, feeling and action, virtue, and moral goodness.[203]

---

[201] Dallas Willard, *The Great Omission* (2009-02-06, HarperCollins, Kindle Edition), p. 124.
[202] Beverly Vos, "The Spiritual Disciplines and Christian Ministry" (Source: Evangelical Review of Theology, 36 no 2 Ap 2012, pp. 100-114, Publication Type: Article ATLA Religion Database with ATLASerials. Hunter Resource Library), p. 113, Accessed 11/5/2014.
[203] Bible Hub, *703. Arête,* http://biblehub.com/greek/703.htm, Accessed 10/23/2015.

Interestingly, the word "virtue" is commonly used in the Bible when referring to character. It's an old English word translated by some newer Bible versions as "excellence." In Scripture, the word "godliness" is also used when referring to character.

Abraham Lincoln said, "Reputation is the shadow. Character is the tree."[204] Another author has stated, "Our character is much more than what we try to display for others to see; it is who we are even when no one is watching. Good character is doing the right thing because it is right to do what is right."[205] And Thomas Babington Macauley claims, "The measure of a man's character is what he would do if he knew he would never be found out."[206]

Character Is Part of God's Essence

God uses the essence of His character as a foundational reason for trusting Him when making covenants and promises with mankind: "The sovereign Lord confirms this oath by his own holy **character**: 'Certainly the time is approaching when you will be carried away in baskets, every last one of you in fishermen's pots'" (Amos 4:2, NET).

The Apostles Spread the Gospel Utilizing Godly Character

When the gospel was spread to the nations, the Apostle Paul said they brought it with deep conviction and character: "We know, brothers and sisters loved by God, that he has chosen you, in that our gospel did not come to you merely in words, but in power and in the Holy Spirit and with **deep conviction** (surely you recall the **character** we displayed when we came among you to help you)" (1 Thess. 1:4–5, NET).

---

[204] Character-training.com/blog, *What is Character?* http://www.character-training.com/blog, Accessed 10/23/2015.
[205] Ibid., Accessed 10/23/2015.
[206] Ibid., Accessed 10/23/2015.

Why Is Character Important in Discipleship?

God elevates character as an essential component of spiritual maturity. Notice that virtually every characteristic listed in 2 Peter 1 is a character trait or an attitude:

> But also for this very reason, giving all diligence, add to your faith virtue [character], to virtue knowledge, to knowledge self-control, to self-control perseverance, to perseverance godliness, to godliness brotherly kindness, and to brotherly kindness love. For if these things are yours and abound, you will be neither barren nor unfruitful in the knowledge of our Lord Jesus Christ (2 Pet. 1:5-8, NKJV).

This is a key passage we must take seriously for discipleship. It outlines a process that leads to spiritual maturity and fruitfulness. It mentions three essential components: (1) virtue (character), (2) knowledge, and (3) attitudes.

Developing Character Takes Time

Character is built over the long haul and is not an overnight process. God uses trials, suffering, persecution, and testing to develop His bedrock character within us. He wants us to be like Him, and He is a God of impeccable character.

Romans 5:3-4 says, "Not only that, but we rejoice in our sufferings, knowing that suffering produces endurance, and endurance produces **character**, and **character** produces hope."

James also speaks of its importance when he says, "Count it all joy, my brothers, when you meet trials of various kinds, for you know that the testing of your faith produces **steadfastness** [character]. And let steadfastness have its full effect, that you may be perfect and complete, lacking in nothing" (James 1:2-4).

Peter echoes the same theme as well: "Such trials show the proven **character** of your faith, which is much more valuable than gold — gold that is tested by fire, even though it is passing away —

263

and will bring praise and glory and honor when Jesus Christ is revealed" (1 Pet. 1:7, NET).

Character Is the Main Quality Required in Leaders

Character is so important that it's the primary quality required in elders and deacons: "Therefore, an overseer must be above reproach, the husband of one wife, sober-minded, self-controlled, respectable, hospitable, able to teach, not a drunkard, not violent but gentle, not quarrelsome, not a lover of money . . . He must not be a recent convert, or he may become puffed up with conceit and fall into the condemnation of the devil" (1 Tim. 3:2–3, 6).

How to Develop Character

Greg S. Baker claims, "Building good character is all about addition, not subtraction. What I mean is this: when it comes to change, our focus is usually on the aspects of our lives that are bad. We try to cut out or cut off these negative or bad qualities. We try to improve by subtraction. That is not how you build good character. It is the process of addition in your life that brings the character. In so doing, you automatically take care of the other negative aspects."[207] Baker adds, "The Bible teaches us this concept in 2 Peter 1:5–9. We are to add things like virtue, patience, love, kindness, faith, and so on. It is the process of adding these things to our lives that we gain the character to be fruitful in life."[208] Baker concludes, "So how do we develop godly character in our lives? You practice it until it becomes part and parcel with you. You diligently focus on what you want to add and then practice it until it becomes a habit."[209]

---

[207] Greg S. Baker, "How to Build Good Character," SelfGrowth.com, www.selfgrowth.com/articles/how_to_build_good_character, Accessed 12/14/2015.
[208] Ibid., Accessed 12/14/2015.
[209] Ibid., Accessed 12/14/2015.

On occasion, however, building character might include ceasing wrong activities in conjunction with building good character. Scripture says that we are to put off our old self and put on the nature of Christ:

> Put off your old self, which belongs to your former manner of life and is corrupt through deceitful desires, and to be renewed in the spirit of your minds, and to put on the new self, created after the likeness of God in true righteousness and holiness (Eph. 4:22–24).

In this passage, we see both putting off and putting on. Therefore, in some situations, we might need to cease certain negative activities in conjunction with building godly character.

Conclusion

Character is a foundational cornerstone upon which discipleship is built. It's part of God's essence and should be part of ours as well. Therefore, we should give utmost importance to developing character, as it's one of the principle components of discipleship. With good character, abilities and knowledge can be acquired, but without it, all of life comes crumbling down.

14. Stewardship and Discipleship

Stewardship is another essential component in the discipleship-making process. There exist three main areas in life in which we are given the responsibility to be stewards, and for which God will hold us accountable: (1) how we use our time, (2) how we use our money and possessions, and (3) how we care for and use our bodies.

What Is Stewardship?

Stewardship is the recognition that "The earth is the Lord's and the fullness thereof, the world and those who dwell therein" (Ps. 24:1). Everything that exists (time, material things, the spiritual world, principalities, and our own souls) are the Lord's. They all belong to Him and are given to us to manage and use for His glory and purposes. A steward is someone who manages what belongs to another. They are not the owners; they are managers who are responsible to the owner.

1. Stewardship of Our Time

Our time on earth is far shorter than most people think. Our lives are like a vapor that appear in the morning and evaporate by midday: "What is your life? For you are a mist that appears for a little time and then vanishes" (James 4:14).

King David aptly pointed out: "O Lord, make me know my end and what is the measure of my days; let me know how fleeting I am! Behold, you have made my days a few handbreadths, and my lifetime is as nothing before you. Surely all mankind stands as a mere breath! Surely a man goes about as a shadow!" (Ps. 39:4–6).

Our lives barely register on the timeline of eternity and how we use our time will determine our eternal state. Moses understood this reality and prayed, "So teach us to number our days that we may get a heart of wisdom" (Ps. 90:12). In addition, Moses, "When he was grown up, refused to be called the son of Pharaoh's daughter, choosing rather to be mistreated with the people of God than to enjoy the fleeting pleasures of sin" (Heb. 11:24–25).

A wise person will realize their days are numbered and will invest them in God's Kingdom rather than in the fleeting pleasures this life has to offer. God warned the Ephesian believers, "Look carefully then how you walk, not as unwise but as wise, **making the best use of the time**, because the days are evil" (Eph. 5:15–16).

Christians and Time Management

We live in unprecedented days where voices are screaming at us at every turn, vying for our attention and time. People's lives are extremely busy with countless activities and stimuli. One author has noted, "There's no doubt that the responsibilities and pressures of this world scream for our attention. The myriad of things pulling us in every direction makes it all too easy for our time to be swallowed up in mundane matters. Those endeavors that have eternal value, then, often are relegated to the back burner."[210] The busyness of our day affects how we spend our time and how much we invest in eternity.

To avoid getting lost in the distractions of life, we need to establish goals and make godly priorities. We must make biblical choices and establish firm convictions that become bedrock, non-negotiable commitments, and then do them regardless of the cost. We must make the essential components of the discipleship-making process priorities in our lives that we cling to daily.

In chapter 2, we talked about heavenly rewards and how the

---

[210] Gotquestions.org, *What Does the Bible Say About Time Management?* www.gotquestions.org/Bible-time-management.html, Accessed 10/24/2015.

use of our time in this life will affect the amount of rewards we will have in the next. If we are wise, we will carefully look at how we spend our time. By the statistics we have researched, the average Christian today needs to do some sober soul-searching and reassess how they are using their time.

2. Stewardship of Our Material Possessions

We will also be held accountable for how we spend our money and use our possessions. Stewardship reflects our commitment to God and our spiritual condition. We should never separate money and possessions from our spiritual life, for they are directly linked. How we manage what God has given us is one way of measuring our level of spiritual maturity.

If we use our money and possessions primarily for our own purposes, then that indicates we are still spiritually immature. It matters little how much Scripture we know or how faithful we are in attending church, if we disobey God in stewarding the resources He has given us, then we are still infants spiritually in this area. We see this affirmed in the Parable of the Talents (Matt. 25:14) and the Parable of the Rich Man (Luke 12:16).

Giving to the Lord Financially

A spiritually mature believer should be faithful in stewarding what God has entrusted to them. In the Old Testament, God required a minimum of 10% to be given to Him in tithes (tithe means 10%). In addition to the tithe, the Israelites gave free will offerings, temple offerings, and offerings for the poor. Some have estimated that the Israelites gave around 25% of their income to the Lord in some way or another. In addition to their giving to God, they also had taxes to pay, just like us today.

In the New Testament, we don't see a required amount of money that should be given to the Lord, but rather a principle encouraging generosity:

268

The point is this: whoever sows sparingly will also reap sparingly, and whoever sows bountifully will also reap bountifully. Each one must give as he has decided in his heart, not reluctantly or under compulsion, for **God loves a cheerful giver**. And God is able to make all grace abound to you, so that having all sufficiency in all things at all times, you may abound in every good work (2 Cor. 9:6–8).

A spiritually mature believer will be generous toward God, realizing they are His stewards and everything belongs to Him.

If in the Old Testament 10% was the minimum required to be given to God, then certainly in the New Testament He wouldn't expect less. I believe the principle of generosity encouraged in the New Testament would suggest we give beyond 10%.

For the person who fails to tithe and spends what they are stewarding primarily on themselves, God likens this to robbery. This was God's accusation to the Israelites in the Prophet Malachi's day. God said they were robbing Him, which is a serious crime. It's one thing to rob a person, but to rob God is entirely different! That's a crime of drastic proportions. God says:

Will man rob God? Yet you are robbing me. But you say, "How have we robbed you?" In your tithes and contributions. You are cursed with a curse, for you are robbing me, the whole nation of you (Mal. 3:8–9).

We are not the owners of what we possess, but God is. If we are not faithful in stewarding what belongs to Him, then we can actually be robbing God. If we are faithful in stewarding God's resources, then He will bless us beyond measure.

After accusing the Israelites of robbing Him, God gave them this promise if they would obey:

Bring the full tithe into the storehouse, that there may be food in my house. And thereby put me to the test, says the Lord of hosts, if I will not open the windows of heaven for you and pour down for you a blessing until there is no more need. I will rebuke the devourer for you, so that it will not destroy the fruits of your soil, and your vine in the field shall not fail to bear, says the Lord of hosts. Then all nations will call you blessed, for you will be a land of delight, says the Lord of hosts (Mal. 3:10–12).

3. Stewardship of Our Bodies

A topic neglected in stewardship, but spoken of repeatedly in Scripture, involves how we use and take care of our bodies. God takes this matter seriously: "Do you not know that you are God's temple and that God's Spirit dwells in you? If anyone **destroys** God's temple, God will **destroy him**. For God's temple is holy, and you are that temple" (1 Cor. 3:16–17). These are strong and sobering words—words to be taken thoughtfully! We can debate what "destroy" means in this context, but one thing is certain, it's not positive or something to be taken lightly.

Our Bodies Belong to God

God reiterates the importance of being good stewards of our bodies in 1 Corinthians 6:19–20: "Or do you not know that your body is a temple of the Holy Spirit within you, whom you have from God? You are **not your own**, for you were bought with a price. So glorify God in your body."

Our Bodies Are to Be Used for Good, Not Evil

One way we can be good stewards of our bodies is by using them for good and not evil: "Let not sin therefore reign in your mortal body, to make you obey its passions. Do not present your members to sin as instruments for unrighteousness, but present yourselves to God as those who have been brought from death to life, and your members to God as instruments for righteousness"

270

(Rom. 6:12–13).

Our bodies are to be used for God, not for sin or our own purposes: "I appeal to you therefore, brothers, by the mercies of God, to present your **bodies** as a living sacrifice, holy and acceptable to God, which is your spiritual worship" (Rom. 12:1).

Sexuality and Stewardship

A common way we can misuse our bodies is sexually: "The body is not meant for sexual immorality, but for the Lord, and the Lord for the body" (1 Cor. 6:13). Misusing our bodies sexually is a serious sin that is rampant in our day. Even many Christians are guilty of sex outside of marriage, adultery, and homosexuality.

Sexual sin is unlike other sins. When we sin sexually, we actually sin against and damage our own body: "Flee from sexual immorality. Every other sin a person commits is outside the body, but the sexually immoral person sins **against his own body**" (1 Cor. 6:18).

Dressing Our Bodies and Stewardship

How we use our bodies can also apply to how we dress or mark them. This is important as it can affect our testimony for Christ. In fact, God warns us that doing things that cause others to stumble is unloving (1 Cor. 8). When we dress or do things to our bodies that are extreme or uncommon, then we can damage our testimony and lose influence before others. For example, if we dress in a strange and extreme fashion, then Christians (and non-Christians) may dismiss our attempts to influence them for Christ due to our manner of dress. God wants us to have the widest audience and the largest platform as possible to minister to others. By dressing in extreme ways or doing questionable behavior, we can lose much of our testimony and influence for Christ.

A trend that is growing widely today is that of tattooing our bodies. There's a verse in the Old Testament I think we should carefully wrestle with before we casually mark our bodies: "You shall not make any cuts on your body for the dead or **tattoo** yourselves: I am the Lord" (Lev. 19:28). While Christians today are not under the Law given to the Israelites in the Old Testament, this verse nonetheless conveys, in some sense, God's feelings about marking our bodies.

I think we should also consider how marking our bodies might affect our testimony as well.

Taking Care of Our Bodies and Stewardship

We also should be good stewards of our bodies by taking care of them. Today, obesity is at an all-time high, over-the-counter drug consumption is unparalleled, junk food consumption is off the charts, and exercise is at an all-time low.

According to recent studies by the U.S. Department of Health and Human Services, many Americans are abusing their bodies. Consider the following statistics:

- More than 2 in 3 adults are considered to be overweight or obese.
- More than 1 in 3 adults are considered to be obese.
- More than 1 in 20 adults are considered to have extreme obesity.
- About one-third of children and adolescents ages 6 to 19 are considered to be overweight or obese.
- More than 1 in 6 children and adolescents ages 6 to 19 are considered to be obese.[211]

Today, we are abusing our bodies (God's temple) and little thought is given to how God feels about it. We look around, see the majority of people overweight, and think it's the new norm.

[211] U.S. Department of Health and Human Services, *Overweight and Obesity Statistics*, www.niddk.nih.gov/health-information/health-statistics/Pages/overweight-obesity-statistics.aspx, 2009, 2010, Accessed 10/24/1015.

Eating and Stewardship of Our Bodies

According to the previous stats, the majority of Americans are not good stewards of their bodies. What does God say about eating and stewardship of our bodies?

God is not silent on the issue and mentions it quite a bit in Scripture. The biblical term for overeating is "gluttony." Interestingly, God frequently uses gluttony and drunkenness together as sinful activities. Consider the following verses:

- **Proverbs 23:20–21:** "Be not among drunkards or among gluttonous eaters of meat. For the drunkard and the glutton will come to poverty, and slumber will clothe them with rags."

- **Proverbs 28:7:** "The one who keeps the law is a son with understanding, but a companion of gluttons shames his father."

- **Proverbs 23:2:** "Put a knife to your throat if you are given to gluttony."

- **Deuteronomy 21:20:** "And they shall say to the elders of his city, 'This our son is stubborn and rebellious; he will not obey our voice; he is a glutton and a drunkard.'"

- **Philippians 3:19:** "Their end is destruction, their god is their belly, and they glory in their shame, with minds set on earthly things." God says a gluttonous person makes food their god and has an earthly focus on life.

- **Titus 1:12-13:** "One of themselves, a prophet of their own, said, 'Cretans are always liars, evil beasts, lazy gluttons.' This testimony is true. For this reason, reprove them severely so that they may be sound in the faith."

As these verses reveal, God considers overeating a sin and calls it gluttony.

What Is Gluttony?

One author has commented, "Gluttony is generally defined as 'excessive eating.' In the Bible, the word 'glutton' and its variants are often mentioned alongside drunkenness. Therefore, it's clear that a glutton is someone who eats more than is healthy or eats excessively, and that such behavior is considered sinful. Gluttony is presented as an ongoing practice, not typically as a one-time activity."[212] In other words, gluttony is not overeating on occasion, but overeating regularly, and it's overeating regularly that leads to being overweight.

Why Is Gluttony Ignored Today?

S. Michael Houdmann contends, "Gluttony seems to be a sin that Christians like to ignore. We are often quick to label smoking and drinking as sins, but for some reason, gluttony is accepted or at least tolerated. Many of the arguments used against smoking and drinking, such as health and addiction, apply equally to overeating. Many believers would not even consider having a glass of wine or smoking a cigarette, but have no qualms about gorging themselves at the dinner table. This should not be!"[213]

As mentioned, gluttony and drunkenness are mentioned together in Scripture as sinful activities. We are quick to condemn drunkenness but tend to overlook gluttony. No pastor or church leader would be accepted in any church if they were a drunkard, yet they can be a glutton, and no one thinks a thing about it. The straight truth is that we have a double standard. We are biblical in one area and unbiblical in another.

---

[212] Compelling Truth, *What Is the Sin of Gluttony?* Compellingtruth.org, www.compellingtruth.org/gluttony-sin.html, Accessed 10/24/2015.
[213] S. Michael Houdmann, *Is Gluttony a Sin? What Does the Bible Say About Overeating?* http://www.gotquestions.org/gluttony-sin.html, Accessed 02/27/2016.

Overeating and Self-Discipline

S. Michael Houdmann weighs in again and states, "Physical appetites are an analogy of our ability to control ourselves. If we are unable to control our eating habits, we are probably also unable to control other habits, such as those of the mind (lust, covetousness, anger) and unable to keep our mouths from gossip or strife. We are not to let our appetites control us, but we are to have control over our appetites."[214]

Consequences of Overeating

- When we are overweight and do not take care of our bodies, we have less energy, strength, stamina, and ability to serve God. Productivity is lowered and money spent on poor health will result in poor stewardship of both our time and money. We also run the risk of dying prematurely, which shortens our time for serving God.
- Failing to be good stewards of our bodies can also sideline us from ministry, causing unnecessary pain in our lives and those around us.
- Being overweight is a symptom of a lack of self-discipline. It communicates to others a message of an undisciplined life. This is especially important for pastors and church leaders to understand because self-discipline is a foundation of the Christian life. When a pastor or church leader is a glutton, they are preaching by their lifestyle an undisciplined and unbiblical way of living to their congregants.

Houdmann asserts, "God has blessed us by filling the earth with foods that are delicious, nutritious, and pleasurable. We should honor God's creation by enjoying these foods and by eating them in appropriate quantities. However, God calls us to

---

[214] Ibid., Accessed 02/27/2016.

control our appetites, rather than allowing them to control us."[215]

Drug Use and Stewardship of Our Bodies

Over the counter drug use is at an all-time high. Estimates suggest 60% of Americans take at least one medication.[216] While much of the medication used today is useful and needed, we can still damage and abuse our bodies by using medication that's not entirely important. Just because a medication might be helpful, doesn't mean it's needed.

Also, it seems many Christians today believe drugs are the answer for all ailments, both physical and spiritual. Anti-depressant drug use is at an all-time high, and the concern is that many Christians are trying to treat their spiritual problems with drugs. I believe we need to be very careful about taking medication for emotional problems.

Our bodies are the temple of God, and He expects us to care for them. His words are quite harsh for those who don't: "Do you not know that **you are God's temple** and that God's Spirit dwells in you? If anyone destroys God's temple, God will destroy him. For God's temple is holy, and you are that temple" (1 Cor. 3:16–17).

Conclusion to Chapter 4

In this chapter, we looked at 14 essential components that must be understood and practiced in order to attain spiritual maturity. In chapter 5, we're going to get real practical! We'll take self-assessment tests to measure our level of spiritual maturity in each category, and provide practical ideas for how to grow in Christ and attain spiritual maturity.

---

[215] Ibid., Accessed 02/27/2016.
[216] Jessica Firger, *Prescription Drugs on the Rise: Estimates Suggest 60 Percent of Americans Take at Least One Medication,* Newsweek, 2015, http://www.newsweek.com/prescription-drugs-rise-new-estimates-suggest-60-americans-take-least-one-390354, Accessed 11/17/2015.

Chapter 5

How to Grow in Christ: Self-Assessment Tests and Practical Help

In This Chapter

In chapter 1, we analyzed the state of discipleship and spiritual maturity today, concluding that they're in critical condition and being grossly neglected. In chapter 2, we investigated the key factors contributing to the neglect of discipleship and spiritual maturity. In chapter 3, we defined biblical discipleship by examining key phrases Christ used in calling people to follow Him. In chapter 4, we discovered 14 essential components for the discipleship-making process that must be understood and obeyed in order to fulfill the Great Commission Mandate and attain spiritual maturity.

In this chapter, we'll talk about how to apply the essential components of discipleship to our lives in order to grow in Christ and attain spiritual maturity. This chapter is a "how-to" chapter. It will be very practical and provide help in the following ways:

1. It will have a spiritual growth assessment test for each of the essential components of discipleship in order to help you discover your spiritual maturity level in each category.

2. It will contain charts and graphs for visualizing and measuring your spiritual maturity in each category.

3. It will provide practical ideas for moving toward spiritual maturity.

4. It will provide action steps that can be chosen for applying the ideas for growth in each category.

5. It will build on the premise that a comprehensive approach to discipleship is the only way to attain spiritual maturity. This means we must grow in all the categories of the essential components of discipleship in order to be spiritually mature.

Now, let me briefly explain how each of the above suggestions function so you can get the most out of this book and begin accelerating your growth to spiritual maturity.

1. Spiritual Growth Self-Assessment Tests

God says in 2 Corinthians 13:5 to "**Examine yourselves**, to see whether you are in the faith. **Test yourselves**. Or do you not realize this about yourselves, that Jesus Christ is in you? — unless indeed, you **fail to meet the test!**" God expects us to analyze and examine ourselves to ascertain our level of spiritual maturity. For this reason, self-assessment tests are provided for each category, and an overall spiritual maturity test is provided at the end of this chapter.

At the beginning of each section dealing with an essential component of discipleship, a short self-assessment questionnaire is provided to help you see your level of spiritual maturity in that category. Please answer the questions honestly and then ask a close loved-one to answer it for you as well. Between all responses, you should get a good idea of your level of spiritual maturity for that category.

Please do this for all categories. At the end of this chapter, there will be a chart for adding up all your scores to see your overall spiritual maturity level. It is recommended to focus your efforts first on strengthening your weakest areas.

2. Charts and Graphs for Visualizing and Measuring Your Spiritual Maturity

The following chart provides an example overview of all the essential components necessary for attaining spiritual maturity. At the end of this chapter, a blank one is provided for you to mark on in order to see your spiritual maturity in each area and keep track of your progress.

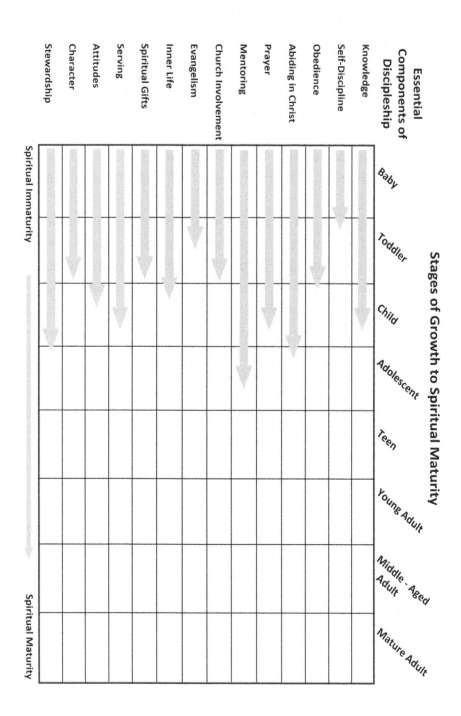

The next chart shows eight stages of spiritual growth: baby, toddler, child, adolescent, teen, young adult, middle-aged adult, and mature adult.

Please note that these labels have nothing to do with your own age. For example, you could be a "mature adult" in physical age, but a "baby" in your spiritual maturity. Similarly, you could be a "teen" physically, but be a "middle-aged adult" in your spiritual maturity. These labels are used solely for the purpose of identifying your spiritual maturity level, not your actual physical age.

Stages of Growth to Spiritual Maturity in (Example Chart)

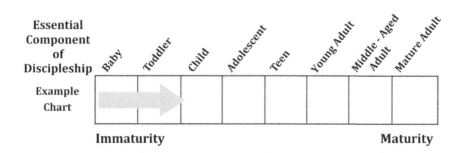

In addition, a similar chart (like the one above) is provided at the beginning of each essential component for discipleship to help you visualize your spiritual maturity in that category.

There will also be a blank chart provided after each self-assessment test for you to mark on so you can see your level of spiritual maturity for that category.

Nature of the Questions for the Self-Assessment Tests

In order to accurately discover your spiritual maturity level in each category, the self-assessment test questions must be asked from the highest level possible, or they won't provide accurate results. Therefore, the questions reflect what I believe should be the characteristics of a spiritually mature believer. There are only 10 questions per test, so there are many other great questions that could be asked but aren't.

3. Practical Ideas for Attaining Spiritual Maturity

After you've taken the self-assessment test for discovering your level of spiritual maturity in a particular category, then you'll find practical ideas for growth in that area.

4. Action Steps to Put into Practice

After taking the self-assessment test and looking at the practical ideas for growth in that category, then it's important to choose at least one of the ideas and begin doing it right away. Growth in Christ doesn't happen by merely knowing what to do, but by **doing** what we know we should do!

5. A Comprehensive Approach to Discipleship

The premise of this book is that in order to attain spiritual maturity we must approach discipleship from a comprehensive perspective. In other words, we need to grow in all the essential components of the discipleship-making process in order to become spiritually mature.

It was noted in chapter 1 that discipleship has been approached from a single-pronged or several-pronged perspective for much of modern day history, which has resulted in an unbalanced and weak outcome. Themes like knowledge, prayer, serving, and church attendance have been highlighted, while other themes like attitudes, character, spiritual gifts, and self-discipline have been overlooked.

A comprehensive approach to discipleship claims that we need to grow in all the essential areas in order to reach spiritual maturity. Spiritual maturity, therefore, is defined as being mature in all areas, not just a few.

For example, one can be strong in knowledge, but weak in their attitudes or character; this is not maturity. A comprehensive approach to discipleship advocates that we assess each category of discipleship to determine what level of spiritual maturity we have attained, and then give special attention to our weakest areas first. Then afterward, we can focus on all the other areas simultaneously.

God's Blessings Are Waiting!

What would change in the average Christian's life if they rightly understood the essential components of the discipleship-making process and practiced them? What if, instead of a single or a several-pronged approach to discipleship, we addressed it from a comprehensive angle? How might our lives be changed? How might our homes be transformed? How might the church be strengthened? How might the Kingdom of God be advanced? And moreover, how might God be honored and glorified?

Now, let's discover our spiritual level of maturity in each category of the essential components of discipleship and consider ideas we can begin to do in order to attain spiritual maturity.

It's time to grow! God's blessings are waiting! Are you ready to attain them and become spiritually mature?

1. How to Grow in the Knowledge of God

"For I desire steadfast love and not sacrifice, the **knowledge** of God rather than burnt offerings" (Hos. 6:6).

"But grow in the grace and **knowledge** of our Lord and Savior Jesus Christ" (2 Pet. 3:18).

Stages of Growth to Spiritual Maturity in Knowledge

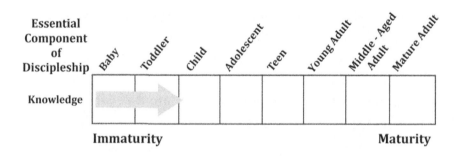

Self-Assessment Test for the Knowledge of God

Please take a moment to answer the following 10 questions to discover your spiritual maturity level regarding your knowledge of God. Answer each question using the following response options. Mark down your points earned for each question and then tally them up at the end to see your level of spiritual maturity in this category. As you take the test, avoid rushing. Answer the questions prayerfully and honestly. After you've taken the test, you might ask a loved one to take it for you as well. This will give you a broader perspective.

Points Possible per Answer

Never....................... 0 Points

Rarely .... 2 Points

Occasionally .... 4 Points

Frequently............... 6 Points

Almost Always ...... 8 Points

Habitually............... 10 Points

1. I read the entire Bible at least once every year. _____

2. I memorize Scripture regularly. _____

3. I have a daily quiet time with God. _____

4. I study the Bible. _____

5. I read the Bible daily. _____

6. I can give a detailed overview of the Bible. _____

7. I know the overview of each book of the Bible. _____

8. I know and can defend the major doctrines of the Bible with clarity and precision. _____

9. I read Christian non-fiction books. _____

10. I read theological books. _____

Total Score _____

Now check your score against the following chart to determine your spiritual maturity level for the knowledge of God.

Spiritual Maturity Grade from the "Knowledge" Test

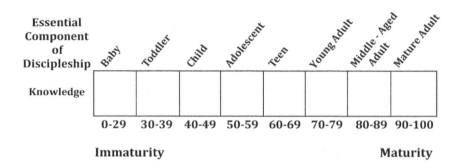

Essential Component of Discipleship	Baby	Toddler	Child	Adolescent	Teen	Young Adult	Middle-Aged Adult	Mature Adult
Knowledge								
	0-29	30-39	40-49	50-59	60-69	70-79	80-89	90-100

Immaturity   Maturity

My spiritual maturity grade for the knowledge of God:

I am a _____ spiritually.

Ideas for Growing in Your Knowledge of God

1. Establish a Bible reading plan for reading the entire Bible every year. You might consider the following options:

   - Reading the Bible chronologically.
   - Reading the Bible from beginning to end.
   - Dividing the Bible into three sections (Genesis–Psalms, Proverbs–Malachi, and Matthew–Revelation). Then read a chapter consecutively from each section daily.
   - Reading two chapters daily from the Old Testament and one chapter daily from the New Testament.
   - Reading the Old Testament once in a year and the New Testament twice in a year.

2. Start a Bible memorization plan. You can memorize selected verses, passages, chapters, and even entire books. It works great to get a 3x5 card, write your verse(s) down, and carry it with you. It's handy this way for memorization. You'll be surprised how much Scripture you can memorize in a year by

just memorizing a verse or two a week.

3. Read all the introductions to the books of the Bible in a Study Bible, on the Internet, or from other sources. This will rapidly give you an overview of the whole Bible.

4. Do a Bible study on the knowledge of God.

5. Read an Old Testament survey book. This will give you an overview of the entire Old Testament.

6. Read a New Testament survey book. This will give you an overview of the entire New Testament.

7. Read a solid, lengthy, systematic theology work. Systematic theology takes each major doctrine of the Bible and looks at all the verses that deal with that doctrine. It's indispensable for understanding the major doctrines of the faith. It's good to read several different systematic theology books to get a balanced view. Here are some suggestions:

   - Wayne Grudem's *Systematic Theology*
   - Charles Hodge's *Systematic Theology*
   - Louis Berkhof's *Systematic Theology*
   - Lewis Sperry Chafer's *Systematic Theology*
   - Gordon Lewis and Bruce Demarest's *Integrative Theology*
   - Millard Erickson's *Christian Theology*
   - Charles Ryrie's *Basic Theology*
   - Henry Thiessen's *Systematic Theology*

8. Read Old and New Testament theology works. These will aid you in understanding the big message and theme of both the Old and New Testaments (these are different from Old and New Testament survey books mentioned above).

9. Join an in-depth Bible study or start one of your own.

10. Read several books on how to correctly interpret the Bible (hermeneutics).

11. Take online Bible classes or even consider seeking an online Bible degree. There are many options available today, and

some are even free.

12. Purchase a good Study Bible, and read the introductions and commentaries it offers.

13. Listen to Bible college lectures. Many Bible colleges now have many of their Bible class lectures online and are free. Great options are Biola/Talbot Bible College and Seminary, and Dallas Theological Seminary. Their lectures can be accessed via YouTube or iTunes.

14. Read other theological books.

15. Read Christian, non-fiction books.

16. Look for someone in your church who is deeply knowledgeable in God's Word and theology and ask him or her to mentor you in this area.

Action Steps for Growing in Your Knowledge of God

Now prayerfully look back over this list, choose at least one idea, and make plans to begin doing it today. Then continually return in the future for implementing other ideas for your growth in the knowledge of God.

2. How to Grow in Self-Discipline

"Have nothing to do with irreverent, silly myths. Rather **train yourself for godliness**; for while bodily training is of some value, godliness is of value in every way, as it holds promise for the present life and also for the life to come" (1 Tim. 4:8).

"It is for **discipline** that you have to endure. God is treating you as sons. For what son is there whom his father does not discipline?" (Heb. 12:7).

Stages of Growth to Spiritual Maturity in Self-Discipline

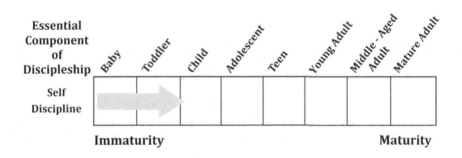

Self-Assessment Test for Self-Discipline

Please take a moment to answer the following 10 questions to discover your spiritual maturity level regarding self-discipline. Answer each question using the following response options. Mark down your points earned for each question and then tally them up at the end to see your level of spiritual maturity in this category. As you take the test, avoid rushing. Answer the questions prayerfully and honestly. After you've taken the test, you might ask a loved one to take it for you as well. This will give you a broader perspective.

Points Possible per Answer

Never .... 0 Points
Rarely .... 2 Points
Occasionally .... 4 Points
Frequently............... 6 Points
Almost Always ...... 8 Points
Habitually .... 10 Points

1. I am a highly disciplined person. _____

2. I manage my time effectively. _____

3. I finish tasks I've started. _____

4. I bring every thought into obedience to Christ and His Word. _____

5. I stick to commitments without giving up. _____

6. I make myself do what I know I should do. _____

7. I put my responsibilities first and pleasures last. _____

8. I am a hardworking person. _____

9. I display godly attitudes despite how I feel. _____

10. I keep my inner heart and exterior surroundings extremely neat, clean, and organized. _____

Total Score _____

Now check your score against the following chart to determine your spiritual maturity level for self-discipline.

Spiritual Maturity Grade from the "Self-Discipline" Test

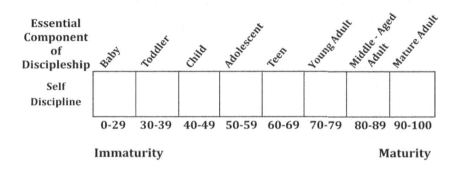

Essential Component of Discipleship	Baby	Toddler	Child	Adolescent	Teen	Young Adult	Middle-Aged Adult	Mature Adult
Self Discipline								
	0-29	30-39	40-49	50-59	60-69	70-79	80-89	90-100

Immaturity   Maturity

My spiritual maturity grade for self-discipline:

I am a _____ spiritually.

Ideas for Growing in Self-Discipline

1. Acknowledge your weaknesses.
2. Pray and ask God for His grace and help.
3. Tell others about your goal to be more self-disciplined.
4. Read books and articles about self-discipline.
5. Memorize Scripture that deals with self-discipline (self-control).
6. Establish spiritual disciplines in your life that you do regularly such as:

   - Reading Scripture
   - Praying
   - Fasting
   - Memorizing Scripture
   - Reading non-fiction, Christian books
   - Giving
   - Serving

7. Remove unnecessary activities and distractions in your life.
8. Make yourself the boss of your body and will, not vice-versa.

9. Practice tolerating physical and emotional discomfort.
10. Visualize the long-term benefits of being self-disciplined.
11. Share your desire to be more disciplined with a loved one and ask them to hold you accountable for developing specific self-disciplines.
12. Set clear, measurable goals and deadlines.
13. Complete unfinished tasks.
14. Start an exercising program.
15. Establish routines in your life.
16. Acquire, or make, a self-discipline logbook and record the start and end times of your tasks and projects.
17. Replace bad habits with good ones.
18. Get up and go to bed at regular times.
19. Plan out your days, weeks, months, and years in advance.
20. Start the habit of using "To-do" lists to get things done and be more efficient in your life.
21. Clean up and organize your surroundings.
22. Reward yourself for your victories and accomplishments.
23. Penalize yourself when you fail.
24. Make a "Checklist Chart" of your commitments and check them off daily in order to build good habits in your life.
25. Find an accountability partner to hold you accountable for your goals.
26. Do a Bible study on self-discipline.
27. Look for someone in your church who is spiritually self-disciplined and ask him or her to mentor you in this area.

Action Steps for Growing in Self-Discipline

Now prayerfully look back over this list, choose at least one idea, and make plans to begin doing it today. Then continually return in the future for implementing other ideas for your growth in self-discipline.

3. How to Grow in Obedience

"And by this we know that we have come to know him, if we **keep** his commandments. Whoever says, 'I know him' but does not **keep** his commandments is a liar, and the truth is not in him, but whoever **keeps** his word, in him truly the love of God is perfected" (1 John 2:3–5).

Stages of Growth to Spiritual Maturity in Obedience

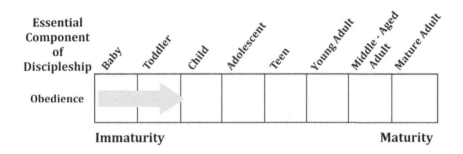

Self-Assessment Test for Obedience to God

Please take a moment to answer the following 10 questions to discover your spiritual maturity level regarding your obedience to God. Answer each question using the following response options. Mark down your points earned for each question and then tally them up at the end to see your level of spiritual maturity in this category. As you take the test, avoid rushing. Answer the questions prayerfully and honestly. After you've taken the test, you might ask a loved one to take it for you as well. This will give you a broader perspective.

Points Possible per Answer

Never .... 0 Points
Rarely .... 2 Points
Occasionally .... 4 Points
Frequently............... 6 Points
Almost Always ...... 8 Points
Habitually .... 10 Points

1. I read my Bible daily. _____

2. I walk close to God throughout the day. _____

3. I pray daily for at least 20 minutes. _____

4. I am deeply involved in a church. _____

5. I regularly share the gospel with others. _____

6. I am highly self-disciplined. _____

7. I maintain a clear conscience. _____

8. I have a ministry where I serve God and others. _____

9. I display excellent, Christ-like attitudes. _____

10. I manage my time, finances, and body, excellently. _____

Total Score _____

Now check your score against the following chart to determine your spiritual maturity level for obedience to God.

Spiritual Maturity Grade from the "Obedience" Test

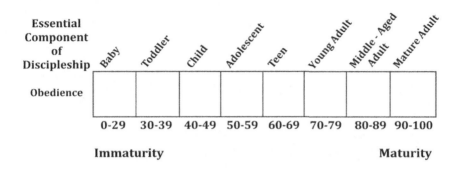

Essential Component of Discipleship	Baby	Toddler	Child	Adolescent	Teen	Young Adult	Middle-Aged Adult	Mature Adult
Obedience								

0-29 30-39 40-49 50-59 60-69 70-79 80-89 90-100

Immaturity   **Maturity**

My spiritual maturity grade for obedience to God:

I am a _____ spiritually.

Ideas for Growing in Obedience to God

1. Prayerfully ask yourself how obedient you are to God and His Word.
2. Ask loved ones and close friends to rate you in how obedient you are to God and His Word.
3. If you are not faithfully reading your Bible, begin now. Choose a Bible reading plan and make a commitment to obey God in this area (see ideas from the "Knowledge of God" section).
4. If you struggle in staying close to God throughout the day, consider setting your watch or smart phone to notify and remind you of God.
5. Put physical reminders up that remind you of God.
6. If you are struggling in obeying God in the area of prayer, commit to a set time and a set amount of time for prayer each day.
7. If you don't share the gospel much, look at the section in this chapter called "How to Grow in Evangelism" and study what the gospel is and how to share it. Then pray and look for

opportunities to share your faith.

8. If you don't have a regular quiet time, make a commitment to do it faithfully each day.
9. If you don't give at least 10% of your income to the Lord's work, make a commitment to do so.
10. If you struggle in obedience in time management, finances, or taking care of your body, look at the section in this chapter called "How to Grow in Stewardship" and choose some ideas to help you be more obedient in these areas.
11. Prayerfully ask yourself if you allow Christ to control what you watch, read, hear, or think about, and commit to allowing Him more control over what you're putting into your mind.
12. Read books and articles about how to obey God.
13. If you have broken relationships and need to ask forgiveness, or need to forgive someone, make a commitment to be obedient in this area.
14. If you are not serving God, make a commitment to get involved in some ministry within your church or community.
15. Do a Bible study on obedience.
16. Look for someone in your church who faithfully obeys God in all areas of their life and ask him or her to mentor you.

Action Steps for Growing in Obedience to God

Now prayerfully look back over this list, choose at least one idea, and make plans to begin doing it today. Then continually return in the future for implementing other ideas for your growth in obedience to God.

4. How to Grow in Abiding in Christ

"**Abide** in me, and I in you. As the branch cannot bear fruit by itself, unless it **abides** in the vine, neither can you, unless you **abide** in me. Whoever **abides** in me and I in him, he it is that bears much fruit, **for apart from me you can do nothing**" (John 15: 4–5).

Stages of Growth to Spiritual Maturity in Abiding in Christ

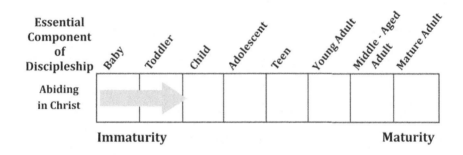

Self-Assessment Test for Abiding in Christ

Please take a moment to answer the following 10 questions to discover your spiritual maturity level for abiding in Christ. Answer each question using the following response options. Mark down your points earned for each question and then tally them up at the end to see your level of spiritual maturity in this category. As you take the test, avoid rushing. Answer the questions prayerfully and honestly. After you've taken the test, you might ask a loved one to take it for you as well. This will give you a broader perspective.

Points Possible per Answer

Never .... 0 Points
Rarely .... 2 Points
Occasionally .... 4 Points
Frequently .... 6 Points
Almost Always ...... 8 Points
Habitually .... 10 Points

1. I have a daily quiet time with God. _____

2. I seek earnestly to live in the presence of God. _____

3. I pray to God throughout the day. _____

4. I think of God throughout the day. _____

5. I make all my decisions based upon God's Word. _____

6. I bring every thought into obedience to Christ. _____

7. I display godly attitudes and character. _____

8. I live with eternity in mind. _____

9. I trust Christ and remain strong in trials and hardships. _____

10. I carefully listen for God's voice throughout the day. _____

Total Score _____

Now check your score against the following chart to determine your spiritual maturity level for abiding in Christ.

Spiritual Maturity Grade from the "Abiding in Christ" Test

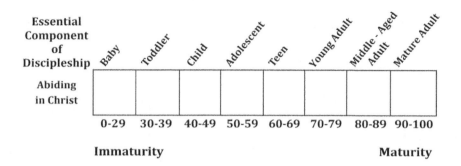

Essential Component of Discipleship	Baby	Toddler	Child	Adolescent	Teen	Young Adult	Middle - Aged Adult	Mature Adult
Abiding in Christ								
	0-29	30-39	40-49	50-59	60-69	70-79	80-89	90-100

Immaturity   **Maturity**

My spiritual maturity grade for abiding in Christ:

I am a _____ spiritually.

Ideas for Growing in Abiding in Christ

1. Start or be more faithful in a daily quiet time.
2. Consider some kind of reminder that causes you to check in with God throughout the day to be more in tune with Him. You might set a timer on your smartphone, put a picture somewhere, or establish a habit of praying and thinking about God more often. Daniel set aside a time to pray three times a day; maybe you might consider doing the same.
3. Seek an accountability partner to help you set your mind upon God more frequently.
4. Memorize Scripture that speaks of abiding in Christ (John 15:1–11; Col. 3:1–4; Ps. 1; Gal. 5:16–25).
5. Read books and articles on abiding in Christ.
6. Pray daily for God's help in learning how to abide in Him.
7. Saturate your mind more with Scripture, which will help greatly in causing you to think more about God.
8. Listen to Christian radio.
9. Listen to Christian music.
10. Listen to sermons on abiding in Christ.

11. Give up the activities in your life that are standing in the way of your full commitment to Christ.
12. Fast and pray to train yourself to abide in Christ better.
13. Reflect or journal on the activities of your day, thinking about how you used your time, how you walked with God, and what you could have done differently.
14. Do a Bible study on abiding in Christ.
15. Look for someone in your church who faithfully abides in Christ and ask him or her to mentor you in this area.

Action Steps for Growing in Abiding in Christ

Now prayerfully look back over this list, choose at least one idea, and make plans to begin doing it today. Then continually return in the future for implementing other ideas for your growth in abiding in Christ.

5. How to Grow in Prayer

"Rejoice always, **pray** without ceasing, give thanks in all circumstances; for this is the will of God in Christ Jesus for you" (1 Thess. 5:16–18).

"Continue steadfastly in **prayer**, being watchful in it with thanksgiving" (Col. 4:2).

Stages of Growth to Spiritual Maturity in Prayer

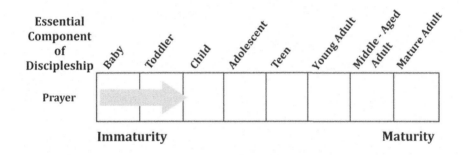

Self-Assessment Test for Prayer

Please take a moment to answer the following 10 questions to discover your spiritual maturity level regarding prayer. Answer each question using the following response options. Mark down your points earned for each question and then tally them up at the end to see your level of spiritual maturity in this category. As you take the test, avoid rushing. Answer the questions prayerfully and honestly. After you've taken the test, you might ask a loved one to take it for you as well. This will give you a broader perspective.

Points Possible per Answer

Never...................... 0 Points
Rarely .... 2 Points
Occasionally .... 4 Points
Frequently............... 6 Points
Almost Always ...... 8 Points
Habitually............... 10 Points

1. I have a designated prayer time daily. _____

2. I confess my sins and pray for forgiveness daily. _____

3. I maintain an attitude of prayer throughout the day. _____

4. I pray daily for at least 20 minutes. _____

5. I thank God for His blessings daily. _____

6. I pray for others daily. _____

7. I pray for God's help to walk closely with Him daily. _____

8. I listen for God's voice during my prayer times. _____

9. I pray with others for the needs of God's Kingdom. _____

10. I pray for my needs daily. _____

Total Score _____

Now check your score against the following chart to determine your spiritual maturity level for prayer.

Spiritual Maturity Grade from the "Prayer" Test

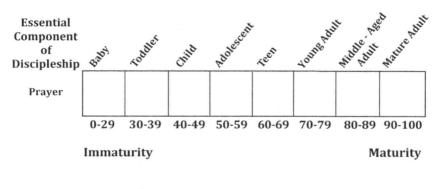

Essential Component of Discipleship	Baby	Toddler	Child	Adolescent	Teen	Young Adult	Middle-Aged Adult	Mature Adult
Prayer								
	0-29	30-39	40-49	50-59	60-69	70-79	80-89	90-100

Immaturity   Maturity

My spiritual maturity grade for prayer:

I am a _____ spiritually.

Ideas for Growing in Prayer

1. Set aside a fixed time for daily prayer.
2. Make prayer a daily habit.
3. Set aside a fixed place for prayer that is free from distractions.
4. Establish prayer topics to help you during your prayer time. Here are some ideas to include:
   - Confess your sins to God and ask Him to reveal unknown sin in your life, or things that are displeasing to Him. This may include broken relationships, wrong activities, mismanagement of time, neglect of God, laziness, allowing sinful things into your mind, and apathy.
   - Pray for the filling of God's Spirit in your life.
   - Pray for help in walking with God and setting your mind on Him.
   - Thank God for all His blessings in your life.
   - Praise God for who He is and what He's done for you.
   - Pray for family members.
   - Pray for unsaved loved ones and friends.

- Pray for missionaries, pastors, churches, Christian organizations, etc.
- Pray for your own needs.
- Pray for your ministry or ministries.
- Pray for government leaders.
- Pray for guidance and direction in your life.
- Pray for opportunities to evangelize.
- Pray for the pastors and leaders of your church.

5. Consider doing a "prayer walk" around some ministry, church, neighborhood, or place that needs Christ.
6. Join your church's prayer team and pray for needs that arise.
7. Start a prayer meeting.
8. Start a prayer journal and keep track of your own prayer requests and those of others. Your faith will be strengthened as you see God faithfully answer prayer.
9. Create a "prayer wall" and post your prayer requests on it.
10. Put prayer requests on your fridge.
11. Set aside meditative prayer times by going to the beach, going on a hike, going to a lake, or going for a walk.
12. Give up something this week to spend more time in prayer.
13. Make a commitment to fast and pray, setting aside a meal, or a full day.
14. Read books and articles on prayer.
15. Do a Bible study on prayer.
16. Look for someone in your church who faithfully prays and ask him or her to mentor you in this area.

Action Steps for Growing in Prayer

Now prayerfully look back over this list, choose at least one idea, and make plans to begin doing it today. Then continually return in the future for implementing other ideas for your growth in prayer.

6. How to Grow in Mentoring

"And what you have heard from me in the presence of many witnesses **entrust to faithful men** who will be able to **teach others also**" (2 Tim. 2:2).

"What you have **learned and received and heard and seen in me** — practice these things, and the God of peace will be with you" (Phil. 4:9).

Stages of Growth to Spiritual Maturity in Mentoring

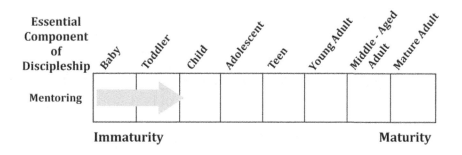

Self-Assessment Test for Mentoring

Please take a moment to answer the following 10 questions to discover your spiritual maturity level regarding mentoring. Answer each question using the following response options. Mark down your points earned for each question and then tally them up at the end to see your level of spiritual maturity in this category. As you take the test, avoid rushing. Answer the questions prayerfully and honestly. After you've taken the test, you might ask a loved one to take it for you as well. This will give you a broader perspective.

Points Possible per Answer

Never...................... 0 Points
Rarely .... 2 Points
Occasionally .... 4 Points
Frequently............... 6 Points
Almost Always ...... 8 Points
Habitually............... 10 Points

1. Currently, I am mentoring someone. _____

2. Currently, someone is mentoring me. _____

3. I have close friends who I allow to hold me accountable for spiritual growth. _____

4. I listen to feedback from others with open arms. _____

5. I am careful to admit my errors and ask forgiveness promptly when I've offended others. _____

6. I respond well to criticism. _____

7. I am skillful in teaching and mentoring others. _____

8. I know exactly what to teach others in mentorship. _____

9. I model what I teach. _____

10. I know God's Word thoroughly in order to give counsel and wisdom to those I teach. _____

Total Score _____

Now check your score against the following chart to determine your spiritual maturity level for mentoring.

Spiritual Maturity Grade from the "Mentoring" Test

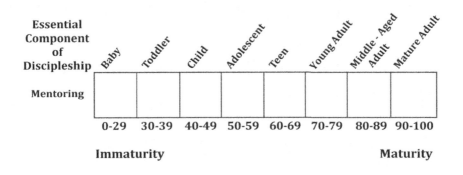

My spiritual maturity grade for mentoring:

I am a _____ spiritually.

Ideas for Growing in Mentoring

As mentioned in chapter 4, biblical mentoring is an informal relationship wherein a more spiritually mature person teaches and models godly, life-skills to others who are generally less spiritually mature. Mentoring can be formal, informal, take place in a group setting, take place in an individual setting, can be regular, or somewhat sporadic.

Examples of mentoring include small group Bible studies, Sunday School classes, youth group, one on one discipleship studies, accountability partners, and so on.

It should be noted, however, that the most effective mentoring takes place in a one on one setting, or in a small group where specific truths and life-skills are intentionally passed on. The following are ideas to consider for mentoring:

1. Pray that God would lead you to someone He desires for you to mentor.
2. Pray that God might lead you to someone who can be your mentor.

3. Develop a discipleship plan of the essential components you would use in mentoring someone (maybe this book would provide this for you).
4. Develop your own spiritual maturity so you can be a mentor who honors God and models what you plan on teaching.
5. Develop your understanding of what a good mentor or coach is and be a mentor who:

- Leads by example
- Has seasoned experience in order to share skills, knowledge, and expertise
- Has integrity
- Listens well
- Has a good reputation for developing others
- Has time and energy to devote to mentoring
- Has a learning attitude
- Demonstrates spiritual maturity
- Knows the strengths and abilities of their mentees
- Wants their mentees to succeed
- Communicates hope and optimism
- Provides guidance and constructive feedback
- Is respected
- Sets and meets ongoing goals
- Values the opinions of others
- Motivates by setting a good example
- Is skillful in teaching
- Provides insight
- Is accessible
- Criticizes constructively
- Is supportive
- Is specific
- Is caring
- Is admirable

6. Ask your pastor to encourage mentorship in your church.
7. Ask your pastor if you can start a mentorship program in your church.
8. Offer to teach a class in your church on mentorship.
9. Ask your pastor if you can put a sign-up sheet in your church lobby for those interested in being mentored, and another for those interested in mentoring.
10. Ask your pastor if he might preach about the role of mentorship in the context of discipleship.
11. Read books and articles on mentorship.
12. Develop a mentorship guide for training others in how to mentor.
13. Do a Bible study on mentoring.
14. Read again carefully the section "Discipleship in the Time of Christ" in chapter 3, which shows how mentorship functioned between Jesus and His disciples.

Action Steps for Growing in Mentoring

Now prayerfully look back over this list, choose at least one idea, and make plans to begin doing it today. Then continually return in the future for implementing other ideas for your growth in mentoring.

7. How to Grow in Church Involvement

"And let us consider how to stir up one another to love and good works, **not neglecting to meet together**, as is the habit of some, but encouraging one another, and all the more as you see the Day drawing near" (Heb. 10:24–25).

Stages of Growth to Spiritual Maturity in Church Involvement

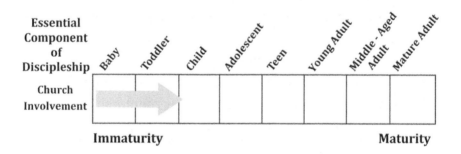

Self-Assessment Test for Church Involvement

Please take a moment to answer the following 10 questions to discover your spiritual maturity level regarding church involvement. Answer each question using the following response options. Mark down your points earned for each question and then tally them up at the end to see your level of spiritual maturity in this category. As you take the test, avoid rushing. Answer the questions prayerfully and honestly. After you've taken the test, you might ask a loved one to take it for you as well. This will give you a broader perspective.

Points Possible per Answer

Never...................... 0 Points
Rarely .... 2 Points
Occasionally .... 4 Points
Frequently............... 6 Points
Almost Always ...... 8 Points
Habitually............... 10 Points

1. I attend a Bible believing church. _____

2. I have a ministry in my church. _____

3. I have accountability partners in my church. _____

4. I am deeply involved in my church. _____

5. I attend a small group meeting. _____

6. I am open and honest with others about who I am. _____

7. I maintain a clear conscience with others. _____

8. I forgive others who have wronged me. _____

9. I am connected with others in my church. _____

10. I give financially to my church. _____

Total Score _____

Now check your score against the following chart to determine your spiritual maturity level for church involvement.

Spiritual Maturity Grade from the "Church Involvement" Test

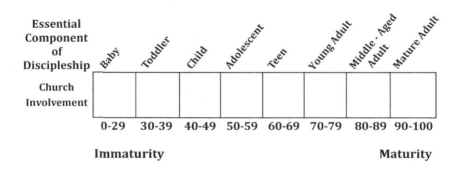

Essential Component of Discipleship	Baby	Toddler	Child	Adolescent	Teen	Young Adult	Middle-Aged Adult	Mature Adult
Church Involvement								
	0-29	30-39	40-49	50-59	60-69	70-79	80-89	90-100

Immaturity   **Maturity**

My spiritual maturity grade for church involvement:

I am a _____ spiritually.

Ideas for Growing in Church Involvement

1. If you can't fully support your church because it doesn't preach or follow God's Word, look for a Bible believing church you can be a part of and support with all your heart.
2. If you're not a member of your church, and they offer membership, join your church.
3. Look for a ministry where you can serve using your gifts and abilities.
4. Pray about starting a new ministry in your church.
5. Pray for your pastor and church leadership.
6. Get to know your church leadership team.
7. Give of your finances faithfully to support your church and obey God.
8. Be more faithful in church attendance.
9. Be careful about being critical and tearing the church down if you haven't been a part of building it up. Tearing down is easy, but building something up is hard work.
10. Commit yourself to loving and encouraging others in your church.

11. Pray about getting more involved in shouldering the load in your church.
12. Apply what you learn to your life. Don't just be a hearer of God's Word, but a doer of it.
13. Learn your spiritual gifts and use them.
14. Be a part of solving problems, not being one of them.
15. Be punctual.
16. Smile, be positive, and be warm to others.
17. Be friendly by greeting visitors and others in your church.
18. Be hospitable and invite people into your home for fellowship.
19. Read books and articles on church health and growth.
20. Do a Bible study on the purpose and role of the church.
21. Look for someone in your church who is faithfully involved in church and ask him or her to mentor you in this area.

Action Steps for Growing in Church Involvement

Now prayerfully look back over this list, choose at least one idea, and make plans to begin doing it today. Then continually return in the future for implementing other ideas for your growth in church involvement.

8. How to Grow in Evangelism

"For I am not ashamed of the gospel, for it is the power of God for salvation to everyone who believes, to the Jew first and also to the Greek" (Rom. 1:16).

"And he said to them, 'Go into all the world and proclaim the gospel to the whole creation'" (Mark 16:15).

Stages of Growth to Spiritual Maturity in Evangelism

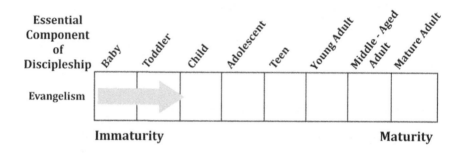

Self-Assessment Test for Evangelism

Please take a moment to answer the following 10 questions to discover your spiritual maturity level regarding evangelism. Answer each question using the following response options. Mark down your points earned for each question and then tally them up at the end to see your level of spiritual maturity in this category. As you take the test, avoid rushing. Answer the questions prayerfully and honestly. After you've taken the test, you might ask a loved one to take it for you as well. This will give you a broader perspective.

314

Points Possible per Answer

Never...................... 0 Points

Rarely .... 2 Points

Occasionally .... 4 Points

Frequently............... 6 Points

Almost Always ...... 8 Points

Habitually............... 10 Points

1. I know each aspect of the gospel. _____

2. I have verses memorized for sharing the gospel. _____

3. I share the gospel regularly. _____

4. I look for opportunities to build relationships with those who don't know Christ. _____

5. I pray for unsaved loved ones and friends. _____

6. I am confident in my ability to share the gospel. _____

7. My heart is full of compassion for the lost. _____

8. I am willing to go anywhere to share the gospel. _____

9. I have a heart for missions. _____

10. I am involved in missions by either praying for missionaries, serving missionaries, or by giving to missions. _____

Total Score _____

Now check your score against the following chart to determine your spiritual maturity level for evangelism.

Spiritual Maturity Grade from the "Evangelism" Test

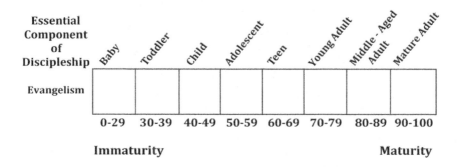

Essential Component of Discipleship	Baby	Toddler	Child	Adolescent	Teen	Young Adult	Middle-Aged Adult	Mature Adult
Evangelism								
	0-29	30-39	40-49	50-59	60-69	70-79	80-89	90-100

Immaturity   **Maturity**

My spiritual maturity grade for evangelism:

I am a _____ spiritually.

Ideas for Growing in Evangelism

1. Write out your testimony about how you received Christ.
2. Practice sharing your testimony with loved ones or friends.
3. Share your testimony at church, in a small group, in a Bible study, etc.
4. Practice sharing the gospel.
5. Pray for opportunities to share your testimony and the gospel.
6. Read and study other Bible verses that focus on the gospel.
7. Read books on apologetics (how to defend your faith).
8. Get to know God's Word better so you are not embarrassed when sharing your faith and are more confident (2 Tim. 2:15).
9. Get to know the missionaries of your church.
10. Pray for missionaries you know.
11. Encourage the missionaries you know by sending them cards, giving them a phone call, etc.
12. Give financially to missionaries you know.
13. Consider serving as a missionary (either short-term or long-term).

14. Read books on great missionaries and the sacrifices they've made for God.
15. Read books and articles on evangelism.
16. Do a Bible study on evangelism.
17. Look for someone in your church who shares the gospel regularly and effectively, and ask him or her to mentor you in this area.
18. Study (memorize if possible) the following biblical presentation of the gospel so you can share it with precision and clarity:

Step 1: God loves us and wants to have a relationship with us, to save us from hell, to give us life now, and that we would spend eternity in heaven with Him.

John 3:16: "For God so loved the world, that he gave his only Son, that whoever believes in him should not perish but have eternal life."

Step 2: Our sin and rejection of God separates us from Him, the life He wants to give us now, and a future in heaven with Him.

Genesis 2:15-17: "The Lord God took the man and put him in the Garden of Eden to work it and keep it. And the Lord God commanded the man, saying, 'You may surely eat of every tree of the garden, but of the tree of the knowledge of good and evil you shall not eat, for in the day that you eat of it you shall surely die.'"

Isaiah 59:2: "But your iniquities have made a separation between you and your God, and your sins have hidden his face from you so that he does not hear."

Romans 3:23: "For all have sinned and fall short of the glory of God."

Summary of steps 1 and 2: We have lost our relationship with God our Creator, and as a result, have a sinful heart. We do not desire to please God and are selfish and sinful. Our greatest sin is that of not having a relationship with God and loving Him as our Father and Creator. If the greatest command in the Bible is to love the Lord our God with all our heart, soul, mind, and strength, then our greatest sin is not to love and have a relationship with Him. This is our primary sin (Matt. 7:21-23).

Step 3: The price for practicing sin and rejecting God is separation from God in eternal torment in hell.

Romans 6:23: "For the wages of sin is death, but the free gift of God is eternal life in Christ Jesus our Lord."

Matthew 13:49–50: "So it will be at the end of the age. The angels will come out and separate the evil from the righteous and throw them into the fiery furnace. In that place there will be weeping and gnashing of teeth."

Revelation 21:8: "But as for the cowardly, the faithless, the detestable, as for murderers, the sexually immoral, sorcerers, idolaters, and all liars, their portion will be in the lake that burns with fire and sulfur, which is the second death."

Step 4: God's remedy for our sin is a relationship with Him now, abundant life, and eternal life through Christ's death on the Cross and resurrection from the dead.

Isaiah 53:5: "But he was pierced for our transgressions; he was crushed for our iniquities; upon him was the chastisement that brought us peace, and with his wounds we are healed."

Romans 5:8: "But God shows his love for us in that while we were still sinners, Christ died for us."

Romans 6:23: "For the wages of sin is death, but the free gift of God is eternal life in Christ Jesus our Lord."

Ephesians 2:8–9: "For by grace you have been saved through

faith. And this is not your own doing; it is the gift of God, not a result of works, so that no one may boast."

Step 5: Would you like to receive Christ and His gift of having a relationship with Him now, forgiveness of sins, abundant life now, and eternal life in heaven with Him?

John 1:12: "But to all who did receive him, who believed in his name, he gave the right to become children of God."
John 3:36: "Whoever believes in the Son has eternal life; whoever does not obey the Son shall not see life, but the wrath of God remains on him."
Acts 4:12: "And there is salvation in no one else, for there is no other name under heaven given among men by which we must be saved."

Step 6: How to receive Christ as your Lord and Savior.

1. Admit that you are a sinner in need of a Savior.
2. Believe that Christ died on the Cross to pay for your sins and rose from the dead to give you eternal life.
3. Believe that without Christ's payment for your sins you deserve hell.
4. Repent and confess your sins to God, asking for His forgiveness and grace.
5. Pray to receive Christ and His gift of salvation.
6. Give your heart and will to Christ.

Action Steps for Growing in Evangelism

Now prayerfully look back over this list, choose at least one idea, and make plans to begin doing it today. Then continually return in the future for implementing other ideas for your growth in evangelism.

9. How to Grow in Your Inner Life

"But the Lord said to Samuel, 'Do not look on his appearance or on the height of his stature, because I have rejected him. For the Lord sees not as man sees: man looks on the outward appearance, but the **Lord looks on the heart** '" (1 Sam. 16:16).

"So I always take pains to have a **clear conscience** toward both God and man" (Acts 24:7).

Stages of Growth to Spiritual Maturity in the Inner Life

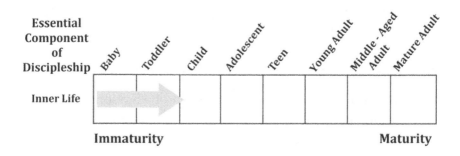

Self-Assessment Test for Your Inner Life

Please take a moment to answer the following 10 questions to discover your spiritual maturity level regarding your inner life with Christ. Answer each question using the following response options. Mark down your points earned for each question and then tally them up at the end to see your level of spiritual maturity in this category. As you take the test, avoid rushing. Answer the questions prayerfully and honestly. After you've taken the test, you might ask a loved one to take it for you as well. This will give you a broader perspective.

Points Possible per Answer

Never...................... 0 Points
Rarely .... 2 Points
Occasionally .... 4 Points
Frequently............... 6 Points
Almost Always ...... 8 Points
Habitually............... 10 Points

1. I am the same in public as I am in private. ____

2. Others can see that God is my highest priority. ____

3. There's nothing in my life I haven't fully surrendered to God. ____

4. I walk closely with God throughout the day. ____

5. I am highly concerned about obeying all of Scripture. ____

6. I replace sinful, impure thoughts with God's truth. ____

7. I maintain a clear conscience before God and others. ____

8. I confess all known sin promptly and ask God and others to forgive me right away. ____

9. I forgive others who hurt me and keep my heart clean of bitterness and resentment. ____

10. I read and meditate on God's Word to better understand His will and keep my life and heart pure. ____

Total Score ____

Now check your score against the following chart to determine your spiritual maturity level for your inner life.

Spiritual Maturity Grade from the "Inner Life" Test

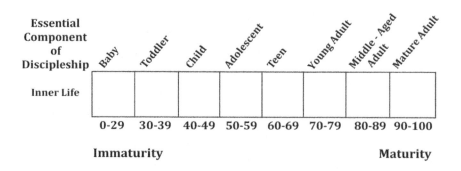

My spiritual maturity grade for my inner life:

I am a _____ spiritually.

Ideas for Growing in Your Inner Life with Christ

1. Prayerfully ask yourself how much of your Christian life and service to God tilts toward looking good before others instead of God.
2. Prayerfully ask yourself if you're more concerned with what others think of you instead of what God thinks of you.
3. Prayerfully ask yourself if you're guilty of the same tendencies as many of those during Christ's day who were hypocritical.
4. Give careful attention to starting or being more faithful in a daily quiet time where you:

   - Pray
   - Read your Bible with purpose
   - Memorize Scripture

5. Do a Bible search for the phrase "selfish ambition" and then meditate on Scripture that speaks of our tendency to be people pleasers rather than God pleasers.
6. Read the "Sermon on the Mount" (Matt. 5–7) that speaks of

doing our service to please God rather than others.

7. Ask loved ones or close friends to truthfully evaluate your life to see if you have selfish ambition.
8. Memorize Scripture that deals with pride and selfish ambition.
9. Prayerfully ask God to show you areas in your life where you are displeasing Him.
10. Read a book on the inner life that deals with how you can develop a heart that focuses on pleasing God and being a genuine follower of Christ.
11. Prayerfully ask yourself why you do what you do in your service to God and others. Is it to gain recognition or to please God?
12. Ponder over your life and prayerfully ask yourself if you have taken stands on biblical truths despite what others think of you.
13. Prayerfully ask yourself if some of your beliefs are held due to what others believe instead of what God's Word says.
14. Do a Bible study on the inner life.
15. Look for someone in your church who displays mature characteristics in their inner life and ask him or her to mentor you in this area.

Action Steps for Growing in Your Inner Life

Now prayerfully look back over this list, choose at least one idea, and make plans to begin doing it today. Then continually return in the future for implementing other ideas for your growth in your inner life.

10. How to Grow in Spiritual Gifts

"Now there are varieties of gifts, but the same Spirit; and there are varieties of service, but the same Lord; and there are varieties of activities, but it is the same God who empowers them all in everyone. To each is given the manifestation of the Spirit for the common good" (1 Cor. 12:4-7).

Stages of Growth to Spiritual Maturity in Spiritual Gifts

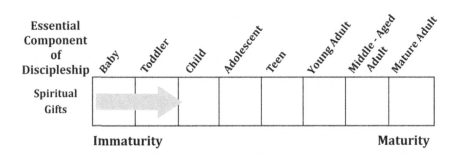

Self-Assessment Test for Spiritual Gifts

Please take a moment to answer the following 10 questions to discover your spiritual maturity level regarding spiritual gifts. Answer each question using the following response options. Mark down your points earned for each question and then tally them up at the end to see your level of spiritual maturity in this category. As you take the test, avoid rushing. Answer the questions prayerfully and honestly. After you've taken the test, you might ask a loved one to take it for you as well. This will give you a broader perspective.

Points Possible per Answer

Never...................... 0 Points

Rarely .... 2 Points

Occasionally .... 4 Points

Frequently.............. 6 Points

Almost Always ...... 8 Points

Habitually.............. 10 Points

1. I know what all the spiritual gifts are in the Bible.   _____

2. I know what each spiritual gift means and how God intends it to be used.   _____

3. I know what my spiritual gifts are.   _____

4. I am currently using my spiritual gifts.   _____

5. I know the doctrinal positions on the spiritual gifts.   _____

6. I am a master at using my spiritual gifts.   _____

7. I am studying and learning more about how to better use my spiritual gifts.   _____

8. I often think about new ways I could use my gifts.   _____

9. I encourage others to use their spiritual gifts.   _____

10. Using my spiritual gifts give me a deep sense of purpose in life.   _____

Total Score   _____

Now check your score against the following chart to determine your spiritual maturity level for spiritual gifts.

Spiritual Maturity Grade from the "Spiritual Gifts" Test

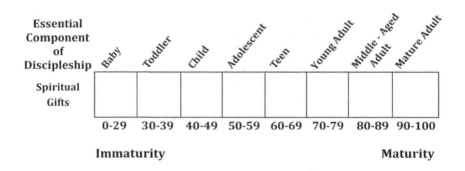

Essential Component of Discipleship	Baby	Toddler	Child	Adolescent	Teen	Young Adult	Middle-Aged Adult	Mature Adult
Spiritual Gifts								

0-29   30-39   40-49   50-59   60-69   70-79   80-89   90-100

Immaturity   **Maturity**

My spiritual maturity grade for spiritual gifts:

I am a _____ spiritually.

Ideas for Growing in Your Spiritual Gifts

1. Do a Bible study on the spiritual gifts.
2. Take a self-assessment test to discover your spiritual gifts (there are many online from which to choose).
3. Take a Bible class on the spiritual gifts.
4. Ask your pastor to offer a class on the spiritual gifts.
5. Lead a Bible study on the spiritual gifts.
6. Write down your spiritual gifts and memorize them.
7. Ask others what they think your spiritual gifts are.
8. Pray and seek out how you can develop your spiritual gifts.
9. If you're not already doing so, offer to use your gifts within your church.
10. Do an in-depth Bible study on your particular gifts.
11. Seek out others who have your similar gifts and ask them to share with you about how they use their gifts.
12. Observe those who are mature in their use of the same gifts you have and watch how they use them.
13. Read books and articles on the spiritual gifts.
14. Read several theological books about the different doctrinal

positions on the spiritual gifts in order to understand all views (some believe all the gifts are for today while others believe not all of them are for today).

15. Pray about how you can develop your spiritual gifts in order to be highly skilled at using them.

16. Look for someone in your church who is faithfully using their spiritual gifts and ask him or her to mentor you in this area.

Action Steps for Growing in Your Spiritual Gifts

Now prayerfully look back over this list, choose at least one idea, and make plans to begin doing it today. Then continually return in the future for implementing other ideas for growth in your spiritual gifts.

11. How to Grow in Serving

"But Jesus called them to him and said, 'You know that the rulers of the Gentiles lord it over them, and their great ones exercise authority over them. It shall not be so among you. But whoever would be great among you must be your servant, and whoever would be first among you must be your slave, even as the Son of Man came not to be served but to serve, and to give his life as a ransom for many'" (Matt. 20:25–28).

Stages of Growth to Spiritual Maturity in Serving

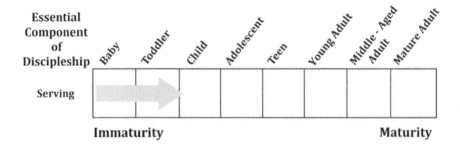

Self-Assessment Test for Serving

Please take a moment to answer the following 10 questions to discover your spiritual maturity level regarding serving. Answer each question using the following response options. Mark down your points earned for each question and then tally them up at the end to see your level of spiritual maturity in this category. As you take the test, avoid rushing. Answer the questions prayerfully and honestly. After you've taken the test, you might ask a loved one to take it for you as well. This will give you a broader perspective.

Points Possible per Answer

Never........................ 0 Points
Rarely .... 2 Points
Occasionally .... 4 Points
Frequently............... 6 Points
Almost Always ...... 8 Points
Habitually............... 10 Points

1. I have a ministry where I serve God and others. _____

2. I am a serving person. _____

3. I enjoy meeting the needs of others without expecting anything in return. _____

4. I see my painful experiences as gifts from God to better serve others. _____

5. I serve God and others through prayer. _____

6. Those close to me would say that my life is more about giving than receiving. _____

7. I am sensitive to the needs of others. _____

8. I volunteer my time on a regular basis. _____

9. Meeting the needs of others gives me great joy and purpose in life. _____

10. I feel deep compassion for those in need. _____

Total Score _____

Now check your score against the following chart to determine your spiritual maturity level for serving.

Spiritual Maturity Grade from the "Serving" Test

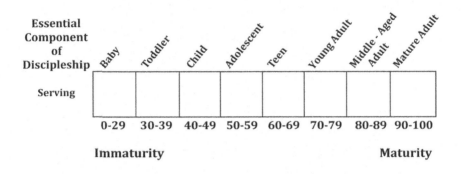

My spiritual maturity grade for serving:

I am a _____ spiritually.

Ideas for Growing in Serving

1. Memorize Matthew 20:25–28 and Philippians 2:5–8.
2. Ask God to reveal any area in your life where you lack a servant's heart.
3. Ask God to give you eyes to see the needs around you.
4. Prayerfully reflect on your desires to lead, and ask yourself if there might be selfish ambition on your part.
5. Instead of focusing on your needs, consider listening more and focusing on the needs of others.
6. If you're not already serving in your church, look for opportunities to get involved.
7. Learn what your spiritual gifts are so you know best how to serve God and others.
8. Pray about the needs of your church and consider talking with your pastor about how to meet those needs.
9. Read Christian books on serving.
10. Sacrifice one hour this week to serve in your church or neighborhood.
11. Look for ways you can serve those in your family.

12. Choose to do a random act of kindness for someone each day this week.
13. Ask for feedback on how you could be a better servant from your pastor, family, and close friends.
14. Ask your neighbors if they need help with something.
15. Look for widows or the elderly who might need a helping hand with projects around their home.
16. Consider serving at a food pantry or kitchen.
17. Serve on a short-term mission trip this year.
18. Serve someone by discipling and mentoring them.
19. Visit the sick in hospitals.
20. Visit shut-ins, the elderly, widows, etc.
21. Do a Bible study on serving.
22. Look for someone in your church who is serving faithfully and ask him or her to mentor you in this area.

Action Steps for Growing in Serving

Now prayerfully look back over this list, choose at least one idea, and make plans to begin doing it today. Then continually return in the future for implementing other ideas for your growth in serving.

12. How to Grow in Spiritual Attitudes

"But the fruit of the Spirit is love, joy, peace, patience, kindness, goodness, faithfulness, gentleness, self-control; against such things there is no law. And those who belong to Christ Jesus have crucified the flesh with its passions and desires" (Gal. 5:22–24).

"You should have the same **attitude** toward one another that Christ Jesus had, who though he existed in the form of God did not regard equality with God as something to be grasped, but emptied himself by taking on the form of a slave, by looking like other men, and by sharing in human nature. He humbled himself, by becoming obedient to the point of death—even death on a cross!" (Phil. 2:5–8).

Stages of Growth to Spiritual Maturity in Spiritual Attitudes

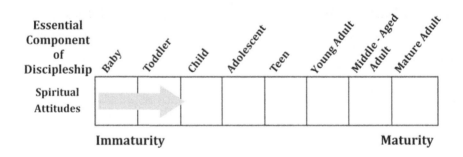

Self-Assessment Test for Spiritual Attitudes

Please take a moment to answer the following 10 questions to discover your spiritual maturity level regarding your attitudes. Answer each question using the following response options. Mark down your points earned for each question and then tally them up at the end to see your level of spiritual maturity in this category. As you take the test, avoid rushing. Answer the questions prayerfully and honestly. After you've taken the test, you might ask a loved one to take it for you as well. This will give you a broader perspective.

Points Possible per Answer

Never......................	0 Points
Rarely	2 Points
Occasionally	4 Points
Frequently...............	6 Points
Almost Always	8 Points
Habitually	10 Points

1. I display Christ-like attitudes. _____

2. I am a loving, kind person. _____

3. I am a joyful person. _____

4. I am a peaceful person. _____

5. I am a patient person. _____

6. I am a friendly person. _____

7. I am a serving person. _____

8. I am a humble person. _____

9. I am a forgiving person. _____

10. I am a thankful person. _____

Total Score _____

Now check your score against the following chart to determine your spiritual maturity level for spiritual attitudes.

Spiritual Maturity Grade from the "Spiritual Attitudes" Test

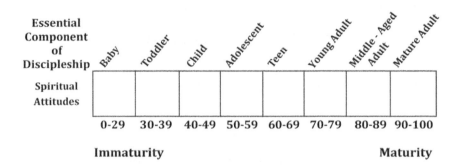

My spiritual maturity grade for spiritual attitudes:

I am a _____ spiritually.

Ideas for Growing in Spiritual Attitudes

1. Identify your default bad attitudes.
2. Identify the good attitudes that should replace your default bad attitudes.
3. Memorize Scripture that addresses your default bad attitudes.
4. Memorize Galatians 5:22–23, Philippians 2:5–8, Philippians 4:8–9, and Romans 12:9–21.
5. Do a Bible study on spiritual attitudes.
6. Identify godly attitudes mentioned in Scripture that we should develop. Here are some examples to consider: we should be loving, joyful, peaceful, kind, forgiving, humble, serving, encouraging, just, obedient, and respectful.
7. Make your quiet time with God a priority.
8. Ask God to help you identify and change your bad attitudes.
9. Share your desire to grow in godly attitudes with a loved one or close friend.
10. Carefully monitor your attitudes and replace them if necessary.
11. Prayerfully ask yourself why you have certain default bad

attitudes.

12. If you are bitter with someone, ask yourself why.
13. Forgive those who have wronged you.
14. Understand that forgiveness is normally both a one-time event and an ongoing process of continual forgiveness.
15. Pray for those who have wronged you.
16. Seek to do something good to bless those who have wronged you (Rom. 12:14–21).
17. Make a list of all the blessings God has done for you and thank Him.
18. Make a list of all the blessings others have done for you and thank them.
19. Thank God daily for His blessings in your life, even the trials (James 1:2–3).
20. Purpose to smile more, reminding yourself that smiling is a way to serve others, regardless of how you feel inside.
21. Get plenty of exercise.
22. Eat healthy food.
23. Get plenty of rest.
24. Find a prayer partner who you can share your needs with and will be faithful in praying for you.
25. Read Christian, non-fiction books on godly attitudes.
26. Look for someone in your church who displays mature, godly attitudes and ask him or her to mentor you in this area.

Action Steps for Growing in Spiritual Attitudes

Now prayerfully look back over this list, choose at least one idea, and make plans to begin doing it today. Then continually return in the future for implementing other ideas for your growth in spiritual attitudes.

13. How to Grow in Character

"But also for this very reason, giving all diligence, add to your faith virtue [character], to virtue knowledge, to knowledge self-control, to self-control perseverance, to perseverance godliness, to godliness brotherly kindness, and to brotherly kindness love. For if these things are yours and abound, you will be neither barren nor unfruitful in the knowledge of our Lord Jesus Christ" (2 Pet. 1:5–8, NKJV).

Stages of Growth to Spiritual Maturity in Character

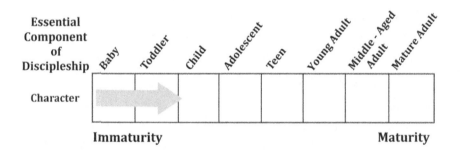

Self-Assessment Test for Character

Please take a moment to answer the following 10 questions to discover your spiritual maturity level regarding your character. Answer each question using the following response options. Mark down your points earned for each question and then tally them up at the end to see your level of spiritual maturity in this category. As you take the test, avoid rushing. Answer the questions prayerfully and honestly. After you've taken the test, you might ask a loved one to take it for you as well. This will give you a broader perspective.

Points Possible per Answer

Never .... 0 Points
Rarely .... 2 Points
Occasionally .... 4 Points
Frequently............... 6 Points
Almost Always ...... 8 Points
Habitually............... 10 Points

1. I am a person of impeccable integrity. _____

2. I do the right thing when no one notices. _____

3. I keep my word even if it cost me money, time, or inconvenience. _____

4. I obey God regardless of the cost. _____

5. I control my tongue. _____

6. I keep my composure when others attack me, irritate me, or say untrue things about me. _____

7. My motive in life is to serve God with all my being. _____

8. I am a truthful person. _____

9. I am a self-disciplined person. _____

10. I am a hardworking person. _____

Total Score _____

Now check your score against the following chart to determine your spiritual maturity level for your character.

Spiritual Maturity Grade from the "Character" Test

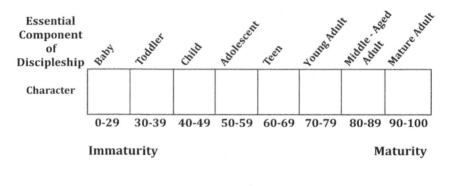

Essential Component of Discipleship	Baby	Toddler	Child	Adolescent	Teen	Young Adult	Middle-Aged Adult	Mature Adult
Character								
	0-29	30-39	40-49	50-59	60-69	70-79	80-89	90-100

Immaturity   Maturity

My spiritual maturity grade for character:

I am a _____ spiritually.

Ideas for Growing in Character

1. Do a Bible study on godly character.
2. Identify godly character traits mentioned in Scripture that we should develop. For example, we should be truthful, trustworthy, honest, loyal, self-disciplined, hardworking, generous, responsible, orderly, cleanly, organized, dependable, faithful, diligent, steadfast, and patient.
3. Identify your character weaknesses by prayerfully analyzing your life and asking trusted loved ones and close friends to help you see your blind spots.
4. Identify the godly character traits you need to develop.
5. Choose your worst character trait and commit to replacing it with the opposite godly character trait.
6. Ask God to supernaturally help you.
7. Practice new godly traits until they become habits.
8. Memorize 2 Peter 1:5–8.
9. Find the verses in Scripture that address your character weaknesses and memorize them.
10. Read a chapter of the Book of Proverbs daily and identify the

godly character traits found in it.

11. Read Christian books and articles on godly character, especially ones dealing with your particular weaknesses.

12. Lead a Bible study on character traits.

13. Make a checklist chart of the practical commitments you are making to develop godly character and check them off daily in order to build good habits in your life.

14. Look for someone in your church who displays mature, godly character and ask him or her to mentor you in this area.

15. Persevere, persevere, and persevere! Character takes time and isn't developed overnight. Be patient with yourself and stay committed to it for the long haul.

Action Steps for Growing in Godly Character

Now prayerfully look back over this list, choose at least one idea, and make plans to begin doing it today. Then continually return in the future for implementing other ideas for your growth in godly character.

14. How to Grow in Stewardship

"O Lord, make me know my end and what is the measure of my days; let me know how fleeting I am! Behold, you have made my days a few handbreadths, and my lifetime is as nothing before you. Surely all mankind stands as a mere breath! Surely a man goes about as a shadow!" (Ps. 39:4–6).

Stages of Growth to Spiritual Maturity in Stewardship

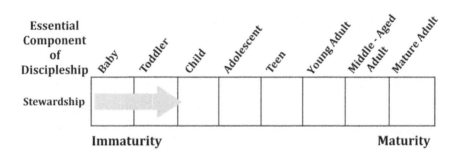

Self-Assessment Test for Stewardship

Please take a moment to answer the following 10 questions to discover your spiritual maturity level regarding stewardship. Answer each question using the following response options. Mark down your points earned for each question and then tally them up at the end to see your level of spiritual maturity in this category. As you take the test, avoid rushing. Answer the questions prayerfully and honestly. After you've taken the test, you might ask a loved one to take it for you as well. This will give you a broader perspective.

Points Possible per Answer

Never...................... 0 Points
Rarely .... 2 Points
Occasionally .... 4 Points
Frequently.............. 6 Points
Almost Always ...... 8 Points
Habitually.............. 10 Points

1. I manage my time well for God's purposes. _____

2. I am heavily invested in building God's Kingdom. _____

3. I am productive and accomplish much for God. _____

4. I let God control what I watch, read, hear, and think. _____

5. I take care of my possessions. _____

6. I am generous with my possessions. _____

7. I give at least 10% of my income to the Lord. _____

8. I am within my weight limit for my body size. _____

9. I exercise in order to take care of my body. _____

10. I eat healthily in order to take care of my body. _____

Total Score _____

Now check your score against the following chart to determine your spiritual maturity level for stewardship.

Spiritual Maturity Grade from the "Stewardship" Test

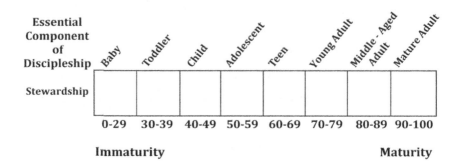

Essential Component of Discipleship	Baby	Toddler	Child	Adolescent	Teen	Young Adult	Middle-Aged Adult	Mature Adult
Stewardship								
	0-29	30-39	40-49	50-59	60-69	70-79	80-89	90-100

Immaturity   **Maturity**

My spiritual maturity grade for stewardship:

I am a _____ spiritually.

Ideas for Growing in Stewardship of Your Time

1. Prayerfully reflect on how much time you spend on average on pleasurable activities each week.
2. Make a chart and keep track of how much time you spend watching TV, on social media, on the Internet, doing fun activities, doing nothing, and so on for a week or two.
3. Look at how you are spending your time and make a decision to be a better steward of it, realizing God will hold you accountable for how you've used this precious talent He's given you.
4. Make a choice to say no to the biggest item that is robbing most of your spare time, and choose to do something instead that is profitable and will serve God, others, or develop yourself.
5. Use a "To-do" list to be better organized.
6. Begin each month, week, and day with a planning time to set goals and log tasks that you should do.
7. Organize your life's activities by using a calendar-planning tool.

8. Cut out unnecessary distractions in your life.
9. Get plenty of rest by going to bed and getting up at regular times.
10. Set up a private zone in your home where you can get away to read, study, pray, meditate, think, and grow.
11. Practice not answering the phone, text messages, emails, etc., after a certain time of the day so you can better utilize your time for rest and personal spiritual growth.
12. Prioritize your goals and give more time to the most important ones.
13. If possible, delegate tasks and responsibilities so you have more free time for spiritual growth and serving.
14. Set a limit to the amount of time you will engage in pleasurable activities per week.
15. Read books and articles on time management.
16. Do a Bible study on time management.
17. Look for someone in your church who is good at time management and ask him or her to mentor you in this area.

Ideas for Growing in Stewardship of Your Possessions

1. Track what percentage of your finances you give to God's work.
2. Make a commitment to give at least 10% of your income to the Lord's work and make it a priority no matter what.
3. Do a Bible study on tithing and giving to God.
4. Read books on financial management.
5. Establish a budget and stick to it.
6. Repair items that are broken instead of buying new ones.
7. Do any needed home repairs that are being neglected.
8. Organize and clean up your surroundings.
9. Commit to getting out of debt.
10. Commit to not spending what you don't have.
11. Cut out needless spending in your life.

12. Eliminate unnecessary spending on pleasure.
13. Read books and articles where faithful Christians have given generously to God and how He has blessed them as a result (George Mueller, etc.).
14. Read Christian books on money management.
15. Look for someone in your church who is good at money management and is faithful in giving to the Lord's work, and ask him or her to mentor you in this area.

Ideas for Growing in Stewardship of Your Body

1. If you are overweight, prayerfully ask yourself why.
2. Commit to getting in shape physically.
3. Commit to a regular exercise program.
4. Commit to eating healthily.
5. Cut out your intake of junk food.
6. Drink water instead of soda, juices, sports drinks, etc.
7. Reduce your eating size portions.
8. Commit to going to bed and getting up at regular times.
9. Find an accountability partner to help you get in shape.
10. Instead of parking close to stores, park far away and walk.
11. Eliminate the poor habits that are causing you to be a poor steward of your body.
12. Read books and articles on how to take care of your body and get in shape.
13. Read the stories of others who have gotten in shape and how they did it.
14. Set clearly defined goals for getting in shape and on how to be a better steward of your body.
15. Do a Bible study on taking care of your body.
16. Make a weekly to-do list for getting in shape that might include the following:

- Workout five days a week
- Eat healthier foods
- Reduce food size portions
- Cut out processed foods
- Drink six large glasses of water daily
- Cut out soda and beverages
- Reduce or eliminate sweets
- Eat dinner before 7:00 p.m.

17. Look for someone in your church who does well at being a good steward of their body and ask him or her to mentor you in this area.

Action Steps for Growing in Stewardship of Your Time, Possessions, and Body

Now prayerfully look back over these three lists on stewardship, choose at least one idea from each category, and make plans to begin doing them today. Then continually return in the future for implementing other ideas for your growth in stewardship.

15. Overall Spiritual Maturity Chart

Now it's time to add up all the scores from each category to discover your overall spiritual maturity level.

Put your score in each corresponding line:

1. Score from Knowledge of God Test   _____

2. Score from Self- Discipline Test   _____

3. Score from Obedience Test   _____

4. Score from Abiding in Christ Test   _____

5. Score from Prayer Test   _____

6. Score from Mentoring Test   _____

7. Score from Church Involvement Test   _____

8. Score from Evangelism Test   _____

9. Score from Inner Life Test   _____

10. Score from Spiritual Gifts Test   _____

11. Score from Serving Test   _____

12. Score from Spiritual Attitudes Test   _____

13. Score from Character Test   _____

14. Score from Stewardship Test   _____

Total score   _____

Total score divided by 14   _____

Now check your score against the next chart to determine your overall spiritual maturity level.

Spiritual Maturity Grade from the "Overall Maturity" Test

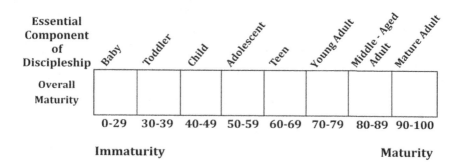

Take your overall adjusted score to find your overall level of maturity in the above diagram.

I am a _____ in my overall spiritual maturity level.

Now look back at the overall spiritual maturity chart and see where you scored the weakest. Next, look at the ideas for that area that you can begin to put into practice for growing toward spiritual maturity. Start with your weakest areas first and then address the next weakest area afterward. Keep doing this for all areas.

Remember, attaining spiritual maturity is a lifelong process so consider rereading this book. Keep focusing and putting into practice the ideas from this chapter in order to grow and attain spiritual maturity in all areas of the essential components of discipleship.

You might even consider using the last two chapters (or even the entire book) for a Bible study or small group resource for teaching others the essential components for attaining spiritual maturity.

On the following page, an overall chart for each category is provided. This will enable you to get an overall view of your spiritual maturity in each area.

Overall Spiritual Maturity Chart

Please put a mark (in pencil) to indicate your present level of spiritual maturity in each category. Consider working on your weakest areas first. Then return regularly to mark your progress and growth toward spiritual maturity in each category.

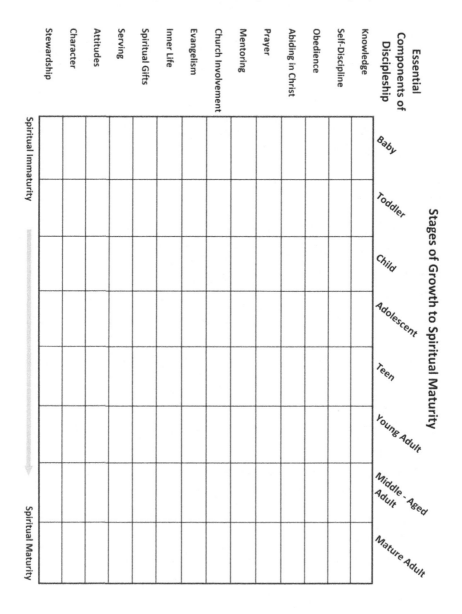

Essential Components for Attaining Spiritual Maturity

Conclusion

Today, we have many ways of defining success in life. Some define it as being a sports hero, others as being wealthy, others as being popular and well liked, and still others as being happy. How does God define success? He defines it as being spiritually mature!

Spiritual maturity is our purpose in life, not happiness, pleasure, possessions, prestige, or the fulfillment of our dreams. A lifelong commitment to discipleship is God's will for our lives and is what enables us to attain spiritual maturity. By neglecting discipleship, we reject God's nature and image, choosing instead to retain the image of sin and remain spiritually immature.

Now it's time to look in the mirror and sincerely ask yourself how much you want to fulfill God's purpose for your life in becoming spiritually mature. Today, there is more competition than ever, and most will get distracted with the cares of this life and remain spiritually immature. As a result, they will have few rewards in heaven. They will spend most of their time and energy focused on this life rather than preparing for their eternal home. How about you? Will you be one of them? I hope not! Are you willing to pay the cost to attain spiritual maturity? I hope so!

In closing, I want to encourage you to take some time to truly ponder and meditate on eternity and your life there. Reflect on how fast time is passing and how short life is. Reflect on eternity and its endless essence. Consider others who have passed away and think about how things are for them now in their eternal state, whether good or bad.

The only thing we're going to take out of this life is who we have become in Christ and our service to Him. We need to reflect prayerfully on the stanza from the poem by C. T. Studd that says:

Only one life, yes only one,

Soon will its fleeting hours be done;

Then, in "that day" my Lord to meet,

And stand before His Judgement Seat;

Only one life, twill soon be past,

Only what's done for Christ will last.[217]

May God truly grant you grace and strength as you strive to attain spiritual maturity and lay up for yourself treasures in heaven.

Thank you for reading this book and may God bless you for your desire to become spiritually mature!

"So teach us to number our days that we may get a heart of wisdom."
Ps. 90:12

"All flesh is like grass and all its glory like the flower of grass. The grass withers, and the flower falls, but the word of the Lord remains forever."
1 Pet. 1:24–25

"What is your life? For you are a mist that appears for a little time and then vanishes."
James 4:14

---

[217] C. T. Studd, *Only One Life Twill Soon Be Past*, http://hockleys.org/2009/05/quote-only-one-life-twill-soon-be-past-poem, Accessed 08/27/2015.

Bibliography

Acts 17:11 Bible Studies. *The Fear of God.* http://www.acts17-11.com/fear.html. Accessed 08/17/2015.

Baker, Greg S. *How to Build Good Character.* SelfGrowth.com. www.selfgrowth.com/articles/how_to_build_good_character. Accessed 12/14/2015.

Barna, George. *Growing True Disciples: New Strategies for Producing Genuine Followers of Christ.* Barna Reports. The Crown Publishing Group. Kindle Edition. 2013.

Barna Group. *The State of the Bible: 6 Trends for 2014.* 2014. https://www.barna.org/barna-update/culture/664-the-state-of-the-bible-6-trends-for-2014#.VdNGKTZRGUk. Accessed 08/18/2015.

Barrier, Roger. *What Does it Mean to "Fear the Lord?"* 2013. Crosswalk.com. http://www.crosswalk.com/church/pastors-or-leadership/ask-roger/what-does-it-mean-to-fear-the-lord.html. Accessed 08/15/2015.

Baucham, Voddie Jr. *Equipping the Generations: A Three-Pronged Approach to Discipleship.* Source: Journal of Family Ministry, 2 no 1 Fall-Winter 2011. Publication. ATLA. Religion Database with ATLASerials. Hunter Resource Library. Accessed 11/5/2014.

Beeksma, Deborah. *The Average Christian Prays a Minute a Day; Prayer by the Faithful Helps Their Relationships.* GodDiscussion.com. 2013. http://www.goddiscussion.com/110131/the-average-christian-prays-a-minute-a-day-prayer-by-the-faithful-helps-their-relationships. Accessed 07/27/2015.

Bible Hub. *703. Arête.* http://biblehub.com/greek/703.htm. Accessed 10/23/2015.

Biblicalhebrew.com. *Hate your Parents: Hate your Father, Matthew 10:37, Luke 14:26.* www.biblicalhebrew.com/nt/lovehate.htm. Accessed 08/08/2015.

Biblestudytools.com. The NAS New Testament Greek Lexicon.
    http://www.biblestudytools.com/lexicons/greek/nas/sozo.htm
    l. Accessed 08/05/2015.

Bloom, Jon. *Let Him Deny Himself.* Desiring God.org. 2010.
    http://www.desiringgod.org/articles/let-him-deny-himself.
    Accessed 7/27/2015.

Blue Letter Bible. BlueLetterBible.org. *Study Resources: Charts and
    Quotes.* www.blueletterbible.org/study/pnt/pnt08.cfm. Accessed
    10/14/105.

Bonhoeffer, Dietrich. *The Cost of Discipleship.* 2011-08-16. SCM
    Classics Hymns Ancient and Modern Ltd. Kindle Edition.

Butt, Kyle. *Hate Your Parents – or Love Them?* Apologeticspress.org.
    2004.
    apologeticspress.org/AllegedDiscrepancies.aspx?article=781.
    Accessed 08/08/2015.

Character-training.com/blog. *What Is Character?*
    http://www.character-training.com/blog. Accessed
    10/23/2015.

Christian Prayer Quotes. *Prayer Quotations.* http://www.christian-
    prayer-quotes.christian-attorney.net. Accessed 10/20/2015.

Cole, Steven J. *Why You Should Hate Your Life.* Bible.org. 2014.
    bible.org/seriespage/lesson-67-why-you-should-hate-your-life-
    john-1224-26. Accessed 08/11/2015.

Compelling Truth. *What Is the Sin of Gluttony?* Compellingtruth.org.
    www.compellingtruth.org/gluttony-sin.html. Accessed
    10/24/2015.

Crockett, Joseph V. *Is There Discipline in Our Discipleship?*
    Source: Living Pulpit. Online. March 1, 2014. ATLA Religion
    Database with ATLASerials. Hunter Resource Library. Accessed
    11/5/2014.

C. S. Lewis Institute. *Sparking a Discipleship Movement in America and
    Beyond.* cslewisinstitute.org.
    http://www.cslewisinstitute.org/webfm_send/210. Accessed
    08/19/2015.

Dyck, Drew. *The Leavers: Young Doubters Exit the Church.* 2010.
ChristianityToday.com.
www.christianitytoday.com/ct/2010/november/27.40.html.
Accessed 09/28/2015.

Edman, Raymond V. *The Disciplines of Life.* Minneapolis, Minnesota.
World Wide Publications. 1948.

Eskridge, Larry. *The Prosperity Gospel Is Surprisingly Mainstream.* 2013.
ChristianityToday.com.
http://www.christianitytoday.com/ct/2013/august-web-
only/prosperity-gospel-is-surprisingly-mainstream.html.
Accessed 08/22/2015.

Fairchild, Mary. *Basics to Prayer.* Christianity.About.com.
http://christianity.about.com/od/prayersverses/a/basicstopra
yer.htm. Accessed 10/16/2016.

Firger, Jessica. *Prescription Drugs on the Rise: Estimates Suggest 60
Percent of Americans Take at Least One Medication.* Newsweek.
2015. www.newsweek.com/prescription-drugs-rise-new-
estimates-suggest-60-americans-take-least-one-390354. Accessed
11/17/2015.

Foster, Richard J. *Celebration of Discipline.* HarperCollins. Kindle
Edition. 2009.

Gotquestions.org. *What Does the Bible Say About the Prosperity Gospel?*
http://www.gotquestions.org/prosperity-gospel.html.
Accessed 08/22/2015.

_____. *What Does It Mean to Abide in Christ?*
www.gotquestions.org/abide-in-Christ.html. Accessed
10/20/2015.

_____. *What Does the Bible Say About Attitude?*
www.gotquestions.org/Bible-attitude.html. Accessed
10/23/2015.

_____. *What Does the Bible Say About Time Management?*
www.gotquestions.org/Bible-time-management.html. Accessed
10/24/2015.

Graham, Billy. *What Did Jesus Mean When He Said We Have to Carry a Cross?* Billy Graham Evangelistic Association. 2006. http://billygraham.org/answer/what-did-jesus-mean-when-he-said-we-have-to-carry-a-cross. Accessed 08/17/2015.

Greenwold, Doug. *Being a First-Century Disciple.* 2007. Bible.org. https://bible.org/article/being-first-century-disciple. Accessed 08/14/2015.

Grudem, Wayne. *Systematic Theology: An Introduction to Biblical Doctrine.* Grand Rapids, Michigan. Zondervan. 1994.

Hayes, Dan. *Motivating Reasons to Pray.* StartingWithGod.com. www.startingwithgod.com/knowing-god/motivating. Accessed 10/20/2015.

Helpmewithbiblestudy.org. *What Did Jesus Mean "Deny Yourself and Take Up Your Cross"?* http://helpmewithbiblestudy.org/9Salvation/SanctifyWhatDoesItMeanToCarryCross.aspx. Accessed 07/27/2015.

Henderson, Daniel. *No Time to Pray.* Praying Pastor Blog. PrayingPastorBlog.blogspot. http://prayingpastorblog.blogspot.mx/2009/02/no-time-to-pray-no-time-to-pray.html. Accessed 10/16/2015.

Herrick, Greg. *Understanding the Meaning of the Term "Disciple."* 2004. Bible.org. https://bible.org/seriespage/2-understanding-meaning-term-disciple. Accessed 08/13/2015.

Houdmann, Michael S. *Is Gluttony a Sin? What Does the Bible Say About Overeating?* http://www.gotquestions.org/gluttony-sin.html. Accessed 02/27/2016.

_____. *What Does the Bible Mean by "Dying to Self"?* http://www.gotquestions.org/dying-to-self.html. Accessed 07/27/2015.

Hull, Bill. *The Complete Book of Discipleship: On Being and Making Followers of Christ.* The Navigators Reference Library 1. 2014. NavPress. Kindle Edition.

Institute in Basic Life Principles. *What Is the Fear of the Lord?* Iblp.org. http://iblp.org/questions/what-fear-lord. Accessed 08/15/2015.

Issler, Klaus. *Six Themes to Guide Spiritual Formation Ministry Based on Jesus' Sermon on the Mount.* Source: Christian Education. Journal Date: September 1, 2010. CEJ: Series 3, Vol. 7, No. 2. ATLA Religion Database with ATLASerials. Hunter Resource Library. Accessed 11/5/2014.

Keathley, Hampton J III. *Church Discipline.* Bible.org. bible.org/article/church-discipline. Accessed 10/08/2015.

Kinnaman, Dave and Lyons, Gabe. *Un Christian.* Grand Rapids, MI. BakerBooks. 2007.

Krejcir, Dr. Richard J. *Statistics on Pastors: What is Going on with the Pastors in America?* 2007. Churchleadership.org. http://www.churchleadership.org/apps/articles/default.asp?articleid=42347&columnid=4545. Accessed 08/06/2015.

_____. *Statistics and Reasons for Church Decline.* 2007. Churchleadership.org. http://www.churchleadership.org/apps/articles/default.asp?articleid=42346&columnid=4545. Accessed 08/07/2015.

LifeWay Research. *Views on Divorce Divide Americans.* 2015. LifeWayResearch.com. http://www.lifewayresearch.com/2015/08/12/views-on-divorce-divide-americans. Accessed 08/19/2015.

Lumina.bible.org. https://lumina.bible.org/bible/Matthew+10. Accessed 08/05/2015.

_____. https://lumina.bible.org/bible/Deuteronomy+10. Accessed 08/16/2015.

MacArthur, John F Jr. *Church Discipline.* Grace to You. www.gty.org/resources/distinctives/DD02/church-discipline. Accessed 10/08/2015.

_____. *The Gospel According to Jesus.* Grand Rapids, Michigan. Zondervan Publishing House. 1988.

_____. *What Does It Mean to "Abide" in Christ?* Gty.org. www.gty.org/resources/Questions/QA161/What-does-it-mean-to-abide-in-Christ. Accessed 10/20/2015.

Martin, Cath. *Evangelicals Admit Struggling to Find Time for Daily Bible Reading and Prayer.* 2014. Christianity Today. www.christiantoday.com/article/daily.bible.reading.and.prayer.is.a.struggle.for.many.evangelicals/36765.htm. Accessed 08/18/2015.

_____. *70 Million Christians' Martyred for their Faith Since Jesus Walked the Earth.* 2014. ChristianityToday.com. http://www.christiantoday.com/article/70.million.christians.martyred.faith.since.jesus.walked.earth/38403.htm. Accessed 08/28/2015.

McGrath, Alister. *The Passionate Intellect; Christian Faith and the Discipleship of the Mind.* Source: Pro Ecclesia. 22 no 1 Winter 2013. Publication Type: Review ATLA Religion Database with ATLASerials. Hunter Resource Library. Accessed 11/5/2014.

Mohler, Albert, R. Jr. *The Scandal of Biblical Illiteracy: It's Our Problem.* Christianity.com. http://www.christianity.com/1270946. Accessed 08/18/2015.

_____. *The Disappearance of Church Discipline–How Can We Recover? Part One.* 2005. AlbertMohler.com. http://www.albertmohler.com/2005/05/13/the-disappearance-of-church-discipline-how-can-we-recover-part-one. Accessed 08/20/2015.

Murray, Andrew. *Power to Change: Great Quotes on Prayer.* http://powertochange.com/experience/spiritual-growth/prayerquotes. Accessed 11/16/2015.

Neverthirsty.org. *Bible Questions & Answers.* http://www.neverthirsty.org/pp/corner/read2/r00664.html. Accessed 08/15/2015.

Ogden, Greg. *Transforming Discipleship: Making Disciples a Few at a Time.* InterVarsity Press. Kindle Edition. 2010.

Pew Research Center. *Evangelical Protestant.* Pewforum.org. http://www.pewforum.org/religious-landscape-study/religious-tradition/evangelical-protestant. Accessed 08/19/2015.

Piper, John. *Prosperity Preaching: Deceitful and Deadly.* 2007. Desiring God. DesiringGod.org. http://www.desiringgod.org/articles/prosperity-preaching-deceitful-and-deadly. Accessed 08/23/2015.

Platt, David. *Follow Me.* Carol Stream, Illinois. Tyndale House Publishers. 2013.

_____. *What It Means to Follow Christ.* LifeWay. http://www.lifeway.com/Article/christian-living-what-it-means-to-follow-christ. Accessed 07-22-2015.

Pratte, David E. *Does God Promise Miracles to Give Us Healing and Prosperity?* 2011. Light to My Path Publications. www.gospelway.com. www.gospelway.com/god/health-wealth.php. Accessed 08/22/2015.

Rankin, Russ. *Study: Bible Engagement in Churchgoer's Hearts, Not Always Practiced.* Nashville. 2012. http://www.lifeway.com/Article/research-survey-bible-engagement-churchgoers. Accessed 07/23/2015.

Reardon, JoHannah. *What Does It Mean to Fear God?* ChristianityToday.com. Accessed 08/15/2015.

Robbins, Dale. *Why Christians Should Attend Church.* Victorious.org. www.victorious.org/pub/why-church-169. Accessed 10/21/2015.

Robinson, Anthony B. The Renewed Focus on Discipleship: 'Follow Me'. 2007. Christian Century, 124 no 18 S 4 2007. Publication Type: Article. ATLA Religion Database with ATLASerials. Hunter Resource Library. Accessed 12/10/2014.

Samra, James G. *A Biblical View of Discipleship.* Bibliotheca Sacra April-June 2003. Publication Type: Article, Database: ATLA Religion Database with ATLASerials. Hunter Resource Library. Accessed 11/5/2014.

Statistic Brain Research Institute. *Television Watching Statistics.* 2015. www.statisticbrain.com/television-watching-statistics. Accessed 08/07/2015.

Struckmeyer, Kurt. *Take Up Your Cross.* http://followingjesus.org/changing/take_up_cross.htm. 2007. Accessed 08/03/2015.

Studd, C. T. *Only One Life Twill Soon Be Past.* http://hockleys.org/2009/05/quote-only-one-life-twill-soon-be-past-poem. Accessed 08/27/2015.

Swindoll, Chuck. *Strengthening Your Grip.* Waco, TX. Word Books. 1982.

U.S. Department of Health and Human Services. *Overweight and Obesity Statistics.* www.niddk.nih.gov/health-information/health-statistics/Pages/overweight-obesity-statistics.aspx. 2009, 2010. Accessed 10/24/1015.

Vander Laan, Ray. *Rabbi and Talmidim.* That the World May Know. www.thattheworldmayknow.com/Rabbi-and-talmidim. Accessed 08/13/2015.

Victory Life Church. VictoryLifeChurch.org. Intercessory Prayer — Praying Always. http://www.victorylifechurch.org/pdf/Intercessory_Praying_Always.pdf. Accessed 08/19/2015.

Vos, Beverly. *The Spiritual Disciplines and Christian Ministry.* Source: Evangelical Review of Theology, 36 no 2 Ap 2012. Publication Type: Article ATLA Religion Database with ATLASerials. Hunter Resource Library. Accessed 11/5/2014.

Whitney, Donald S. *Spiritual Disciplines for the Christian Life.* Colorado Springs, Colorado. NAVPRESS. 1991.

Willard, Dallas. *The Great Omission.* 2009-10-13. HarperCollins. Kindle Edition.

_____. *The Spirit of the Disciplines.* 2009-02-06. HarperCollins. Kindle Edition.

_____. *Transformed by the Renewing of the Mind.* Lecture given at Henry Center for Theological Understanding, 2012. https://youtu.be/jkzeUcnzYbM?list=PLApp3jRh1oAqt64uvfw4 J_Ps2lD8bYokR. Accessed 10/15/2015.

Wilke, Jon D. *Churchgoers Believe in Sharing Faith, Most Never Do.* LifeWay.com. LifeWay Research. http://www.lifeway.com/article/research-survey-sharing-christ-2012. Accessed 08/04/2015.

Willis, Avery T Jr. *MasterLife: Discipleship Training for Leaders.* Source: Theological Educator, no 28 Spr 1984. Publication Type: Article. Subjects: Baptists--Education; Christian life ATLA Religion Database with ATLASerials. Hunter Resource Library. Accessed 11/5/2014.

About the Author

Todd M. Fink is founder and director of Go Missions to Mexico Ministries. He received a Bachelor of Theology Degree from Freelandia Bible College (1986-1990), did studies at Western Seminary (1990-1993), received a Master of Theology Degree from Freedom Bible College and Seminary (2012-2013), and received a Ph.D. degree in Theology from Trinity Theological Seminary (2015).

He served as youth/associate pastor for 12 years at an Evangelical church in Oregon (1987-1998).

 Todd (Mike) is currently serving as pastor and missionary with Go Missions to Mexico Ministries in Mexico (1998-present) and is also an author, speaker, and teacher. He has a deep passion for God's Word and enjoys helping people understand its eternal truths. He is married to his lovely wife, Letsy Angela, and has four grown children.

Ministries of Go Missions to Mexico

HolyLandSite.com ~ Holy Land video teachings and resources

MinisteriosCasaDeLuz.com ~ Spanish resources for pastors

SelahBookPress.com ~ Book publishing

Connect with Todd (Mike)

Email: missionstomexico@yahoo.com

Facebook: Go Missions to Mexico

Websites:

- ToddMichaelFink.com
- SelahBookPress.com
- GoMissionsToMexico.com
- HolyLandSite.com
- MinsiteriosCasaDeLuz.com

Look for More Books Coming Soon by Todd (Mike)

- *Discovering the True Riches of Life*
- *Biblical Sites of the Holy Land: See Where the Bible Took Place*
- *Understanding the Fear of the Lord: How to Receive God's Richest Blessings in Your Life*
- *Understanding Heavenly Rewards: An Overlooked Truth*
- *Biblical Leadership: How to Lead God's Way*
- *Gender Roles in the Family and Church: What Does the Bible Say?*
- *Church Discipline: Intensive Care for Wayward Believers*
- *How to Share Your Faith: A Biblical Approach*

Made in the USA
Monee, IL
10 February 2023

27409682R00218